Food and the Self

Materializing Culture

Series Editors: Paul Gilroy and Daniel Miller

Food and the Self

Consumption, Production, and Material Culture

Isabelle de Solier

BLOOMSBURY

LONDON • NEW DELHI • NEW YORK • SYDNEY

Bloomsbury Academic

An imprint of Bloomsbury Publishing Plc

50 Bedford Square   1385 Broadway
London   New York
WC1B 3DP   NY 10018
UK   USA

www.bloomsbury.com

Bloomsbury is a registered trade mark of Bloomsbury Publishing Plc

First published 2013

British Library Cataloguing-in-Publication Data
A catalogue record for this book is available from the British Library.

ISBN: HB: 978-0-8578-5421-6
        PB: 978-0-8578-5422-3
      ePub: 978-0-8578-5435-3
      ePDF: 978-1-4725-2090-6

Library of Congress Cataloging-in-Publication Data
de Solier, Isabelle.
Food and the self : consumption, production and material
culture / Isabelle de Solier.
pages cm. — (Materializing culture)
Includes bibliographical references and index.
ISBN 978-0-85785-422-3 (pbk.) — ISBN 978-0-85785-421-6 (hardback) —
ISBN 978-0-85785-435-3 (epub) — ISBN 978-1-4725-2090-6 (epdf)
1. Food—Social aspects. 2. Food—Economic aspects. 3. Food supply.
4. Food consumption. 5. Material culture. I. Title.
GT2850.D48 2013
394.1'2—dc23   2013021379

A catalog record for this book is available from the Library of Congress.

Typeset by Apex CoVantage, LLC, Madison, WI, USA.

For Buck

Contents

Acknowledgments

My sincere thanks go to the foodies who participated in my research, for their interest in the project and their generosity in sharing their experiences with me. I am very grateful to Daniel Miller for recognizing the value of this book project and supporting it from its inception. I thank John Frow, Toby Miller, and Robert Stebbins, and the anonymous reviewers for Bloomsbury, for their extremely helpful feedback on drafts of this book. Thanks also to my very good friends and colleagues Meredith Martin and Alison Huber for their excellent editorial eyes at different stages of the manuscript. To my editorial team at Bloomsbury, I thank Louise Butler and Sophie Hodgson for their patience, interest, and constructive guidance throughout the process. This publication was supported by the Faculty of Arts Publication Subsidy Scheme during my tenure as an Honorary Research Fellow in the Faculty of Arts at the University of Melbourne. Parts of this book have previously been published as "Making the Self in a Material World: Food and Moralities of Consumption" in *Cultural Studies Review*. I am very grateful for the support of my friends and my parents, Alex Yarovy and Carol Yarovy. Special thanks go to Naomi Rush and Craig Bourdain for their inspiration and support throughout the project and to Amelia Scurry, Nathan Cherry, Tim Inglefinger, Alyssa Raj, Kaylea Fearn, and Andrew Dawson. Finally, I cannot thank Buck Rosenberg enough for reading and rereading this book and sharing new intellectual insights with me on each occasion. It has lived with us for a long time, and we are both happy for it to finally take on form as a material object and begin a social life of its own.

Introduction

Foodies: Material Culture and the Self in Postindustrial Society

How do we make a meaningful self-identity in a late modern, postindustrial world? Whether it's self-help books telling us how to find our so-called "true" selves, television programs showing us how to style ourselves, or neoliberal rhetoric stressing that we must take responsibility for ourselves, we live in a time where the individual self is increasingly in focus, and we are being made aware that it is our duty to shape it and maximize it. Because we are no longer afforded the comfort (or restriction) of being defined by tradition, in late modernity the burden of creating identity and meaning in life has shifted onto the individual: we must all create "a life of one's own" (Beck and Beck-Gernsheim 2001: 22); we have "no choice but to choose" (Giddens 1991: 81). In postindustrial society, most understandings of this process emphasize the seminal role played by commodities, suggesting that it's through consumption that we make ourselves today (Bourdieu 1984; Featherstone 1991; Baudrillard 1998). We make our selections from the array of goods on offer and combine them to shape who we are or who we want to be: selves, then, are made through things.

As scholars have come to focus on consumption, what was once considered the defining feature of self-identity—our work, or forms of production—has become increasingly obscured from theories of self-formation. In postindustrial societies where most people's work is not materially productive, as it was in the past, does this mean that production no longer matters in self-making? Or alternatively, has production taken on new forms and meanings in people's lives, precisely as a result of this changing nature of work? This book argues that if we think production no longer matters, we may be looking for it in the wrong place. For as production has lost meaning at work, it has found meaning in leisure: it is in our free time that production finds its expression in self-making for many people today in forms of "productive leisure" (Gelber 1999). This may involve actually producing things—such as a dish, dress, or blog. Or it may involve learning things—such as how to cook, sew, or Photoshop digital images. Knowledge and production are integrally linked in productive leisure, for in postindustrial society, new understandings of being productive are bound up with acquiring and expressing knowledge. So if selves today are made through things, I argue that we need to understand how they are shaped not only through consuming things but also through learning and producing things and the values that each of these hold. For there are questions of morality at work here: because of the growing suspicion of consumption in self-making, productive leisure is often regarded as having a higher moral value in this process.

This book intervenes in a range of theoretical debates occurring across the social sciences and humanities, including sociology, anthropology, and cultural studies. I share the concern of recent social theory with questions of self-identity and reflexive individual lifestyles in late modernity (Giddens 1991; Beck and Beck-Gernsheim 2001; Bauman 2008). However, my approach to these questions focuses more directly on the state of life in postindustrial society and how people attempt to create a meaningful and moral individual self through material culture when they no longer produce things at work. In using the term "material culture," I'm drawing on a tradition of material culture studies established in British social anthropology, and in particular, the work of Daniel Miller (1987, 2008, 2010; see also Appadurai 1986; Buchli 2002; Tilley et al. 2006; I. Woodward 2007; Hicks and Beaudry 2010). This field is dedicated to the study of the material things or objects that surround us in our everyday life, from the homes we live in, to the clothes we wear, and the computers we use. In this book, I concentrate on food, an object that has been relatively neglected in this field to date (see Sutton 2001). Indeed, until recently, the subject of food had not attracted significant attention throughout the social sciences and humanities. Despite some important early contributions (Lévi-Strauss 1965; Douglas 1966; Goody 1982; Finkelstein 1989), it was not until the turn of the century that food became more widely recognized as a legitimate object of study, with the growth of the interdisciplinary field of food studies (Bell and Valentine 1997; Counihan and Van Esterik 1997; Warde 1997; Ashley et al. 2004; Belasco 2008; Miller and Deutsch 2009; Albala 2012; de Solier and Duruz 2013).

Where much work in food studies tends to focus on food alone, I am interested in food here as an example of material culture, including how it relates to other objects that make up our world, as well as larger questions of the nature of material culture. Like other scholars in material culture studies, I am not just interested in material things themselves, but more importantly, in the relationship between people and things. Yet unlike most work in this field, my approach to this question focuses on the role material things play in late modern self-identity formation, in the construction of "reflexive" or "DIY selves" (Giddens 1991; Beck and Beck-Gernsheim 2001). In this book, I use ethnographic research to explore the role food plays in the formation of the post-traditional elected self-identity of the *foodie*. While the relationship between food and identity has attracted substantial attention within food studies, most research to date has focused on categories of social identity—such as gender, ethnicity, race, and nation (Gabaccia 1998; Probyn 2000; Ray 2004; Williams-Forson 2006)—leaving the category of the individual self unexplored.

The understanding of *material culture* I develop in this book differs from existing research in the field in that I consider this category to include not only material things themselves but also the cultural products that take them as their focus—in particular, forms of media dedicated to material objects. I refer to these as *material media,* where the term material describes their content rather than their form (although in the case of print media, it may refer to both). Thus, as I understand it, the material culture of food includes not only food itself but also food media, such as television cooking shows, food blogs, and cookbooks. For the material world does not exist in isolation; the media play a key role in the relationship between people and things. Indeed, they are the source of much of our knowledge of material things. It is not just objects that are important in self-making; rather, we need knowledge of objects in order to use them in this process: knowledge of how to consume and produce them. It is through material media that we acquire most of this knowledge, or material education, in a postindustrial world. This is certainly the case for foodies. Food media are central to foodies' relationships with food and to their self-making through it. Thus, in order to gain a comprehensive understanding of the role of material culture in self-identity formation, we need to examine both material objects and material media and the interconnections between the two.

The way I do so is by focusing on what people *do* with objects and material media, on the practices they engage in, such as consumption, production, and education, and the connections between these. I'm interested in the role these material cultural practices play in shaping the self. How do people consume and produce material objects? How do they consume material media in order to learn how to do so? And how do they produce material media in order to share this knowledge? In order to examine the full gamut of foodie self-formation through material culture, the chapters in this book examine the foodie's relationship with food as a material object across a range of social practices, including the food consumed when dining out, purchased when shopping, and produced when cooking. I also examine how foodies learn what food to consume and produce as well as how to do so through material media, such as restaurant guides, cookbooks, and food television, and how they share their knowledge and experience of this material object online through food blogs. Foodie selves are generated through the interactions between the material and mediated dimensions of food.

My approach to studying material culture, then, focuses on the reflexive making of the self through practices of consuming and producing material objects and material media—in this case, food and food media. It is distinct from other recent approaches to materiality in food studies. This includes an increasingly popular approach that developed out of philosophy and focuses on the body, which is concerned with embodiment, the senses, affect, health, and weight (Heldke 1992; Giard 1998; Korsmeyer 1999, 2005; Roe 2006a,b; Mol 2012). This perspective concentrates on the production and consumption of food as integrated embodied practices of cooking and eating. In comparison, following recent work in sociology, in this book I am primarily interested in theorizing food production and consumption as social practices (see Warde 2005). As a result, I am more concerned with consumption in the metaphorical sense of symbolic and economic appropriation than the literal sense of eating. This enables more productive conceptualizations that account for not just the consumption of food but for material objects more generally, as well as material media—that is, it allows me to understand the consumption of material culture in all its forms in self-making. My focus on the consumption and production of material objects and media as social practices also facilitates my understanding of how they are internally differentiated and undertaken as forms of work and leisure in postindustrial self-formation. My approach here is also distinct from the large-scale integrative analysis of food production-consumption networks and commodity chains characteristic of agro-food studies in geography (Goodman 2002; Jackson et al. 2010), as well as celebratory theories of the consumer as an active and resistant "prosumer" or "produser" popular in discussions of digital cultures in media and cultural studies and sociology (Toffler 1980; Bruns 2007; Ritzer and Jurgenson 2010; Rousseau 2012a). While I share the integrative concern of this work in that I bring consumption and production together and show how they overlap, intersect, and connect in late modern self-formation, I argue that these categories are not as blurred as abstract postmodern theorizing may suggest. Rather, my ethnographic fieldwork reveals that the categories of consuming things and producing things are not understood as one and the same but hold different meanings and moral values in postindustrial processes of self-construction. In saying this, I am not suggesting that consumption and production are divided up or separated in people's lives; rather, they are closely interconnected and form part of the same making of the self. However, I am suggesting that ideas of consumption and production hold different values, and social practices are imbued with these meanings in late modern self-making. That is, shopping and fine dining are understood more as consumption, while cooking and blogging are understood more as production. The division of this book into practices of consumption and production functions as a heuristic device intended to highlight these different values and enhance our understanding of them, not to imply that these practices are separated in people's lives.

This book is not only concerned with how we make our self through material culture in postindustrial society but with how this relates to what I see as the new *moralities of self-making* that have emerged in the late modern era. While the term morality is often conflated with ethics, I do not understand them as one and the same. Following other work in material culture studies (D. Miller 2001a), I understand these terms less in relation to abstract philosophy and more ethnographically in relation to the way they circulate in ordinary people's lives, where ethics refers more to a direct concern for others—indeed, putting the interests of others before those of the self—and morality is concerned with more general values of good and bad, or right and wrong behavior. In this sense, ethics is more about others, whereas morality is more about the self. There has been a recent trend toward studying ethics, rather than moralities, driven largely by the growing concern with ethical consumption across the social sciences and humanities (Barnett et al. 2010; Lewis and Potter 2011; Carrier and Luetchford 2012). In contrast, my primary focus in this book is on moralities. While I address the question of ethics, most notably in relation to ethical consumption and shopping, it is not my core concern. Rather, I seek to place ethical consumption within a wider framework of moralities of self-making because the role of ethical and moral questions in self-formation today—and self-making through material culture—is not confined to ethical consumption. In fact, it extends beyond broader moralities of consumption (see Wilk 2001; Slater 2010). For as I have suggested, it is not just through the consumption of material culture that we make the self in late modernity but also through its production, which carries a higher moral value.

Our understanding of the moralities of late modern self-making needs to account for the complex and multifaceted role of production. In postindustrial society, the morality of production is so strong that it actually comes to shape consumption—and indeed, leisure in general—in self-making, as a result of the changing nature of work. In this book, I develop a new conceptual vocabulary to understand these emerging moralities of self-formation. The overarching concept that guides my understanding of the moralities of both consuming *and* producing material culture in postindustrial self-making is what I call the *moralities of productive leisure.* While the idea of work-like "productive leisure" or "serious leisure" has been richly theorized by historians (Gelber 1999) and sociologists (Stebbins 1979, 1992, 2007), its connection to theories of self-identity, material culture, and postindustrial society has not been explored, and its significance has largely been confined to the field of leisure studies.

The new moralities of productive leisure in self-making, I argue, are linked to the different relationship to material culture brought about by the changing nature of work in postindustrial societies. It is not just the lack of materiality

in modern work but also the primacy of knowledge that influences these moralities. For both (old) material production and (new) knowledge production
carry high moral values that infuse leisure. Indeed, the morality of knowledge
is central to postindustrial productive leisure, as it takes the form of what I
call *knowledge-based leisure*. This involves practices of learning and education, formal or informal. For many, it involves a material education; the acquisition and expression of knowledge of material objects, their consumption
and production, from material media. Learning about objects carries a higher
value than simply consuming them in these new moralities. But this morality of knowledge as a productive force comes to shape consumption too in
the form of *serious consumption*. This is considered a moral approach to consuming material objects in postindustrial self-formation because it is deeply
invested in knowledge and takes on work-like characteristics, and is central
to my understanding of contemporary moralities of consumption. But it is the
production of material culture in forms of *creative production* that carry the
highest moral value in self-making. These are both productive in the sense of
being knowledge-based as well as in the sense of actually making something,
whether it be material media or objects. The production of the latter in forms
of *manual leisure* is the most highly prized in late modern self-formation, as it
directly compensates for the loss of material production in work. Thus the moralities of productive leisure *guide* the new forms of self-making through material culture in postindustrial society: productive leisure is considered a *moral
approach* to shaping the self through material culture in a world where we no
longer do so at work. The concept of moralities of productive leisure constitutes an integrative theoretical framework for approaching both production
and consumption and operates as a conceptual bridge to understand how
they connect in new modes of self-making in late modernity. While this concept unites production and consumption, it maintains a recognition of the
different values they hold, which is essential to understanding postindustrial
moralities of self-making, and risks being eradicated by hybrid concepts that
conflate consumption and production.

Because it is so ordinary, material culture is often dismissed as insignifi-
cant. But what this book reveals is that material culture does matter, particularly in postindustrial self-formation. People strive to feel connected to the
material world. Material objects and media, and practices of consuming and
producing them in leisure, are not trivial but highly significant in people's lives
and play a vital role in creating and maintaining a sense of self in a runaway
world. The construction of the self through material culture I explore here is
not a superficial or frivolous process but rather a productive, reflexive, and
serious making of the self, riddled with moral anxieties. It is through their
negotiations with material culture that people face large moral questions of
self-formation in late modernity, of what is the right kind of self to shape. For

many, the production of material culture matters more and is felt to be more substantial and profound than simply its consumption. And for some, certain categories of material culture matter more. These new trends in postindustrial self-identity formation are exemplified by foodies.

FOODIES: AMATEURS, MATERIAL CULTURE, AND SELF-IDENTITY

The foodie is a self-identity that has gained significant popularity in postindustrial society. One might think of foodies as prime examples of consuming selves, as their material commodities of choice are not only consumed economically and symbolically but also literally, and as these goods are assimilated into their bodies, the goods become a material part of foodies' selves. The foodie's potential status as the paradigmatic consumer is further enhanced by the ways in which food cultures have become central to commodity and media cultures in the twenty-first century. This notion of the foodie as a consumer is certainly how this identity has been understood to date within both popular culture and academia.

The term foodie was coined in 1982 in the British style magazine *Harpers & Queen*. The article used the term to refer to a "cuisine poseur" who used sophisticated culinary consumption as a means of social distinction (Woods et al. 1982). Two years later, *Harpers & Queen* published *The Official Foodie Handbook* (1984), written by one of the authors of the original article, journalist Ann Barr, along with Paul Levy, food writer for the *Observer*. It located the foodie boom as spreading across multicultural Western societies, such as Britain, the United States, and Australia, and constructed foodies as consumers who use food as a status symbol in class distinction, as the cover declared: "Food is the opium of the stylish classes."

Josée Johnston and Shyon Baumann put forward a similar perspective in *Foodies: Democracy and Distinction in the Gourmet Foodscape* (2010), which concentrates on foodie discourse. Its main focus is professional food media, which is understood to be "the central point of production of foodie discourse," and is supported by discourse analysis of short questionnaire interviews with people from across the United States (2010: 108, 223). Johnston and Baumann draw on Pierre Bourdieu's (1984) theory of distinction to argue that foodies are consumers who are bound up in the pursuit and acquisition of status through their taste in food. They develop a theory of the foodie as a particular "kind of cultural consumer—the omnivore" (2010: 205). This focus on questions of consumption, taste, and status is an increasingly common approach to the study of food today (Hage 1997; Warde 1997; Warde et al. 1999; de Solier 2005; Naccarato and LeBesco 2012).

In contrast, in this book, I am not primarily concerned with sensational foodie culture as it is represented in the media but with how the identity of the foodie is lived by ordinary people in everyday life. My ethnographic research found that the foodie's self-formation through food could not be reduced to questions of consumption nor the superficial pursuit of status. Rather, it involves a much larger and more substantial process whereby people strive to form a meaningful and moral self through both the production and the consumption of material culture in forms of productive leisure in postindustrial society. This book argues that to understand foodies purely from the perspective of consumption would be to miss what matters to them most: the production of material culture in forms of productive leisure. I examine not just what foodies eat but what they do and why they do it through an in-depth study of their social practices. I explore how their practices of producing material culture (cooking and food blogging) and acquiring knowledge of objects (from material media) carry a higher moral value in their self-making than their practices of consuming material culture (dining out and shopping). This reflects an increasing suspicion of consumption as a form of self-making and also reflects the moralities of productive leisure that guide self-formation through material culture in postindustrial society.

Rather than simply understanding the foodie as a consumer, then, I develop a theory of the foodie as an *amateur*—a type of productive leisure identity—for whom both the production and consumption of material cultures of food are central to their self-formation. These amateurs adopt the work-like approach of professionals to their food leisure practices. Today, there is a blurring between amateurs and professionals in food cultures. Foodies are cooking technical haute cuisine dishes at home, establishing links with the suppliers of their ingredients, making informed judgments of restaurant cuisine, and publishing their recipes and restaurant reviews online. Most don't aspire to actually *be* professionals (unlike those on *MasterChef*, for example) but adopt a serious approach to and exert significant effort in their food practices. They frequently adopt the approach of chefs to their shopping and cooking and the approach of food critics and writers to dining and food blogging. Thus, even their consumption takes on a work-like approach as it too becomes productive leisure in the form of serious consumption, which can function as a way of negotiating the morally suspect status of consumption in self-formation. Of course, foodies are not all the same, and my informants participated in practices of consumption and production to different degrees according to their individual interests. The chapters in this book cover different types of foodies, from restaurant buffs and bloggers to produce enthusiasts and amateur cooks, and many of the most serious foodies crossed all categories. But what united the foodies in my research, regardless of the specific practices they participated in, was their professional approach as amateurs and their morality of productive leisure.

LOCAL FOODIES, GLOBAL IDENTITIES

Melbourne is like New York. It has that culture of foodies that are finicky, hard-ass and very possessive about their city.

—Gordon Ramsay (Linnell 2008)

I'd rather eat in Melbourne than Paris.

—Anthony Bourdain (Northover 2012)

Melbourne reminds me why I do what I do, why I enjoy all this food-related stuff.

—Heston Blumenthal (Blumenthal 2009)

This book makes an empirical contribution to the disciplines of sociology, anthropology, and cultural studies, as well as a theoretical one. It is based on ethnographic fieldwork I conducted with foodies in the city of Melbourne, Australia, between 2007 and 2009. Australia is a multicultural country with a population of 22 million people, 6 million of whom are migrants born in over 200 countries around the world (ABS 2011b). One of those migrants is my father, who was among the hundreds of thousands of people who moved to Australia from Europe following World War II. I grew up in Newcastle, a regional working-class postindustrial city two hours' drive north of Sydney. As an undergraduate student, I moved more than 1,000 kilometers south to Melbourne, where I have lived for the past fifteen years.

The capital of the state of Victoria, Melbourne is Australia's second largest city, with a population of around 4 million people. In 2012, it was judged to be the "world's most liveable city" for the second year running, but it is also one of the most expensive places in the world, with the cost of living about 40 percent higher than New York (Ferguson 2011; Hosking 2012). Melbourne has long been considered the most European of Australia's cities, distinguished from the sun and beaches of cities like Sydney, Perth, and Newcastle by its colder climate, wide Parisian-style boulevards and trademark trams, narrow cobblestone laneways filled with bars and cafes, and a population renowned for wearing black. Both the state and its citizens imagine Melbourne to be the "cultural capital" of Australia: "Our assets are our sophistication, diversity and reputation for cosmopolitan and cultural experiences...Melbourne is ranked as the lead Australian city associated with theatre, shopping, world class restaurants, cafes, bars and nightlife" (State Government of Victoria 2006: 12). It is also a UNESCO City of Literature, one of only five in the world.

Settled by Europeans in 1835, Melbourne's population grew rapidly in the early 1850s following the discovery of gold in Victoria, with an average of

90,000 people arriving from around the world each year during the height of the gold rush, including many from China (City of Melbourne 1997: 21). By the 1880s, it was one of the fastest growing and richest cities in the world, and it became the nation's capital between 1901 and 1927. The cultural landscape of Melbourne was transformed by successive waves of postwar migration, which is often credited with developing the city's food culture. Following World War II, over 160,000 Greeks migrated to Australia, with Melbourne having one of the largest Greek diaspora communities in the world; while by the early 1970s, there were over 120,000 Italians living in Victoria, many in the inner-Melbourne suburb of Carlton, whose main street remains the city's Little Italy, filled with Italian restaurants, delicatessens, and alfresco dining. More recently, much migration has come from Asia, primarily Vietnam, China, and India. In total, over 30 percent of Victorians were born overseas (Museum Victoria n.d.).

Melbourne provided an ideal site for a study of foodies, as it is also widely regarded by the Victorian state, its citizens, and tourists, as the "culinary capital" of Australia (Tourism Victoria n.d.). It has an international reputation as a leading food city among the world's top chefs, as shown by the quotations with which I began this section. Melbourne's gastronomic status is largely based on its number and diversity of restaurants that reflect its multicultural composition, yet it is also home to the nation's largest food festival (which included more than 300 events over twenty days in 2012), has the highest proportion of farmers' markets, and has a well-established system of food evaluation and foodie media. The city's 2011 *Good Food Guide* reviewed 665 fine dining restaurants serving more than thirty different ethnic cuisines (Apelgren 2010), while the 2010 *Foodies' Guide to Melbourne* reviewed more than 400 specialty food stores (Campion and Curtis 2009).

Unlike many scholars who write on food, I am not a foodie myself. This position provides a critical analytical distance from my subject, which scholars have found lacking in existing studies of foodies (see Clark 2011). I also refuse the romanticization, celebration, and even fetishization of food (and its practitioners) that can characterize some work in food studies. In order to understand foodies and how they see the world, I spent three years immersed in foodie culture in Melbourne. In a city of 4 million people, Melbourne's foodie community is large and dispersed. They belong to a "social world" that is "diffuse and amorphous in character," an "internally recognizable constellation of actors, organizations, events, and practices" (Unruh 1980: 277). Daniel Miller argues that when researching modern metropolises, the object of ethnographic inquiry has shifted from societies to individuals and households, where deep immersion is problematic and even gaining access can be difficult (2008: 296; 2009). I used a number of methods to access this dispersed urban community and recruit informants: I was introduced to members by a key contact in the foodie community, I left flyers in bookshops dedicated to food, and the city's chief food critic published a story on my research in the leading news publication targeted to foodies (the *Epicure* food supplement in *The Age* broadsheet). This latter approach may account for the taste for mainstream food media displayed by my informants; however, this proclivity appears to be something they share in common with foodies elsewhere (see Johnston and Baumann 2010). My informants, then, were self-selected and self-identified foodies.

My fieldwork took me into the homes of foodies—in particular, into their kitchens, where they cooked, and to their dining tables, where we ate. The kitchen is one of the most important spaces for foodies, where they make and remake their identities through the productive practice of cooking. It is a space full of memories and meaning, fundamental to their sense of self. My research took me to their bookshelves, which house their often large collections of cookbooks, food magazines, and folders with printouts from food websites and handwritten recipes. It allowed me to see their eyes light up with excitement as they showed me their collections, pulling cookbooks off the shelf one by one, pointing out their favorite recipes, telling me about the chefs who wrote the books, or explaining how they'd come to acquire a particular book—describing the "social lives" of these material things (Appadurai 1986). In addition to exploring how foodie selves were shaped in the private sphere, my fieldwork also explored the foodie's relationship with food in the public sphere. This fieldwork took me to restaurants and cafes with foodies to explore their public consumption and judgments of cuisine; to farmers' markets and food and wine festivals, where Melbourne's large foodie community comes together; and online to foodie blogs and social media, which increasingly connect this community.

Food media, such as cookbooks, restaurant guides, television cooking shows, and food websites, have become popular topics in academia in recent years (Bonner 1994, 2009; T. Miller 2001, 2007; de Solier 2005, 2008, 2010; Polan 2011). Most work on food media—particularly in cultural and media studies and sociology—focuses on the text, using discourse or textual analysis (Hollows 2003a,b; Collins 2009; Johnston and Baumann 2010; Naccarato and LeBesco 2012; Rousseau 2012a,b). In contrast, in this book, I take an ethnographic approach to food media, seeking to understand what people do with media, not just what messages media communicate. My ethnography provides rare data on how people perceive and use a range of food media in their daily lives and practices. I examine how foodies consume a wide array of professional food media, from cookbooks and restaurant guides to television cooking shows and online recipe websites. Where most research focuses on the experts of professional media, such as food writers and TV chefs, I focus on the audiences who use such media and how they use it.

While there is much speculation within the scholarly literature (and popular culture) about the influence of such media on the everyday food decisions and culinary skills of their audiences, my research provides rare empirical evidence of the media's actual impact on people's lives. Professional food media were particularly important to the foodies in my study because such media provided the main way in which they acquired material knowledge of food consumption and production to guide them in their self-formation. In addition to exploring the consumption of professional media, I use the technique of digital ethnography—pioneered in social anthropology in recent years (Miller and Slater 2000; Horst and Miller 2012)—to explore how foodies also produce their own amateur food media in the form of blogs. Finally, rather than considering food media in isolation, in this book, I consider both professional and amateur food media as forms of material media in relation to debates about "lifestyle media" (Brunsdon 2003; Lewis 2008a; Rosenberg 2008b).

In addition to participant observation, my research also included in-depth interviews, which have been advocated as particularly productive for ethnographies of food and urban cultures (see Hockey 2002; Counihan in Miller and Deutsch 2009). Twenty foodies (ten women and ten men) participated in interviews that were semi-structured and conversational, allowing individuals to focus on their particular interests and practices; these interviews lasted for between one and three hours. My questions revolved around meals, cooking, shopping, dining out, and media. They also formed the basis of a qualitative open-ended questionnaire that was completed by a further thirty foodies (twenty-three women and seven men), which plays a supportive role to my primary ethnographic research.

The subjects of this book reveal the foodie to be an elected self-identity that operates across social categories of identity, such as gender, age, race, and ethnicity. Where historical identities such as the gourmand and the gourmet were more masculine, the category of the foodie encompasses both men and women. It is an identity that disrupts normative gender relations in terms of the sexual division of labor in food provision and preparation. The women and men in my research ranged in age from early twenties to late sixties. They also came from a variety of ethnic backgrounds—from Anglo-Australian, British, and American to Italian, Greek, and French to Chinese, Sri Lankan, and Thai—and a significant number were first-generation migrants. Indeed, among the younger generation, Anglo-Australians were the minority. Thus, I found the foodie identity was not exclusive to white people. Where this identity is less diverse, however, is in terms of class. My informants were, in general, middle class, mostly members of the new middle class or knowledge class. As a group, they were highly educated. The large majority had tertiary qualifications, and a substantial minority were undertaking or had completed postgraduate qualifications. They worked in a range of white-collar occupations in government, business and academia. The majority earned incomes above the national average, with a substantial minority earning double. They were predominantly urban, with the large majority living in gentrified inner-city suburbs. In the interest of anonymity, I have replaced their names with pseudonyms. My research findings are conveyed through the presentation of these various individuals, yet as is common in ethnographies, some discussions focus on key informants who played a central role in the fieldwork and are therefore given a more prominent role in my discussion (see Counihan 2004; D. Miller 2009).

While my ethnographic research was conducted in the culturally specific context of Melbourne, and therefore necessarily has local dimensions, this setting nevertheless shares many similarities with urban food cultures in other postindustrial, multicultural Western societies, most notably the United Kingdom and the United States. The trends I examine are not unique to Australia but are a part of global trends in food cultures and identities. Moreover, food is a field in which Australia is recognized as leading current trends and shaping such cultures as global. As the British food writer William Black observes, "the unashamedly cosmopolitan cultures of Australia, the USA and to some extent Great Britain have created a food culture that reflects the decline of the national, or perhaps the dominance of the global" (2007: 3–4).

Likewise, the foodie is not an Australian identity but an increasingly global one found across many countries and cultures. It is a product of globalization and transnational flows of food, tastes, media, capital, and people. This globality is highlighted by the multicultural makeup of the foodie identity in Melbourne, as reflected in the range of ethnicities of my informants. It is also manifested in the cosmopolitan nature of the foodie taste formation that I explore in Chapter 3. This cosmopolitan taste is something that differentiates foodies from other kinds of food enthusiasts—in particular, those whose love of food is an expression of their ethnic, regional or national identity, such as the Tuscans studied by Carole Counihan. She describes how their love of food is confined to their own cuisine, which they consider "the best," and argues that this "culinary chauvinism" is common to the identities of many in Italy (Counihan 2004: 20), as it is in France (Schehr and Weiss 2001). Where food chauvinists express distaste and even revulsion towards other cuisines, foodies embrace these cuisines: I found that foodies' love of food encompasses a diverse range of other ethnic and national cuisines, and their favorite cuisine is generally not that of their cultural heritage. Thus for foodies, their ethnicity or national identity isn't the defining feature of their relationship with food. Yet nor is their cosmopolitanism, as the taste for culinary difference has become increasingly common in multicultural societies, particularly among the middle class. Rather, what distinguishes foodies, I argue, is the productive and professional approach they take to the consumption and production of food and food media as amateurs, which epitomizes the new moralities of self-making in postindustrial society.

OVERVIEW OF THE BOOK

The book incorporates my ethnographic research into each chapter in order to develop a "grounded theory" (Glaser and Strauss 1967) of self-making through material culture, which places the lived experiences of real people at the fore-front. In the opening chapter, I take up the moralities of productive leisure that govern the new approach to both the consumption and the production of material culture in postindustrial self-formation. I contextualize these new moralities within theories of leisure, including the historical development of productive leisure and rational recreation as moral forms of leisure targeted to the working class in industrial modernity. Next, I consider how such work-like leisure has become popular among the middle class in postindustrial modernity—the predicted leisure society—particularly as a moral approach to using material culture in self-making. I explore how, in the case of the foodie, this productive leisure takes the form of the amateur, whose work-like and professional approach constitutes a moral way of shaping the self through the love of a material object, food, and functions as both a form of care of the self and the care of others. I situate contemporary productive leisure within theories of postindustrial society as a knowledge society and argue that the role of knowledge as the new force of production has not only come to define work but also to define postindustrial productive leisure as knowledge-based leisure. I show how the morality of knowledge shapes the approach taken to material culture in self-formation, which involves acquiring a mate-rial education in both the consumption and production of objects, and in the foodie's case, can be considered a *gastronomic education.*

Chapter 2 examines the material media from which people acquire this education in their postindustrial self-making. I theorize material media as a subcategory of lifestyle media—popular media focused upon the individual self—that concentrate on the connection between material objects and the self. I intervene in current theoretical debates about material lifestyle media in general—and food media in particular—that understand these media ei-ther purely as entertainment texts or as texts whose pedagogical functions are limited to educating audiences in material commodity consumption as a moral process of self-improvement. In contrast, I argue that material media are educational texts that not only teach audiences how to consume material objects but how to improve the self by producing objects in productive leisure; I also argue that the latter is represented as having a higher moral value in self-formation. I examine the lifestyle experts of material media, including food experts such as celebrity TV chefs, restaurant critics, and food writers, within theories of expert systems in late modernity, and I argue that people place trust in such experts to guide them in their self-formation through objects because of the decline of traditional social structures, such as the family. I examine which forms of material media foodies use—and trust—in their self-formation through food in productive leisure, exploring their perceptions of print media (such as cookbooks, food magazines, and restaurant guides), television (such as cooking shows and food documentaries), and digital media (such as online recipes, restaurant reviews, and food blogs) as sources of material knowledge in their gastronomic education.

Having established the overall importance of moralities of productive leisure—and the centrality of knowledge and material media within them—to how both the consumption and the production of material culture are used in self-making in postindustrial society, the remainder of the book tackles these latter two processes. Chapters 3 to 5 focus on consumption, which is the key concept through which theories of self-formation have understood our relationship with material culture to date. I argue that the morality of making a self through the consumption of material objects has been placed in question in postindustrial society with the spread of anticonsumerism among the educated middle class, and this has led to an increasing importance for many people on shaping what is felt to be a moral self through the consumption of material culture. I explore how this self is shaped in a variety of ways and social practices.

In Chapter 3, I take up the question of taste, which constitutes the main theoretical framework through which scholars have understood the role of material culture in self-formation in postindustrial consumer society. I argue that the new moralities of self-making involve constructing what people believe to be a moral self through their taste in material objects. For foodies, this involves the construction of the self as an omnivore of food in contrast to snobs such as gourmets, whose elitist taste is considered immoral. However, I argue that most foodies are not true omnivores because they consume highbrow haute cuisine and middlebrow "authentic" ethnic cuisine but repudiate lowbrow industrial and processed foods from supermarket chains and fast food outlets. As well as examining foodies' taste in food, I also examine their taste in food media; I show how they favor print publications and television programs that are also highbrow and middlebrow, as well as instructional and educational, which reflects their moral approach to consuming material media as knowledge-based productive leisure. While existing textual analysis of material lifestyle media has suggested that this form of media teaches audiences good taste, I provide empirical evidence of how foodies actually acquire such taste from the experts of material media rather than the family as a means of self-improvement. However, I argue that while acquiring good taste from the media may make one a better person in these new modes of self-making, acquiring it purely for instrumental purposes of status, and displaying it conspicuously, certainly does not. I show how the foodie's self-formation involves a strong belief in the *immorality of distinction* that is negotiated through moralities of productive leisure by shaping the self as an amateur with a deep and serious commitment to food rather than a consumer in search of status. I conclude that theories of taste and distinction are limited in their ability to understand the new moralities of consumption in self-making, because these moralities are shaped not only by *what* people consume but *how* they consume as productive leisure.

The next two chapters explore this question of modes of consumption by examining different social practices of consuming material culture. In Chapter 4, I examine dining out, which has been relatively overlooked in material culture studies and food studies to date. I explore how people negotiate anxieties over the moral status of consumption in self-formation in a number of ways. The first is through the selection of which categories of material objects are deemed more appropriate for self-making. For foodies, food is seen as holding a higher moral value for self-formation than other objects, such as clothes, which are often perceived as superficial. The second is through the level of consumption that is considered proper. I show how, for foodies, the consumption of food in fine dining restaurants must be restricted through moral regimes of asceticism because it is a luxury product and therefore morally suspect. However, I argue that people negotiate anxieties over consumerism and materialism not only through which objects they consume, and what level they consume, but importantly, through how they consume. I draw on theories of social practice and leisure to develop the concept of serious consumption to describe a moral approach to consuming objects as a form of productive leisure, one which is knowledge-based and work-like, and in the case of amateurs, such as foodies, involves emulating professionals. I show how this knowledge-based serious mode of consuming is central to the moral approach foodies take to the consumption of luxury food in restaurants. This involves the work of acquiring knowledge about both the production and the consumption of such food from material media as well as the deployment of this knowledge in restaurants as foodies shape their selves as amateur restaurant critics rather than conspicuous consumers. I explore this in relation to molecular gastronomy restaurants, where this serious and knowledge-based approach to consumption in dining reaches its zenith.

In Chapter 5, I examine shopping, the practice that has received the greatest scholarly attention in accounts of consumption and self-identity to date. I show how the mode of serious consumption as productive leisure is also deployed by people as a moral approach to consuming objects within this social practice in the new forms of self-making in postindustrial society. I explore how foodies adopt this mode in their food shopping, as they take a work-like approach that emulates professional chefs by going to significant effort to source produce from multiple alternative suppliers and acquire knowledge of food production to guide their consumption. Yet where their serious dining is governed by a moral asceticism designed to restrict consumption and spend less money, their serious shopping is governed by a *morality of quality* that involves a willingness to spend more money, because while both constitute forms of luxury consumption, only fine dining is regarded as such by foodies; in contrast, they consider buying expensive, quality food for the home to not only be right but to be a necessity. I explore this morality of quality in relation to theories of moral, political, and ethical consumption. I show how it is linked to a politics of consumption that is opposed to the global industrial food system and seeks to re-embed shopping in local contexts and social relations, a politics that is associated with the Slow Food movement. I examine how these issues of morality and politics connect to questions of ethical consumption, surrounding concerns for the environment and labor. However, I argue that in the case of foodies, such political and ethical concerns are ultimately subordinated to the morality of quality (food) that governs their serious shopping and its use in their self-making. Thus, while recent research has concentrated on ethical consumption, my research suggests that questions of morality are of utmost importance in the formation of selves through the consumption of material culture in postindustrial society.

But the argument developed in this book is that people do not just shape a reflexive DIY self through the consumption of material culture, as the existing literature suggests. Rather, I argue that if we want to understand how people construct an individual self through material culture in a postindustrial society where they no longer produce objects at work, we also need to examine how people increasingly produce material culture in productive leisure, a process that has been overlooked by scholars to date. The production of material culture is of crucial importance in late modern self-formation because it holds a higher moral value and is considered a more substantial way of connecting to the material world than simply consuming it. Thus, having explored the existing understanding of the relationship between material culture and the self through the realm of consumption, in the final three chapters, I turn my attention to the realm of production. This follows my discussion of consumption because the social practices of the production of material culture that I examine build upon the practices of consumption within self-formation: that is, the production of food in cooking builds upon the consumption of ingredients in shopping, while the production of food media in blogging builds upon the consumption of restaurant cuisine in fine dining (by writing reviews), as well as the production of food in cooking (through documenting recipes).

Before examining these social practices directly, in Chapter 6, I explore how material media promote the production of objects as a means of self-formation and self-improvement and educate audiences in the moralities of productive leisure that guide the new modes of self-making through material culture in a postindustrial world. Where most scholars argue that material media in general—and food media in particular—no longer teach audiences to produce things but merely to consume them, I argue that both producing objects and acquiring the skills to do so are often central to the models of self-improvement and self-actualization such media promote and are represented as having a higher moral value than consumption in this process. Moreover, while it is commonly assumed that audiences no longer acquire practical knowledge or productive skills from such media, I show, through an in-depth analysis of how they use cookbooks and television cooking shows in their everyday lives, that people such as foodies actually *do* acquire a practical education in material production. I argue that such material media are not just forms of "food porn" but are practical educational texts, as my ethnographic research found these texts to be the primary source of culinary education for foodies. Indeed, material media are integral to how many people learn to produce objects in postindustrial society because we no longer acquire such skills in work (or increasingly, the family). These media provide the main way many of us acquire skills in material production to use to craft the self in a late modern world.

The next two chapters explore how people use different social practices of the production of material culture in their self-formation. In Chapter 7, I explore the main form this takes: the manual production of material objects in productive leisure. I argue that this practice is of utmost importance in self-making through material culture for many people in postindustrial society, because they do not have an opportunity to produce objects at work, and they believe it is a more substantial and moral way of shaping the self than simply by consuming objects. For foodies, being a producer of food holds a higher moral value than being a consumer, and the way they achieve this is through cooking. I explore how cooking as a moral practice in foodies' self-making involves not only a belief that one should produce food but also that one should produce it *as* productive leisure—and produce it from scratch—as they emulate the approach of professional chefs to their home cooking. I develop the concept of creative production to describe how practices such as cooking hold significant appeal for people not only because they provide an opportunity to produce things but also because they provide an outlet for creative expression, both of which are felt by many to be missing in postindustrial work. I draw on theories of craft to explore how the particular type of creative production offered by cooking—like other practices such as DIY, gardening, or knitting—is one that allows people to make something material, and make it with their hands. I conceptualize this as a form of manual leisure that people pursue in part as a balance to their mental labor.

In the final chapter, I explore the newest forms of the production of material culture that people are using in their self-formation in postindustrial society: the digital production of amateur material media, such as food blogs, in productive leisure. I argue that like the production of objects, this is of vital importance to many people as a way of connecting to the material world in a nonconsumptive manner, and it holds a higher moral value in self-formation than the consumption of professional media because it involves sharing knowledge, not just acquiring it. I show how it too is experienced as a form of creative production that fulfills a need to engage in such activities missing in postindustrial work—but in this case, it is the digital creative production of material media rather than the manual creative production of material objects. I draw on theories of new media to show how these amateur material media blur the distinction that is commonly made between personal and public blogs because they serve both a personal function of documenting the blogger's self-formation through a material object and a public function of sharing the blogger's knowledge and lifestyle advice on this object with others. Like professional material media, amateur food blogs share knowledge and advice on both the production of objects (culinary blogging) and the consumption of objects (restaurant blogging). Where the former allows foodies to share the knowledge and skills they have acquired in their culinary education, it is in the latter that these amateurs come closest to approximating professionals in their productive leisure, as they shape public tastes and influence consumer behavior. I show how this has led to struggles between amateurs and professionals over expertise in material objects in late modernity.

Finally, in the Afterword, I reflect on what it means to be postindustrial and show how the evidence presented in this book challenges and reconfigures current understandings of postindustrial society as the consumer society, leisure society, and knowledge society. The purpose of this book is to explore how and why people make the self—and increasingly, a moral self—through material culture in postindustrial late modernity.

1

Moralities of Productive Leisure and Material Culture

The commonsense understanding of leisure is that it is the opposite of work. Within this binary distinction, work is associated with production, while leisure is associated with consumption. In the first theory of leisure, Thorstein Veblen defined it as the abstention from productive work. He suggested that pre-industrial feudal societies were separated into a wealthy "leisure class," whose time was spent engaging in "conspicuous consumption," and a working class, whose time was spent in manual labor (1934: 1–2). Cultural historian Steven Gelber (1999), on the other hand, argues that work and leisure were integrated in preindustrial societies, and that the real division between them came with industrialization in capitalist modernity and the separation of time into "work time" and "leisure time." Work time was the time of production in the new industrial factories, and leisure time became the time of consumption in the new commodity cultures.

However, Gelber argues that at the very moment that work and leisure were separated under industrialism, leisure was colonized by the work ethic in the form of "productive leisure." The new leisure time of the industrial working class was perceived as a behavioral and ideological threat by middle-class reformers, who responded by restricting access to "inappropriate" activities and encouraging the "productive use of free time" in forms of work-like leisure (1999: 2–3). Gelber focuses on the case of hobbies—in particular, craft and collecting—as forms of productive leisure, which were promoted by the guardians of public morality in the United States as a means of keeping the working class busy, inside their homes, and out of mischief. The working class was to remain productive in their spare time through making and collecting material objects. Thus productive leisure transfers the Protestant work ethic and its morality across into the sphere of leisure.

Peter Bailey (1978) traces a similar history of the morality of productive leisure in Victorian England. He focuses on the campaign for Rational Recreation, which was part of broader movements for temperance and educational reform that sought the moral and social improvement of the industrial working class. Bailey argues that the leisure time of this class "constituted a problem whose solution required the building of a new social conformity—a play discipline to complement the work discipline that was the principal means of social control in an industrial capitalist society" (1978: 5). Middle-class reformers encouraged the working class to spend their spare time more productively by learning things rather than consuming things—drinking and feasting—and provided "alternative recreations which stimulated and restored the mind rather than merely debilitated the body" (1978: 36). The working class was encouraged to participate in "improving" and educational forms of leisure, such as visiting libraries, museums, art galleries, and reading rooms, which blended "study with recreation," and education with entertainment (1978: 48).

Just as industrialism led to significant shifts in the nature of leisure in the nineteenth century, so postindustrialism was envisaged to lead to major social changes in leisure in the twentieth century. In the 1970s, many predicted that postindustrial society would be a "leisure society"—characterized by shorter work weeks, extra vacations, and job sharing—as a result of a projected decline in the economy and the number of jobs (Jenkins and Sherman 1979). However, in the early twenty-first century—despite the global financial crisis—this leisure society has not materialized in the form predicted. Most people in postindustrial societies continue to work long hours: in 2011, Australians worked an average of 1,693 hours a year, compared with 1,625 in the United Kingdom and 1,787 in the United States (OECD 2012). Yet despite these levels of work, many people are still seeking to engage in productive and work-like forms of leisure in their spare time, as they carry over this work ethic into their leisure. It is productive leisure that has taken hold in postindustrial society rather than play.

Sociologist Robert Stebbins has conducted a significant body of ethnographic research into these work-like forms of leisure in late modernity. He theorizes them as forms of "serious leisure," which includes amateur, hobbyist, and volunteer activities that a person finds so substantial, interesting, and fulfilling that they embark on a project of acquiring and expressing its special knowledge, skills, and experience (2007: 5, 1982). His research includes studies of amateur archeologists, astronomers, actors, musicians, and sportspeople. Stebbins distinguishes serious leisure from "casual leisure" and "project-based leisure." Casual leisure, he argues, is a relatively short-lived pleasurable activity, which is immediately and intrinsically rewarding, and requires little or no special training, such as a stroll in the park. Project-based leisure, on the other hand, is a one-off or occasional short-term creative undertaking that is reasonably complicated, such as redecorating a bedroom, which in some cases leads to a serious leisure career in the activity (2007: 5).

While there are no accurate statistics that measure productive leisure activities, in North America, Stebbins estimates that around 20 percent of people participate in some form of serious leisure (2007: 134), while Gelber suggests that around 10 to 15 percent of adults have hobbies (1999: 31). Charles Leadbeater and Paul Miller suggest the figure may be far higher in the United Kingdom, with up to 58 percent of the population participating in some form of amateur activity (2004: 29). This includes at least 4,500 independent archeologists, tens of thousands of amateur ornithologists, and 387,000 family historians (Finnegan 2005: 4). In Australia, the national Bureau of Statistics found that over 2.7 million adults were involved in hobby activities (ABS 2011a).

Where productive leisure was originally imposed on the working class by middle-class reformers as a means of moral improvement, today it is increasingly the leisure of choice among the middle class themselves (Leadbeater and Miller 2004; Campbell 2005; Stebbins 2007). This stands in contrast to C. Wright Mills's suggestion that because of the seriousness of their work, the leisure of white-collar workers has to be unserious as a form of compensation (1956: 236). It is more likely a result, in part, of the fact that "white-collar workers more often engage in leisure that replicates attitudes and worldviews typical of their vocations" (Gelber 1999: 18). In this sense, productive leisure—in general—can be considered a form of "spillover leisure" (Wilensky 1960: 544) as it carries over the morality of the work ethic, along with workplace skills and values (although the particular forms it takes often have crucial compensatory dimensions, as I will explore). But I would argue that the rise of productive leisure as a means of working on and improving the self is also a response to processes of individualization and the compulsion to create a life of one's own in neoliberal society, where as Nikolas Rose puts it, "the individual is to become, as it were, an entrepreneur of itself, seeking to maximize its own powers, its own happiness, its own quality of life, through enhancing its autonomy and then instrumentalizing its autonomous choices in the service of its lifestyle" (1992: 150–51). In particular, because of its work-like nature, productive leisure provides a moral approach to creating an individual self through material culture in leisure in a postindustrial world where there are few opportunities to do so in work.

AMATOR: ONE WHO LOVES

The etymological root of amateur is *amator,* meaning "one who loves" (Stebbins 1979: 30). Today, it also refers more specifically to someone who pursues as leisure an activity that others perform as work. Both these senses of the term are encapsulated in the self-making of foodies: they are defined by their love of a specific genre of material culture—food—as well as their professional approach to food practices during their leisure time. Amateurism is a particular kind of productive leisure, one which is not just work-like, but actually emulates professional practices. Stebbins distinguishes amateurs from hobbyists on the basis that amateur pursuits have professional counterparts, whereas hobbies do not; indeed, hobbyists often pursue activities that bear little or no resemblance to regular work roles (1992: 11, 2007: 6–8). Not only do amateurs possess professional counterparts, they are strongly influenced by them; they interact with and develop relationships with them, either in person or via media.

While they may not reproduce professional practices as directly as other forms of amateurs, such as those in sport or theater, the foodie's pursuit of food as an amateur activity is characterized by the centrality of professional experts to their leisure and their emulation of the professional approach to this form of material culture in their self-making. Their formation of the self as an amateur is considered a moral approach to material culture—as opposed to simply being a consumer—because it is serious and work-like. Foodies do not just like eating out, but look to professional critics for guidance in the choice of restaurant, adopt the critics' approach to analyzing the quality of the meal, and in some cases, publish their own reviews on the Internet. They do not simply enjoy cooking in their spare time; they enjoy preparing the recipes of haute cuisine chefs and go to significant effort to source their ingredients from multiple suppliers with whom they develop strong relationships. Production is central to their professional approach to material culture, as is knowledge. Like professionals, foodies are driven by the pursuit of food knowledge, and they acquire most of it from such professionals via food media. They are not just interested in learning about their own cuisine, but about all cuisines.

Foodies possess what I call a *productive leisure ethic*, which shapes their approach to material culture in self-formation. This is not simply a "Protestant leisure ethic," the belief that leisure time should not be spent idly but in constructive pursuits (Clarke and Crichter 1985: 5), although this does form its broader foundation. More specifically, the productive leisure ethic refers to the higher moral value placed on producing and learning about material culture over simply consuming it in self-formation, in the context of postindustrial consumer culture and middle-class anxieties over materialism, combined with the decline of material production in work. Yet this concept also describes how the consumption of material culture itself comes to take on productive and work-like forms in leisure as a way of alleviating such anxieties.

Amateurism, as a form of productive leisure, involves high levels of commitment and the investment of large amounts of time and energy. For foodies, this is invested in a particular form of material culture. Just as professionals have a career in food, so do amateurs—what Stebbins (2007: 5) calls a "leisure career," which similarly involves the acquisition and expression of knowledge, skills, and experience over a long span of time. The foodies in my ethnography were all, by and large, what Stebbins would call "pure amateurs" (1979: 36), people who have never seriously held or pursued professional aspirations—as opposed to "pre-professionals," who seek a professional career in food, like many of the contestants on *MasterChef*. While some of my informants expressed a desire to shape the self as a food professional, this desire functioned more as an occupational daydream than as a serious plan. These daydreams covered a variety of occupations, from being a chef (Beth), food critic (Mathew), or restaurateur (Sam), to being a butcher (George), baker (Ruth), or food historian (Jeff). However, the large majority had not made any serious attempt at pursuing professions related to their food interests, as they already had established occupations in other fields. Most were happy to keep these practices as leisure, not work. Becoming a chef, the most common occupational fantasy, was often offset by the recognition of the difficult nature of chefs' work, including long hours and stressful environments, an unromanticized view of those who continue to make the self through material production in work. Yet it may also have been a result of the lower status of this job as a skilled trade, rather than a middle-class profession. Nevertheless, there was a pervasive fear that pursuing their interest in a professional manner would make it "too serious" and take the pleasure out of it. For example, Nick was a marketing analyst in his twenties, who had recently returned to study to undertake his master's degree. After discovering a passion for cooking since completing his undergraduate degree, he had considered changing careers, but ultimately decided that "I enjoy cooking too much to want to ruin that by making it a profession." Rosa, who was in her early thirties, had made the most serious attempt to pursue a career as a chef, undertaking several months of an apprenticeship the previous year, before returning to a career in the public service. As she put it, "I decided that I wanted to keep my obsession as my passion and not my profession." Thus, being a foodie is about developing a moral approach to material culture in self-formation through work-like leisure, rather than work.

For foodies, the material culture of food constitutes what Robert Dubin calls a "central life interest" (CLI). He argues that "a committed gardener, stamp collector, opera buff, jet setter, cook...are all usually devoted to their activity as a central life interest. Give such individuals a chance to talk freely about themselves and they will quickly reveal their CLI through fixation on the subject and obvious emotional fervor with which they talk about it" (1992: 42). This was evident in my encounters with foodies. When I met Sam, a social worker in his early fifties, he described how he had a central life interest in food, saying "my interest, my passion, my obsession in the world—it's not sport, it's not gardening, it's about food and all of the things that are associated with it." He described how this drove him to read cookbooks in bed, take sourdough "mother" (starter dough) on holidays, take responsibility for the cooking in his home, and "hunt for that obscure ingredient which will make a difference to a dish." He said, "I suspect my thirst for food knowledge drives my wife mad in view of the hundreds of cookbooks and recipe cuttings I have accumulated in our spare room over many years." As she had recently said to him, "You're just wired for food, you're wired for food." The intense commitment to an amateur pursuit as a central life interest—whether focused on a form of material culture or otherwise—leads to what Stebbins calls its potential "uncontrollability," where it is so attractive that it threatens to take up more and more of the participant's time and energy (2007: 69–70). Other people, such as partners, friends, or strangers, sometimes find it difficult to understand the commitment amateurs display toward their chosen pursuits. As Sam said when describing his "obsession," "I know I'm starting to sound like a madman." In his ethnographic research, Gary Alan Fine similarly found that amateur mushroomers, who also shaped their selves through the material culture of food, felt they would potentially be perceived by others as mad. He refers to this as "Fine's Law of Shared Madness," whereby "groups often present to observers and one another the knowing claim that they are 'crazy,' 'mad,' or 'addicted,'" as a form of defense (1998: 208).

So why do people spend such time and energy engaging in work-like forms of leisure with material culture, particularly when they work such long hours in their paid jobs? While it may appear "mad" to others, most of my informants felt that their serious commitment to food—as productive leisure—played a central role not just in forming a moral self through material culture, but also in contributing to their sense of personal wellbeing and happiness. Many described being a foodie as "extremely important" to them—not for purposes of social distinction or cache, but for their overall physical and psychological wellbeing. Their food-related productive leisure, I argue, can be considered a form of what Foucault (1986) calls "the care of the self." This involves taking care of, and cultivating, one's soul. As Foucault observes, the goal of the care of the self is to "live most happily" (1986: 45). The positive emotional states linked to the foodie's love of food help to achieve this goal. As Theresa, who was an account manager in her thirties, put it, "being a foodie is part of my life, my personality and my wellbeing. It would be a sadder, greyer existence if I wasn't a foodie." Another informant, John, was in his fifties and worked in property development. He described how he had decided to pursue an interest in food as a form of care of the self at a very difficult and sad point in his life:

When the marriage ended, which was just over a decade ago, I made a conscious decision that I was going to have some fun with food...So it became a hobby really. It was something I could do, you know. I found life hard sometimes being on my own, but it was something I could do, close the world out, and I could do, and feel good about it.

The care of the self, as Foucault observes, involves "doing things"; it involves "the work of oneself on oneself" (1986: 51):

> It takes time...This time is not empty; it is filled with exercises, practical tasks, various activities. Taking care of oneself is not a rest cure. There is the care of the body to consider, health regimens, physical exercises without overexertion, the carefully measured satisfaction of needs. There are the meditations, the readings, the notes that one takes on books or on the conversations one has heard, notes that one reads again later, the recollection of truths that one knows already but that need to be more fully adapted to one's own life. (1986: 50–51)

The various activities that foodies participate in based around the material culture of food, such as cooking, sourcing produce, eating, reading, note-taking, and thinking about food, all contribute to this care of the self. The pursuit of knowledge is central to this regime. As Foucault argues, "educating oneself and taking care of oneself are interconnected activities" (1986: 55). This is highlighted in the words of Amelia, who was in her early twenties and worked in communications. She said, "I think I know heaps. But I don't go on and on about it, so my friends wouldn't necessarily know how much I knew—or care. I just like knowing about restaurants, chefs, recipes, ingredients etcetera for myself." This is considered a moral approach to material knowledge in self-formation. Likewise, Anne stressed how this education was important just for herself, as she said: "I seem to retain the most trivial information if it's food-related, like all the names of unusual vegetables, or chefs' names...It is important to me but I think to a lot of people, it's not." The acquisition of a material education, then, is seen as central to the care of the self. While Foucault examines the care of the self in the early Roman Empire, the incitement that one must "take care of the self" assumes particular force today within the privatized Do-It-Yourself philosophy of neoliberal governance, in which the care of the self is increasingly one's own responsibility, not that of the state (see Rose 1992; Beck and Beck-Gernsheim 2001; Rosenberg 2005, 2011b; T. Miller 2007).

However, despite this increasing trend toward privatization and individualization, central to the morality of the foodie's productive leisure approach to material culture is that it operates not only as a form of care of the self, but in many cases, it is also a form of care for others. For as Daniel Miller argues, the decline of the social has not led, as many critics have feared, to a situation of "isolated individuals, defined through choices—whether of commodities or of a political party" (2008: 285). His ethnographic research on modern life in London finds "limited evidence of any belief in, or cult of, the individual *per se*" (2008: 285). Instead, the decline of the social has led to the importance of significant and fulfilling relationships: relationships with other people and relationships with material things. Indeed, he argues that the two are inseparable: objects are central to our relationships with other people in late modernity (2008: 287).

For foodies, the material culture of food is central to their relationships with other people and to their systems of care. As Olivia put it, foodies are "interested in food as a social medium for interaction with others." My informants used food as a medium to develop relationships with food professionals and fellow foodies, as well as to enhance their personal relationships. Several of them had formed or joined dining groups with fellow foodies— some via Twitter—where they would regularly visit restaurants together. This included Nick, who formed a group that would go to a restaurant every few weeks, visiting one expensive restaurant and then two less expensive to balance the spending and retain a moral approach to consumption. It also included Lynette, a retiree in her sixties, who organized a dining group among her friends. While wealthy herself, the group included a friend who had fallen on hard times, so they established a set budget of twenty-five dollars for two courses, and Lynette used her knowledge of local restaurants and researched special lunch menus at fine dining restaurants to work within this budget.

In addition to consuming food together, or commensality, producing food for others was an important form of sociability for those in my research, and similarly central to their moral approach to food in self-formation. As Sam put it, "it's the connection and the relationship—the cooking is a medium that brings people together, whether it be friends, or whether it be your partner." Since her husband had died, Olivia—who was in her early sixties and worked as an executive assistant—cooked regularly for friends, both entertaining them in her own home and taking food to them in theirs. Cooking was seen as a form of care for others, as Celina said: "putting a lot of effort into a meal prepared for someone is an expression of love and caring towards them, in my opinion." A senior manager, she spent around an hour after work each night preparing dinner to share with her husband. For some, it was not just cooking for others, but cooking *with* them, that was central to their relationship. This was the case for John in his new marriage (to his childhood sweetheart), where food was no longer just part of the care of the self, but as he described it, "an important part of the shared pleasure of being together." His wife, Elena, said "we have a lot of fun cooking together." She compared this to her previous marriage, where she cooked alone. While she enjoyed cooking then, she said:

> It wasn't like what John and I do. Because we interact, we chat...John gets home from work before I do, and when I come home, he sort of has planned what we're having for dinner. And then we have a glass of wine, a glass of soda water, and

we sit down and talk about the day, and I chop, and you know, it's just part of what we do!

Another informant, Ruth, regularly stayed up late at night baking food to take in to work the next day, which she saw as a form of care for her colleagues, and a way of creating a sense of community and belonging in the workplace (a government department). She would send an email around to her colleagues when she arrived at work, inviting them to come to the "bakery table" next to her desk to share the food and hear about the "history of the dish." For example, one of her emails announced that "today we have freshly made Cinnamon and Cardamom Buns (Finnish), Yoghurt, Semolina and Rose Water Cake (Cyprus), and Bourekia (Deep fried ricotta, cinnamon and orange blossom water pastries) (Cyprus)." For many of the female foodies in my study who were mothers, cooking was also seen as a form of nurturing children. Of course, this notion of expressing love and care through cooking has been ideologically ingrained in women, particularly through the media. However, it highlights the fact that the foodie's love of food does not come at the expense of a love of people. The moralities of productive leisure that guide the use of material culture in self-formation, then, are not just about the individual self, but are also central to establishing and maintaining relationships with others through material culture.

PRODUCTION, MATERIAL CULTURE, AND KNOWLEDGE: WORK AND KNOWLEDGE-BASED LEISURE

When productive leisure emerged in industrial modernity, most people's work involved producing material objects. Today, this is no longer the case. While it may not have led to a post-work leisure society, postindustrialism has led to significant changes in the nature of work. The obvious links between work and production have been deteriorating, as more and more people no longer make or produce things at work. It is often assumed that production matters less in self-formation as a result, its place usurped by consumption (Featherstone 1991; Lury 1996; Baudrillard 1998). However, I argue that production matters more in different ways, as these changes in the relationship to material culture in work explain the increasing resonance and particular modalities of productive leisure in postindustrial self-formation. Productive leisure takes on new force and meaning in people's lives today because of the changing nature of work and production—in particular, the decline of material production work.

In postindustrial societies, work is not defined by the absence of production but by a different type of production—not of material things but of knowledge. As Jean-François Lyotard argues, "knowledge has become the principal force of production" (1984: 5). For this reason, postindustrial society is often thought of as the "knowledge society" in which notions of production and productivity are increasingly tied to knowledge rather than materiality. The composition of the workforce has changed significantly in postindustrial societies, with the shift away from manual labor and material production toward mental labor and knowledge production. As well as outsourcing manufacturing to developing countries, the knowledge society developed on the back of changes in the distribution of knowledge—in particular, the rise of mass tertiary education. In Australia, this was fuelled by the abolition of university fees from the mid-1970s to the late 1980s, after which subsidized fees and a government loan system were implemented. Australia now has one of the highest rates of tertiary graduation in the world at 50 percent in 2006, compared to 39 percent in the United Kingdom and 36 percent in the United States (OECD 2010). The rise of tertiary education fuelled the expansion of the new middle class, or what John Frow has termed the "knowledge class," made up of people with tertiary qualifications whose work is based upon "the possession and exercise of knowledge" (1995: 111).

This raises the issue of what counts as knowledge. For knowledge itself is not a neutral term (Finnegan 2005) but is invested in systems of power and exclusivity, attaching different values to different types of knowledge and their possessors. Frow argues that the designation of workers as members of the knowledge class depends on what is socially defined as knowledge and knowledge work (1995: 90). Applied technical knowledge, or skill—while clearly a specialized form of expertise in late modernity—is not included in this formulation, for as Frow observes, the "ideology of rationalized, 'scientific' management was decisive in this respect in that it defined 'manual' workers as lacking in relevant knowledge" (1995: 119). Therefore practical knowledge of material production does not count as socially recognized "knowledge." Nicos Poulantzas argues that the distinction between mental and manual labor is ideological, for "every kind of work includes 'mental activity,'" but "not every kind of work is located on the mental labour side in the politico-ideological division between mental and manual labour" (1975: 254). Thus, although manual occupations clearly involve mental labor (for example, problem solving in carpentry) and mental occupations clearly involve skills (for example, skills in information technology), a hierarchy of value exists between knowledge and skill in which "knowledge" is that possessed by the middle class of mental laborers, and "skill" is that possessed by the working class of manual laborers. Knowledge, then, is central to class politics in postindustrial society.

While research on the knowledge society has concentrated on this realm of knowledge work, the changing nature of work and production in postindustrial society has also had a significant effect on leisure. It is not just the decline of the material from work but also the rise of knowledge that is central to shaping the particular forms taken by postindustrial moralities of productive leisure in self-making. Indeed, the primacy of knowledge in notions of production today has taken hold in productive leisure as well as work: the central characteristic of postindustrial productive leisure, I argue, is that it is *knowledge-based leisure*. The morality of acquiring and expressing knowledge is carried over from work into leisure, particularly among the knowledge class. This is the spill-over dimension. The compensatory dimension is the type of knowledge that is acquired and expressed in leisure, as opposed to work. Much of this takes the form of material knowledge, which is not found in work. Knowledge-based leisure includes learning about material culture, acquiring a *material education*. This is essential to the formation of the self through material culture. We must learn about material objects if we are to incorporate them in self-making, and the main way we do so is via material media. These media teach us how to consume material objects, and, importantly, they also teach us how to produce them, as we no longer acquire such knowledge in work. This is a key difference between my concept of knowledge-based leisure and that of knowledge work. Where knowledge work excludes manual skill, knowledge-based leisure includes it, for this form of practical knowledge carries a high moral value in productive leisure, particularly among the knowledge class.

But knowledge-based leisure, as I understand it, does not just include the acquisition of knowledge—of how to consume and produce material culture—in these practices of material education. It also includes the expression of knowledge in practices of consuming and producing material culture. This is central to the morality of such practices in self-formation. As I will explore, the consumption of material culture takes on a moral form in self-making through serious consumption that is knowledge-based and work-like. The production of material culture in forms of creative production is similarly knowledge-based, yet it carries additional moral value because it is also productive in a more literal sense of making things and compensates for the lack of opportunity to do so in postindustrial work. In particular, the production of material objects in forms of manual leisure carries an especially high value in postindustrial moralities of productive leisure because it is felt to compensate for the loss of material production in work. Thus the effect of changes in the nature of work on postindustrial productive leisure includes not only the rise of knowledge-based leisure but the rise of creative production and manual leisure. Production carries meaning in productive leisure both in the old sense of materiality and in the new sense of knowledge. But before considering these practices of consumption and production in self-formation, we need to understand the practice of material education that provides the foundation for both.

MATERIAL EDUCATION: FOOD FOR THOUGHT

Foodies pursue a particular type of material education based around food, which I call "gastronomic education" (see also de Solier 2010). In the early nineteenth century, the amateur food scholar Jean-Anthelme Brillat-Savarin defined gastronomy as the knowledge of everything related to food (1970: 52). It is in this sense that I use the term here to describe the education of foodies as a leisure pursuit, which is the same sense in which it has recently been used to describe formal education in food studies in universities (Santich 2002). I use the term gastronomic to highlight the variety of knowledge that foodies acquire, both theoretical and practical, which relates to both the production and consumption of material cultures of food. In addition to culinary skills and taste formations, it includes knowledge of restaurants, chefs, cuisines, ingredients, producers, suppliers, food history, anthropology, and food media, as well as skills such as judging or photographing food, writing restaurant reviews, or designing and maintaining a food blog.

The pursuit of knowledge is central to the foodie's morality of productive leisure as an amateur and to their care of the self, as we have seen. This gastronomic education was something that was shared by all the informants in my research, regardless of the particular practices of consuming or producing material cultures of food in which they deployed such knowledge. For example, Surat was one of only two of my informants who did not regularly cook; rather, his self-formation as a foodie was shaped through the consumption of food in fine dining and the production of food media through blogging. While he did not acquire practical knowledge and culinary skills, he nevertheless spent a significant amount of his spare time reading cookbooks and magazines in order to understand how dishes were made, and then he applied this knowledge to analyze and interpret the dishes he consumed in restaurants, in the manner of a critic. Thus, the morality of acquiring and deploying material knowledge was central to his self-formation through food in productive leisure. Almost all of my informants, however, also acquired manual culinary skills, which they applied in cooking. Unlike in the labor market, there is not a hierarchy between knowledge and manual skill in the foodie's productive leisure, or if there is, it is weighted in favor of the latter, as culinary skills are highly prized by those who possess them.

This project of gastronomic education was thought about reflexively by many foodies in terms of its role in their self-formation through material culture. For example, as Madeleine put it: "By calling myself a foodie, I'm referring to the fact that I take a particular interest in food, and that I think about it in a constructive way, with a desire to become more educated about it, rather than just eating for the sake of it." This educational approach to food as material culture is framed as a more moral approach than simply consuming food.

Madeleine felt that this education, and being a foodie more generally, was "critically important" in her life. It provided a stable basis and identity where she had yet to develop one in work. After graduating with an arts degree, she had worked as a manager in administration but had recently resigned and returned to further study. Now in her late twenties, she was:

> spending a lot of time pondering what it is I want to do. I still don't know the answer to that from an employment perspective, but when I think about what I'm interested in, food is number one on the list. The consumption and preparation of it, being knowledgeable about how it's sourced, are really significant to me.

It was important for Madeleine to spend her spare time in food-related productive leisure pursuits, which at this point were more significant to her self-identity than work.

Sam also thought reflexively about his material education in food. For him, as for many foodies, it was a process of "lifelong learning"; a lifelong project of the self. He described how he began this gastronomic education and his career as a foodie as a young boy in the 1960s:

> I think I was actually aware of, I already had an awareness of an interest in food—probably my earliest memory was around ten years old, because I was already cooking then. And I mean given that I'm fifty-three now, when you think about boys cooking in those days, it was actually a bit odd. It was a bit like, you know, boys doing ballet, or boys doing sewing, or boys—it wasn't something—I mean my parents were okay with it, but it wasn't something that I necessarily advertised.

Sam went on to describe the four decades that he has invested in this leisure career so far and his anticipation of the years to come, in what he considers his unfinished (or unfinishable) project of gastronomic education:

> It's a work in progress, there will never be an end, I'll probably continue to be, in all likelihood, learning things until the day I drop off the earth. And that's exciting, knowing that it's never going to get to the point where I know it all, but it's a fantastic point in my life where I have a level of confidence that I can put my hand to pretty well anything I want to cook.

For Sam, as for many foodies, this project of material education in food is clearly a "project of the self" (Giddens 1991: 5), as it is intimately tied to his sense of self and his life—past, present, and future. His project of gastronomic education is one of self-development and self-improvement through food and knowledge. Sam is reflexive about the significant time and effort he has had to invest in this project. This leads to a sense of satisfaction and achievement with the time and labor expended when his knowledge is validated. For example, when discussing a television cooking show, Sam described how, while the host "presents it in three and a half minutes, it might have taken me twenty-five years to get there, but it's still validating knowing that I've got it."

Another informant, Anne, was in her mid-thirties and worked as an e-media specialist. She described how she understood her gastronomic education as a form of knowledge-based leisure: "I think that it's an education that sits outside of work and career...It's not necessarily professional training, you're self-taught. And I think that when you have a passion for it you often do teach yourself through reading, or trying different recipes, things like that." Some of the knowledge foodies possess may be acquired through adult education, such as cooking classes, as well as from friends and fellow foodies. However, most of their gastronomic education is acquired from professionals via material media.

2

Learning Things: Material Media and Gastronomic Education

The media are among the central forces shaping individual selves in late modernity. This is particularly the case for "lifestyle media", a category of popular media that focuses on the self, and more specifically, the moral process of self-improvement. It operates as a neoliberal "technology of the self" (Foucault 1988) that offers citizens guidance and instruction in how to make and maximize individual selves. Lifestyle media trains people to construct a "reflexive project of the self" (Giddens 1991: 5), requiring continual self-examination and self-improvement. This mode of individual identity formation is highly valorized in neoliberal capitalist societies. In such privatized societies where the state is increasingly reluctant to govern, the "management and care of the self becomes an imperative in different, and arguably more urgent ways... in terms of obliging citizens to actualize and 'maximize' themselves" (Ouellette and Hay 2008: 12). The neoliberal subjects that are the target—and product—of lifestyle media are "more responsible for creating their own individuality than ever before," as reflexive self-fashioning has increasingly become not a choice but "a requirement of personal and professional achievement" amongst the middle class (T. Miller 2006: 112, 116). Lifestyle media guide us in the moral process of self-improvement, in "what we should be, who we should *become* and how we should manage our lives" (Raisborough 2011: 5; original emphasis). They are part of a dispersed network of technologies of neoliberal citizenship geared to self-actualization and self-improvement, which aid audiences with techniques for shaping and guiding themselves (Ouellette and Hay 2008: 3–4).

Material objects are central to this process. One of the main subcategories of lifestyle media is what I call *material media*. These media focus on material objects, such as food *(The Naked Chef)*, clothes *(What Not to Wear)*, homes *(Changing Rooms)*, gardens *(Ground Force)*, and cars *(Top Gear)*. They guide audiences in how to make and improve the self through material objects in postindustrial society. Such media have been overlooked in material culture studies to date, being the focus instead of lifestyle media studies, as the former field has tended to concentrate on the relationship between people and material objects themselves. In contrast, I include material media alongside objects as part of my understanding of material culture in late modernity, as I argue that these media are central to how objects are used in postindustrial self-formation, playing a crucial role in guiding individuals in this process and educating them in material knowledge. Rather than focusing on food media in isolation, then, as is common in food studies (Johnston and Baumann 2010; Naccarato and LeBesco 2012; Rousseau 2012a,b), in this book, I examine food media as a form of material media within wider debates on lifestyle media in order to explore broader social questions regarding material culture and the self. I also examine it ethnographically, in contrast to the textual and discourse analysis of existing work on food media. Here, I begin by interrogating debates about material media within lifestyle media studies; I then examine how foodies use different forms of material media—print food media, food television, and digital food media—in their gastronomic education and self-formation.

Most research and debates about material lifestyle media have occurred in relation to television, and I focus on this literature here. The key debates circulate around two interconnected issues: first, the role of such media as forms of entertainment or education, and second, their promotion of models of selfhood and self-improvement based around the consumption or the production of material objects. There is a particular focus on how contemporary material media in postindustrial society differ from their antecedents in industrial society in these two respects. Charlotte Brunsdon's work provides a good overview of these debates for my purposes here. She places the origins of material lifestyle television in the "hobby programming" or productive leisure programming of industrial society in the 1950s and 1960s (2003: 6). She identifies a broad generic shift from traditional informational hobby television—screened during the daytime—to the newer forms of lifestyle television that have taken over prime-time schedules in postindustrial society since the turn of the century. Brunsdon describes the traditional type of hobby programming as employing a "realist mode," which was more explicitly instructive, and targeted an audience of amateur enthusiasts whom it sought to educate in skills of material production, such as cooking, gardening, dressmaking, and DIY (2003: 10; 2004: 119).

While Brunsdon observes that this realist mode is continued in some contemporary programs, she argues that most of the newer material lifestyle programs operate in a "melodramatic mode" that focuses on entertainment and spectacle and addresses viewers as consumers (2003: 10). In this new mode, self-improvement as a moral process is to come through consuming material objects rather than acquiring practical skills and producing objects. This melodramatic mode is epitomized by the makeover format, which has received the greatest amount of scholarly attention (Moseley 2000; Heller 2006, 2007; Jones 2008; Palmer 2008; Lewis 2009; Weber 2009; Raisborough 2011).

In contrast to the more realist mode, where an expert delivers advice directly to viewers, makeovers are a form of reality television in which experts transform the material possessions or bodies of "ordinary people", following a narrative structure of before and after, with the melodramatic climax of the reveal scene.

Thus the material lifestyle media of postindustrial society are commonly understood to differ from the earlier informational or hobby media of industrial society in two key ways: first, in their focus on entertainment over education, and second, in their focus on the consumption of material objects as opposed to their production in models of self-formation and self-improvement. This suggests that in industrial society, such media sought to educate us in material production, whereas in postindustrial society, they seek to entertain us with material consumption. In terms of food television, this has been summed up by Michael Pollan (2009) as the "historical drift of cooking programs—from a genuine interest in producing food yourself to the spectacle of merely consuming it." I want to unpack these two intersecting claims about material lifestyle media more closely in relation to "culinary television" (de Solier 2005).

MATERIAL MEDIA: ENTERTAINMENT OR EDUCATION?

The claim that postindustrial material lifestyle programs are more concerned with entertainment and spectacle than they were in the industrial past has been made quite vehemently in relation to cooking shows, within academia and the media alike. Phebe Chao, for example, argues that "cook shows have become entertainment; the cooks, stars with recognizable personalities and names," and that such programs "belong with the category of spectator sports; they are no longer really about viewers becoming better cooks" (1998: 19, 27). Similarly, Signe Rousseau argues that postwar TV cookery is characterized by "a move from the educational and informative to the entertaining and vicarious," and that "food channels have become the perfect platforms for manufacturing celebrity chefs and for turning food into a spectator sport" (2012b: 13, 17; see also Adema 2000; Chan 2003; Pollan 2009).

The field of food television as a whole has certainly become more entertainment-driven since the 1990s, yet this is largely due to its diversification through hybrid formats, such as game shows *(Ready Steady Cook)*, reality docu-soaps *(Jamie's Kitchen)*, and reality culinary contests *(MasterChef)*. Interestingly, it is these hybrid formats that have transformed the face of food television in postindustrial society rather than the makeover, which has transformed—and all but replaced—other genres of material television, such as DIY and gardening programs (Moseley 2000; Brunsdon 2003; Rosenberg 2008a,b). In contrast to gardening and DIY makeovers, such as *Ground Force* and *Changing Rooms,* most cooking shows still conform to a version of the traditional format where an expert delivers instructions directly to viewers. Cooking shows do operate through what I have previously called a "transformative aesthetic" that displays the transmutation of food not merely from raw ingredients into a cooked dish (Lévi-Strauss 1969) but, importantly, from raw ingredients into a *stylized* dish (see de Solier 2005: 467). However, cooking shows are distinctly different to makeover shows, as they are generally not reality formats built around ordinary people or their material belongings but formats built around the expert figure of the TV chef.

As I have explored in depth elsewhere (de Solier 2005, 2008), some recent cooking shows have placed a high emphasis on entertainment, often through focusing on the personalities of presenter-experts and processes of celebritization. Graeme Turner argues that "celebritization" refers to the process whereby attention shifts from a person's public role to their private life (2004: 8). In cooking shows, this involves the inclusion of scenes of the TV chef's personal life, such as in the programs of Jamie Oliver and Nigella Lawson from Britain and Kylie Kwong and Bill Granger from Australia (see Moseley 2001; Hollows 2003a,b; de Solier 2005). Such culinary television overlaps with makeover television in its use of drama and personal narratives.

However, this emphasis on entertainment and celebrity in cooking shows is not new or unique to postindustrial society; rather, it was a central feature of some of the earliest cooking programs in industrial modernity. As Frances Bonner has observed, programs organized around the personality of the TV chef have been screening since soon after television began (2005: 39). Fanny Craddock's program *Fanny's Kitchen* began in Britain in 1955. Craddock was famous for cooking while wearing ball-gowns and for her extroverted personality. Her program also featured her husband Johnnie, which "gestured to the inclusion of family members we think of as a recent trend" (Bonner 2005: 39). Dana Polan argues that cooking shows mediated education through strategies of entertainment from the start (2011: 9). Julia Child's *The French Chef,* which debuted in the United States in 1963, was clearly instructional and educational, yet as Polan argues, it was also humorous, wacky, and fun through "the larger-than-life, entertaining spectacle bound up in the dynamic figure of Julia Child" (2011: 4). Australia's earliest cooking show, *Entertaining with Kerr,* also placed a high emphasis on entertainment and celebrity, as its name suggests. It screened during prime-time on commercial television from 1965 and was hosted by British-born Graham Kerr, described in the program's advertisements as an "entertaining raconteur" (Bonner 2009: 349). When Kerr moved to Canada in 1969, his show was renamed *The Galloping Gourmet,* which incorporated his private life through scenes with his wife Treena where they sought to entertain audiences through dramatic sketches. It was filmed in front of a live studio audience—which is also thought of as a recent trend with shows such as America's *Emeril Live*—and screened in thirty-eight countries, including Australia, the United States, and the United Kingdom, as Kerr became the best known internationally of all early TV chefs (Bonner 2005: 39). While some contemporary cooking shows in postindustrial society continue this tradition, others are far less entertainment-driven than Kerr's programs in the 1960s. This includes programs such as those of Delia Smith and Rick Stein in the United Kingdom, Ming Tsai and Lidia Bastianich in the United States, and Maggie Beer and Donna Hay in Australia (see also de Solier 2008). Thus, while the notion of a straightforward historical trajectory from instructional programming in industrial modernity to entertainment programming in postindustrial modernity may hold true for other genres of material lifestyle television, such as gardening and DIY, it does not for cooking.

Following the claim that contemporary cooking shows are more concerned with entertainment and spectacle, there is an assumption that audiences in postindustrial society no longer learn—or even want to learn—from these material media but simply want to be entertained by celebrities (Chao 1998; Adema 2000; Pollan 2009). For example, Chao argues that "the audience watches cook shows for entertainment," and that learning "how to cook specific dishes, honing one's own culinary abilities, or becoming an accomplished cook no longer seem of primary importance to many cook-show viewers" (1998: 27, 23). Caroline Dover and Annette Hill, some of the few scholars to have conducted research amongst audiences of material lifestyle television, argue that such research is particularly valuable for "challenging assumptions of lifestyle viewers based on textual analysis" (2007: 24). For as de Certeau argues, we cannot assume from the text itself what audiences want from it or do with it; rather, we need to conduct ethnographic research to understand the uses to which texts are put: "The presence and circulation of a representation...tells us nothing about what it is for its users. We must first analyze its manipulation by users who are not its makers. Only then can we gauge the difference or similarity between the production of the image and the secondary production hidden in the process of its utilization" (1984: xiii).

In contrast to Chao's claim, my ethnographic research found that foodies *do* watch cooking shows primarily to learn; education, not entertainment, was of utmost importance in material media for these postindustrial individuals. Moreover, this knowledge-based approach was considered a moral approach to consuming these forms of material media in foodies' self-formation. As Tim summarized, "I enjoy watching TV cooking shows, but I am more interested in facts than being entertained." In a similar manner, Raymond declared, "I don't watch to be entertained"; rather, he watched such programs for "relaxation and information"—as a form of productive leisure. While for some of my informants entertainment was secondary, to others, such as Raymond, entertainment and celebrity were not liked at all: "Jamie doesn't appeal to me . . . nor does Nigella. I'm more a Rick Stein or Maggie Beer type. They are more interested in the food than themselves." For foodies, the material object is of prime importance in material media rather than the celebrity self. Leah, who also liked Rick Stein, was highly critical of other TV chefs, such as Jamie Oliver and Nigella Lawson, whose emphasis on the celebrity self she found immoral: "I'm not interested in their kids or their baby! That's nice! Good for them, really, but it's just self-promotion and they are too self-absorbed."

As I explore further in the following chapter, while most of my informants watched the instructional realist mode of cooking shows, only some watched the more entertainment-oriented programs. For those who did, however, the focus on the material object was still more important than the celebrity self, as Emma—a fan of Jamie Oliver—put it: "I am interested in what and how they cook, not their private lives." Similarly, Madeleine, who also watched Jamie Oliver's programs, said, "I'm not so interested in learning about his life as I am in learning about how he prepares food." In terms of de Certeau's distinction, these responses by foodies highlight the difference between the production of the text as entertainment-oriented and celebritized and the secondary production in its utilization by foodies who incorporate it into their moralities of productive leisure and pursuit of material education. This evidence stands in contrast to the perspective of critics such as Chao, who assume that in order for material media, such as cooking shows, to educate their viewers, these media need to be couched in explicitly instructional—rather than entertaining—modes of representation, as if they cannot both entertain *and* educate. My informants acquired material knowledge of food from both more instructional programs, such as those of Rick Stein, and more entertainment-oriented programs, such as those of Jamie Oliver. Thus, in postindustrial society, material media, such as cooking shows, are not just entertainment texts but educational texts. However, what exactly do their audiences learn?

MORALITIES OF MATERIAL MEDIA: IMPROVING THE SELF THROUGH CONSUMING OR PRODUCING THINGS?

The second argument about material lifestyle media in postindustrial society suggests that if these media do educate viewers, it is only, or primarily, in how to construct and improve the self through consuming material objects rather than through producing them, like the hobby media of industrial modernity. Much of the recent research on material lifestyle television has focused on the issue of consumption (Bell and Hollows 2005, 2006). Scholars have highlighted how such programs address their audiences as consumers rather than citizens, or as hybrid consumer-citizens (Bonner 2000; Moseley 2001; T. Miller 2007). Most material lifestyle programs either implicitly or explicitly promote commodity consumption and the idea that selves are formed—and improved—through consuming material things. Guy Redden argues that such programs depict a "moral vision of consumption," as an act leading to self-improvement (2007: 152). The acquisition of "good taste" and its deployment in commodity consumption is central to the ideology of self-improvement within such media (see de Solier 2005). The promotion of material consumption as a means of improving the self is particularly strong in makeover television in which one's body, clothes, home, or garden is improved through commodities (Moseley 2000; Heller 2006, 2007; T. Miller 2008; Rosenberg 2008b). Product placements are central to such programs, which some argue function primarily as platforms to advertise goods and services (Deery 2006). However, while most material lifestyle programs are invested in a logic of consumption, this is not to say that they all promote rampant consumerism and materialistic forms of selfhood. As Buck Rosenberg argues, most home makeover programs "work not within a sphere of uncontrolled consumption but within a discourse of thrift," by offering guidance on "renovation on a budget" (2008b: 508).

Cooking shows may not use the makeover format, yet they still advance the idea that one can become a better person through the consumption of the "right" ingredients. While product placements have been central to some cooking shows—Delia Smith and Jamie Oliver's commercial relationships with Sainsbury's in the United Kingdom, for example, or Iain Hewitson's relationship with Bi-Lo supermarkets in Australia—most programs increasingly promote a middle-class taste for nonbranded fresh ingredients. Indeed, taste is one of the main forms of consumer knowledge in which food programs educate their viewers (de Solier 2005). For they do not promote consuming food indiscriminately; rather, they advocate disciplined and selective modes of consumption in self-formation (de Solier 2008). While many cooking shows advocate the selective consumption of expensive gourmet ingredients as the path to self-improvement, others promote an ideology of thrift (de Solier 2005). In addition, the incorporation of scenes of the TV chef shopping for food—their representation as a consumer—promotes the belief that leisure time should be spent consuming and that consumption is fundamental to modern lifestyles and identities. Moreover, commodification is central to cooking shows, through the release of spin-off merchandise such as cookbooks, DVDs, cookware, gourmet food lines, and other commodities by TV chefs, who become what Turner (2004: 34) calls "celebrity-commodities."

However, this logic of material consumption was also common to some postwar hobby media in industrial modernity. It was in this era that hobbies became commercialized, as "the center of hobby activity shifted from education, government, and employee recreation programs to companies that made hobby supplies and hobby shops that sold them for a profit...what made the post-war hobby world new was the intense commodification of the process" (Gelber 1999: 53). Indeed, the logic of consumption as a path to self-improvement was also central to postwar cooking shows, as one of their main goals was to advertise products to viewers. Dana Polan argues that a constant concern of postwar food shows was how to integrate product placements with the cookery demonstration. In some cases, the hosts affixed brand names to every ingredient and every appliance; in others, they dramatized fictional scenarios in which the host narrated his or her personal discovery of the branded product (2011: 52). Toby Miller has highlighted how Julia Child's hobby programs began as product platforms: "Her first appearance in 1962 was an attempt to promote sales of her book *Mastering the Art of French Cooking,*" while later the "San Francisco station KQED sold her cooking knives as its first membership gifts" (2007: 125). Teaching viewers to consume, then, as a means of self-formation and self-improvement, is not an innovation of contemporary material media.

Moreover, I argue that in postindustrial society, some forms of material media—in particular, those focusing on cooking, gardening, and DIY—continue to teach audiences to construct and improve the self through the production of material objects, as well as their consumption. These material media address audiences as producers, not just consumers, and advocate the idea that leisure time should also be spent participating in creative production: in building a shed, growing vegetables, or cooking a meal. They encourage audiences to engage in these activities as forms of productive leisure, to spend their spare time not just consuming material things, but also producing them, and acquiring the knowledge and manual skills required to do so. They not only promote the values of consumption, then, but also those of industriousness and productivity, which are integral to contemporary capitalism, as they encourage viewers to carry over their work ethic into their leisure time. Hence, while consumption is represented as leading to self-improvement during leisure, I argue that producing material things—such as cooking a meal from scratch—and acquiring the skills to do so, is represented as morally superior to simply consuming things—such as takeaways or ready-made meals—and if you can grow your own ingredients, even better. The notion of self-improvement in these material media thus remains one of skill acquisition: if you learn to cook, or to cook *this* dish, you will be a better person. In the case of culinary television, then, there is greater continuity between the hobby media of industrial modernity and the material lifestyle media of postindustrial modernity than is commonly thought to be the case. The production of material objects such as food is represented as a way of connecting with the material world that is more substantial than just consuming it. Hence, material media, such as cooking shows, promote the new moralities of productive leisure that guide self-formation through material objects in postindustrial society.

Thus, where existing understandings of material lifestyle media suggest that it teaches audiences to construct and improve the self through the consumption of material objects, I argue that it also teaches them to do so through the production of material objects, and that this productive leisure is represented as carrying a higher moral value in self-formation than consumption. My ethnography found that foodies acquire knowledge and skills related to both the consumption and production of food from material media in their project of gastronomic education. I explore this in detail in the chapters that follow; in particular, Chapter 3 examines how foodies acquire knowledge of material consumption and taste, and Chapter 6 explores how they acquire knowledge of material production and practical skills. Here, I examine who it is that foodies learn from via material lifestyle media, before exploring which forms of media they use in their gastronomic education.

GASTRONOMES AND FOODIES: EXPERTS, AMATEURS, AND MEDIATED RELATIONSHIPS

A central feature of lifestyle media is the figure of the expert. It is these lifestyle experts who teach audiences how to shape and maximize individual selves through material objects. Giddens has highlighted the expansion of "expert systems" in late modernity. He argues that modern systems of expertise depend on the possession of specialized knowledge and skills. With the abundance of information in postindustrial knowledge society, one can only "be an expert in one or two small corners of modern knowledge systems" (1991: 30). The rise of professionals is linked to such systems of expertise, as they "hold wide knowledge of a specialized technique," and are recognized by laypeople and amateurs as having authority based on such knowledge (Stebbins 1979: 24).

Giddens emphasizes the pervasiveness of systems of expertise in late modernity as these systems come to govern more areas of our everyday life, from personal relationships to food and cooking (1991: 18). Tania Lewis (2008a) has focused on the development of such "ordinary" forms of expertise. She suggests that in the past, the term "expert" was generally reserved for individuals such as scientists, doctors, and lawyers whose specialized professional knowledge was far removed from the realm of ordinary, lay knowledge. However, Lewis observes that in late modernity, "skills and knowledges associated with everyday life and with 'ordinary people'...are becoming valued as forms of expertise in their own right" (2008a: 2). She argues that there has recently been a proliferation of such forms of "popular" or "ordinary" expertise in the media, and more specifically, lifestyle media. This is epitomized by the mediated lifestyle expert, a "familiar and seemingly reliable figure" who "offers easy how-to guides to choosing between and managing optimal lifestyles in a context of growing complexity and information overload" (Lewis 2008a: 12; see also Smith 2010).

The experts of material lifestyle media are experts in particular genres of material objects. In this book, I use the term "gastronome" to refer more specifically to mediated food experts, such as TV chefs, food writers, and restaurant critics. This is a broader sense than that of Stephen Mennell (1996: 267), who uses it to describe a person who possesses refined taste in food and educates others in such taste via print publications. My conception of the gastronome extends this expert beyond print media to television and digital media. It also extends the gastronome's role beyond taste education to include an education in food production as well as consumption, for gastronomy refers to the knowledge of everything to do with food.

Expert guidance becomes central to the construction of reflexive or DIY selves in late modernity. As traditional social structures decline, people increasingly look to experts for advice and instruction in everyday living, whether it is the guidance of therapists or TV chefs. Such experts take on crucial importance in postindustrial societies dominated by information, commodities, and risk: expert advice functions as a risk-minimization mechanism that guides people toward the best—or most reliable—information (recipe) or goods (food). Experts perform an important ordering function, clearing a path for people through the forest of knowledge and commodities.

Mediated food experts, or gastronomes, play an integral role in people's self-formation as foodies, and in particular, in their material education, as they constitute the main professionals from whom foodies acquire knowledge and skills. While the relationships amateur foodies have with these food professionals may be mediated, they are nonetheless experienced by my informants as meaningful relationships that are crucial to their self-making through material culture. These relationships are characterized by a sense of intimacy; my informants often referred to such experts by their first name in conversations—as simply "Jamie" or "Nigella"—as one refers to friends. This sense of intimacy is a common feature of relationships with celebrities in late modernity, as one feels a connection with such individuals, however one-sided (Turner 2004).

Like interpersonal relationships, these mediated relationships with experts are based on trust. Because expert systems are "abstract systems" that disembed knowledge from local social relations and face-to-face interactions and rearticulate them across time and space, trust is integral to interacting with such systems, as it "generates that 'leap into faith' which practical engagement demands" (Giddens 1991: 3). Many scholars have highlighted the lack of trust in—and increasing skepticism toward—experts in late modernity, as a result of the decline of grand narratives, competing voices of authority, and continually revised "truths" (Lyotard 1984; Bauman 1987; Giddens 1991). However, my research found that foodies run counter to this trend, as they display a significant amount of trust and faith in experts, whom they rely on for their material education. This expertise may be based on qualifications and training, such as that of the credentialed haute cuisine chef, or on generations of experience—and often the mediation of tradition—such as that of the uncredentialed family-taught professional chef. The experts of material media thus play a key role in guiding self-formation through material objects such as food in late modernity.

Yet it is important to note that foodies do develop their own amateur "local knowledge" (Geertz 1983) of food, through the adoption, negotiation, co-optation, and rearticulation of professional expert knowledge. For while one can only be an expert in one or two small corners of modern knowledge systems, one may develop this expertise in leisure, as well as work. Foodies develop forms of amateur-expertise in food that depend on lengthy training and specialization during their leisure time. Indeed, some even become mediated food experts, or amateur gastronomes, sharing their knowledge of this object with others by producing their own material media in the form of a food blog.

FOODIES, MATERIAL MEDIA, AND GASTRONOMIC EDUCATION

What forms of material media do foodies use? Which forms are central to their self-formation through food and their education in this material object? Are some considered more respectable than others? Where most research on lifestyle media concentrates on only one medium—and in most cases, on television—throughout this book, I explore foodies' use of a wide variety of material lifestyle media: of print media, television, and digital media. Here, I introduce these different mediums and consider how foodies perceive them in terms of their gastronomic education, before exploring the specific roles they play in foodie self-formation in the chapters that follow.

PRINT FOOD MEDIA

The print medium is the oldest form of mass food media. It is also the only form of this category of material media that is also a material object. Cookbooks were among the earliest printed books (Mennell 1996). They began to target home cooks as early as the mid-eighteenth century with Hannah Glasse's *The Art of Cookery, Made Plain and Easy* (1747), but it was *Beeton's Book of Household Management* (1861) by Isabella ("Mrs.") Beeton that achieved mass popularity, selling 60,000 copies in its first year (Langland

1995: 32). The profession of food journalism stretches back to the work of Alexandre Balthazar Laurent Grimod de la Reynière in early nineteenth-century Paris, whose original *Almanach des Gourmands* (1803) contained the first restaurant guide and sold out at 20,000 copies (Gigante 2005: 2). Later, in 1825, came Brillat-Savarin's amateur monograph *La Physiologie du Gout,* translated as *The Physiology of Taste* (1970), which combined lifestyle guidance with a more scholarly philosophy of food. As well as being the oldest, print publications are also generally the most respected, and "respectable", food media, less "popular" than television programs and digital media—yet they have received less academic attention than television, perhaps for this reason.

Print publications, such as cookbooks, food magazines, restaurant guides, and food newspaper supplements, played a central role in foodies' self-formation through material cultures of food for all the participants in my research. Most of my informants used print publications in combination with food television, and to a lesser extent, digital food media. The exception, here, were John and Elena, a married couple in their early fifties. They almost exclusively used print publications in their productive leisure and self-formation. This included food supplements in newspapers, food magazines, and cookbooks, which they used to acquire knowledge about different ingredients, suppliers, and recipes. While their television sat neatly in the corner of their open-plan lounge and dining room adjacent to the kitchen, and they used the Internet for emails and work, they did not use television or digital media regularly in their material education in food. Instead, they preferred to use print publications, with their favorite and most used cookbooks being stored on a bookshelf in the kitchen above the fridge. They put this preference for print media partly down to their age, saying that they had formed their habits before the recent boom in food television and the emergence of digital food media. But also, and perhaps more importantly, they felt it was a result of the advantage of print publications in terms of acquiring and applying "the complex information that underpins much of our home cooking," as John put it. "The beauty of the printed word," he said, "is that you can slowly take it in, and refer back to it." The permanence of these media as material objects was seen as superior to the ephemeral nature of food media on television and online.

Like John and Elena, almost all of my informants used cookbooks, whether it was in their everyday cooking, when entertaining guests, or when learning how to cook a new dish. The majority also read food magazines, such as *Gourmet Traveller, Vogue Entertaining + Travel, delicious,* or *Donna Hay,* to learn about trends in food, get ideas of restaurants to visit, and find new recipes to cook. Reading the weekly *Epicure* food supplement in Melbourne's broadsheet *The Age*—from which some informants were recruited—was a must for most, to keep up-to-date with news on the local food scene, such as new restaurants or suppliers. Many also used *The Age's* annual *Good Food Guide* for restaurant reviews. Some foodies spent a significant amount of time reading these print publications on a regular basis. For example, Ruth and Pippa were filled with excitement at the publication of *Epicure* every Tuesday, when they would buy the newspaper and begin to read the articles before work, often texting one another to comment on a particular opening of a new supplier, or which recipe they planned to cook for dinner that night. Others, such as Leah, worked full-time as an accountant, but dedicated at least half an hour of her spare time each day to reading about food, and she made a habit of preparing at least one new recipe from these sources each week.

I explore how foodies use cookbooks in their culinary education in Chapter 6, so here I want to highlight some of the other ways they learn from and engage with such material media in their productive leisure. While the foodies in my research primarily used cookbooks as practical texts to cook from, some of my informants also enjoyed the experience of simply reading them. For example, Tess, a public relations agent in her late twenties, preferred to pick up and read a cookbook than a novel. This is partly due to her central life interest in food. Yet it is also a response to the literary quality of some cookbooks. Susan Leonardi highlights the way in which cookbooks that embed recipes in personal narratives and intertextual references to literary texts and authors develop a discourse that is itself akin to literary discourse, with a social context and a cast of characters (1989: 342). This explains some of the pleasure gained from simply reading such cookbooks. As Maureen, a housewife in her mid-sixties, put it, "I rather like the ones with a story interspersed with recipes"; "I read them like novels." Similarly, Sam described how he loved "reading stories of other people's experience of food. I really enjoy some of the older—I mean go back to the ubiquitous Elizabeth David, she was a good writer in being able to take you to another place and time."

Some of my informants enjoyed reading historical cookbooks to expand their material education. Due to the lack of accurate measurements and sometimes strange ingredients, many older cookbooks are not particularly useful as practical texts; however, foodies read them to learn about the types of foods and dishes that were eaten in various times and places in the past, to acquire a historical culinary education. For example, George was a Cypriot-Australian who had a particular passion for traditional British cuisine. One of his cherished possessions was a copy of Mrs. Beeton's *Book of Household Management* (1861). He had tried to prepare some of the recipes on a few occasions but said they were hard to "get right." Yet he still referred to the book often, to get an understanding of the style of food in Victorian Britain. Another informant, Jeff, had a passion for food history. A nurse in his early fifties, he had invested a significant amount of his spare time in this historical material education over the past ten years. He also owned a copy of *Mrs. Beeton's,* but like George, he used it mostly to acquire historical knowledge, as "generally the recipes in those cookbooks aren't really accurate enough." Jeff particularly enjoyed reading historical Australian cookbooks in order to learn about the evolution of food and how waves of immigration had affected culinary tastes and cultures. As he described, "I've got a real interest in the history of cuisine as a definer of culture. There's some fascinating stuff that's been written on how food actually structures a culture, and indelibly leaves its mark on people." In addition to his material education through primary texts, Jeff engaged in secondary readings in the history of certain foods, such as caviar, eels, potatoes, and curry. He used his interest in food as a form of material culture as a way of learning about the world, about different times, places, and cultures, or as he put it, "just the desire to know what everything is, where it came from, where—both in terms of history and geography and—you know, what is the future."

Some foodies who were more interested in the future of food undertook reading about the science of cooking, such as molecular gastronomy. For example, Raymond, a semiretired real-estate agent in his early sixties, described Harold McGee's *On Food and Cooking* (2003) as "one of the best food books ever." He said he constantly read these sorts of books "for inspiration." Another informant, Adam, was also fascinated by McGee's book, as well as Hervé This's *Molecular Gastronomy* (2006). A Chinese-Australian in his late thirties, Adam now worked in sales but put this interest down to his background in science as well as his passion for food. He was particularly interested in how molecular gastronomes used science to test historical beliefs and myths about food and cooking:

> The interesting thing was, they conducted all these experiments to see whether all these beliefs about food were true. It's like the thing about sealing the meat, and they said, "Well, you know, sealing the juices, it doesn't happen because it's just this sort of myth, and the important thing is actually the caramelization, that's where the flavour comes from. But the entire thing about, you seal in the juices by doing this, it's just not true, the juices still leak out." So I find things like that really intriguing...There are these conclusions that have been set over hundreds of years, and some of them might turn out to be wrong! I just find it very interesting.

Thus, foodies use print publications to acquire not just a practical education in food but also a historical and scientific education, which they use in their self-formation through this material object.

Lastly, the materiality of print publications enables another practice to form around these objects, that of collecting. Some of my informants, particularly serious amateur cooks, had large collections of cookbooks, numbering in the hundreds. Others, particularly restaurant buffs, collected the annual *Good Food Guide,* keeping it as a historical document to look back at the restaurants that have come and gone and the changes in culinary taste. For example, Lynette was a Welsh-Australian in her sixties, who had migrated to Australia in the late 1950s. She had collected every edition of the city's *Good Food Guide* since 1984, which she described as "a history of Melbourne." The collection of restaurant guides is the form of foodie collecting that comes closest to notions of "hobby collections," representing what Gelber refers to as "secondary collections" (1999: 59) composed of items that were originally designed to be used (as opposed to "primary collections" of objects made simply to be collected, such as baseball cards). For Gelber argues that the defining feature of collecting as a hobby is that the things collected are *not* used by collectors, as they "create new meaning for objects by collecting rather than using them" (1999: 78). The other characteristics he cites of collectible objects are that they are both rare and desirable, as they are often traded with fellow collectors and possessed in part for their economic value. The collection of cookbooks by foodies does not fit this notion of hobby collecting because the collections continue to be used for their original purpose (unlike the outdated editions of restaurant guides), and none of the cookbooks are generally traded or sold—they are collected for their use-value, not their exchange-value. Rather, foodie cookbook collections constitute a form of what Nicky Gregson and Louise Crewe call "collections-in-use," which appear to be increasingly common among individuals (2003: 187). Using the cookbooks, rather than simply collecting them, also reduces the potentially consumerist connotations of owning so many books. Yet Russell Belk (1995) argues that collecting, in general, is considered a more morally acceptable form of consumption, one that allows people to escape the shame or guilt often associated with the accumulation of material goods.

FOOD TELEVISION

Food television is a much more recent innovation than print food media, but as my discussion showed earlier, it has a history that stretches back for more than half a century. Due to its recent proliferation, it has attracted the greatest amount of scholarly attention of all food media (Bonner 1994, 2005; T. Miller 2001, 2007; Hollows 2003a,b; de Solier 2005, 2008; Polan 2011; Rousseau 2012b). Yet where existing research has examined it through discourse or textual analysis, in this book I use ethnography to explore how people use food television in their daily lives. While television was not used by all of the informants in my research (unlike print publications) it was still central to the self-formation of the large majority of foodies. Those who did not watch food programming regularly tended to avoid television in general; it was not their medium of choice. There was little variation in food television viewership according to demographics of gender or age among my informants, as both women and men of all ages watched such programs. The foodie viewer, then, differs from the typical lifestyle program viewer found by Dover and Hill (2007) in the United Kingdom. Their large-scale quantitative survey research found the lifestyle viewer was more likely to be a woman in her twenties or thirties (2007: 36). While Dover and Hill found that retirees hardly watched any life-style programming (2007: 31) at all, all of my retired informants watched food television.

Some foodies described how they liked watching food television precisely because of the nature of the moving image. This was tied to their education in the material production of food. For example, Winona was a human resources manager in her late forties. As she put it, you can "imagine making it when you see it, as opposed to just reading the recipe." This echoes the words of Sian, a retired teacher, who said, "I enjoy watching how something is done, as books can only tell." For many foodies like Winona and Sian, print publica-tions and television programs have their respective virtues; the former offer more detailed and complex information to which one may continually refer, while the latter offer the opportunity to see *how* something is done, in action, before trying it oneself.

I explore the types of television programs foodies watch and how they ac-quire a material education in food consumption and production in the chapters that follow. Here, I want to briefly highlight the broader gastronomic education foodies acquire from food television. One of the main forms of this is anthro-pological knowledge about the food practices of different cultural groups. For example, Amelia was a communications worker in her early twenties, who was something of a food television fan. In relation to her favorite kinds of food television, she said, "I like when there is an insight into home cooking from different cultures." Television provided a way for foodies to acquire knowledge of a range of different cultures and cuisines, a global understanding of this type of material culture and its use in the formation of different identities, which was central to their cosmopolitan approach to food. This may be through pro-grams that feature the home cooking of migrants in Australia, or food travel programs that show the culinary practices of people in different countries. Television, then, is one of the ways in which foodies learn about the cuisines of other cultures, and in some cases, it challenges their assumptions about such cuisines. For example, Anne was also a keen food television viewer, something she shared in common with her partner. After work, they would often come home and watch a food program together, and then go into the kitchen to cook side-by-side. Anne described a program about Lebanese cuisine she had watched the previous evening, saying:

> I really got an insight about Lebanese food that I didn't have before. Because I always thought it was very meat-based, but it's actually not. They have so many different vegetables; it was so much more colourful than I'd ever seen before, because I haven't eaten out in many Lebanese places. So that was just learning something new as well, which was quite fascinating. I really like that aspect of constantly learning and evolving my own knowledge.

Anne emphasizes the morality of knowledge and the educational approach to material media in her own self-formation through food. Her comment demonstrates how we learn about material objects like food not just through engaging with them directly but also through material media. Yet it also highlights how material media, such as food television, can be used to develop a global connection to food as a way of forming the self through material culture in a globalized world.

DIGITAL FOOD MEDIA

The newest forms of food media, based around the Internet, have only begun to gain momentum over the past decade. They have attracted less academic attention to date, and again no ethnographic attention (de Solier 2006, 2010; Naccarato and LeBesco 2012; Rousseau 2012a). While digital media were not used as commonly as print publications or television programs, the substantial majority of my informants did use some form of online food media, regardless of demographics of age. The most common thing they use the Web for is to find recipes. This is mostly done by performing a Google search for a particular dish or ingredient rather than frequenting a specific recipe website, such as *epicurious* or *allrecipes.* Indeed, this appears to be a widespread cultural practice, as around 1 percent of all searches on Google are for recipes, which led to the launch of the Google Recipe Search in 2011 (see Rousseau 2012a: 63). Some of my informants, however, also accessed recipes on the websites of television cooking shows. Such sites reflect the contemporary "convergence culture, where old and new media collide" (Jenkins 2006: 2). As Henry Jenkins defines it, convergence refers to "the flow of content across multiple media platforms, the cooperation between multiple media industries, and the migratory behavior of media audiences" (2006: 2). Other sites of convergence used by my informants included the online delivery systems of traditional print publications, such as newspapers and food magazines, particularly international publications, such as the *New York Times* and the

Guardian, as well as podcasts related to food. Some also used more interactive Web 2.0 media, such as blogs and the forums on the website *eGullet,* that provide a key space for foodies to engage in discussions with professionals, including high-profile international experts such as Anthony Bourdain or Ferran Adrià. Toward the end of my research, some foodies had increasingly begun to use social networking and microblogging sites, such as *Twitter* (and today, *Instagram*), that provided greater scope for both instantly sharing information and photos with fellow foodies as well as interacting with food professionals.

The reasons why foodies do not use digital media as much in their self-making as they do print publications and television programs revolve around issues of risk and trust. For many, there is a lack of trust in digital media because the sources of much of the information online are unknown and therefore cannot be confirmed as expert and legitimate, or are considered lay or amateur and therefore illegitimate. This comes back to the high levels of trust most foodies place in professional experts in their material education. The Web, for many foodies, is seen as a site of risk: it is an abstract system that disembeds knowledge from known personalities, whether celebrities or friends. Such knowledge is not embedded within local face-to-face relations of trust, such as those with friends or family, nor in mediated relations of trust with known experts.

As Leonardi (1989) has observed, recipes have historically been an "embedded discourse" bound up in relationships of giving or sharing, particularly between family and friends. Because of the lack of personal relationships between mediated food experts and their audiences, gastronomes often embed their recipes in their own personal narratives in order to create a persona whom their audiences can "identify and trust" (1989: 347). Leonardi writes: "Even the root of *recipe*—the Latin *recipere*—implies an exchange, a giver and a receiver. Like a story, a recipe needs a recommendation, a context, a point, a reason to be" (1989: 340). The problem with recipes found on unknown websites via Google is that foodies do not know who the giver is. They wonder: Who wrote this recipe? Someone on the other side of the world, who I don't know personally, or abstractly as an expert; how can I trust their knowledge? This is an abstract, anonymous system of exchange that is laden with risk, the risk to one's reputation as a cook. Giddens argues that trust presumes "a leap to commitment, a quality of 'faith' which is irreducible. It is specifically related to absence in time and space" (1991: 19). Anne described how she made such a leap to commitment once, but would not do so again: "No-one's ever let me forget a recipe I got off the Internet for Panforte, a fruit and nut cake. I wanted a traditional recipe and I couldn't find one anywhere in my cookbooks. So I Googled it, got one up, and I made it, and it was rock hard, it was a complete disaster!" For Anne, the risk posed to her reputation by such bad knowledge from the Web means she will not place trust in this abstract system again but will rely on the knowledge of experts she knows.

The disembedded nature of online knowledge was also a reason why some foodies did not trust online restaurant reviews, combined with a lack of trust in the opinions of (unknown) laypeople. Sarah, for example, was a veterinarian in her twenties. She said:

> I guess I don't trust the layman's opinion, you know. If I know the person—like if a friend recommends it to me, I'll listen to them, but if someone on the Internet, just "Tom" from down the street has gone to such and such and recommends it I'm like "Well what do you know?," you know?...Experts, friends and family, I'll listen to strongly—anyone else, I'm like "nuh!"

Many foodies place a large amount of trust in experts and little trust in the (disembedded) knowledge of laypersons. It was for this reason—the lack of confirmable expertise—that such foodies saw the information on the Web as risky and untrustworthy. A key issue in terms of foodies and digital media, then, revolves around the distinctions between experts and laypersons, professionals and amateurs, that becomes even more important in the context of blogs.

Most of my informants did not read food blogs regularly. The main reason, again, was the lack of trust in the unknown sources, who were not culturally recognized as experts, and the blogger's status as amateur. For example, Tess, who was an avid user of both print media and television, said, "I don't know who they are written by and if they have the same expectations of food that I do." Katarina, a credit manager in her forties, was also a food television fan like Tess. She highlighted the amateurism of blogs as her main reason for not reading them, saying,"they're a bit rambly, I suppose, and I guess that's what they are, they're just amateur writings aren't they?...No, it's never appealed." She also criticized the quality of the photography, showing that these amateur productions are judged by and compared to professional standards.

In contrast, those of my informants who did read amateur food blogs liked them precisely because they were *not* professional media; these foodies enjoyed the blogs' amateur nature and the creative freedoms that came with it. Maureen, for example, said she read blogs because she was "interested in different opinions of non-professionals." Anne described how she was constantly amazed by the effort and work that amateurs put into their food blogs, such as taking photos that document all the stages of preparing a dish. In contrast to ideas of disembeddedness, Mary highlighted the embedded, personal narratives of food bloggers as one of the attractions of these amateur media: "It gives you an idea of what they were feeling and what they get out of food, from what they put down on their blog. And it's how emotive they make it, because that's what food is, or that's why you go to a blog usually." A business manager by day, Mary was in the process of setting up her own food blog. As I explore in Chapter 8, it is in this practice of blogging that new media takes on greater importance in foodie self-making, not in terms of acquiring knowledge—like old media—but in terms of sharing knowledge.

It is not just through material objects, then, that we form individual selves through material culture in postindustrial modernity. Rather, material media are fundamental to this process. In a late modern world dominated by risk, we need guidance in how to incorporate objects into the reflexive project of the self, and increasingly, this guidance comes not from traditional social structures, such as the family, but from the experts of material media. It is through these media that we acquire a material education and learn about objects such as food. Acquiring such an education is part of the moralities of productive leisure that guide our self-formation through material culture in postindustrial society. It forms part of a serious knowledge-based approach to material culture in self-making. The use of different forms of material media in this process is based on trust. Old media are trusted because the knowledge they communicate comes from professional experts. New media, on the other hand, are riskier, and are not trusted by many for the material education that is central to their self-formation.

3

Consuming Things: Material Cultures and Moralities of Consumption

Questions of morality are central to consumption, both to scholarly understandings of it and to how people negotiate it in their practices of self-making. Daniel Miller argues that consumption has been viewed negatively throughout history as an "intrinsic evil." A higher moral value has historically been placed on production, which "creates the world," than consumption, "whereby we use it up" (2001b: 227). This morality is epitomized by the work ethic and abstention from consumption on the part of middle-class puritan Protestants that Weber explored in *The Protestant Ethic and the Spirit of Capitalism* (1930). Miller highlights how this suspicion of consumption and the moral stance against it continues today and has dominated scholarly work on the topic. This stance is embodied in the theory of consumption as materialistic, which suggests that people in postindustrial societies are bound up in the excessive accumulation of material goods—either for their own sake or for purposes of distinction—and that these goods, while never satisfying consumers, are more important to them than their relationships with people. Material goods are viewed as "intrinsically bad" and "superfluous," as "pure individuals or pure social relations are sullied by commodity culture"; what is required is an "ascetic repudiation of the need for goods per se," the "liberation" of people from things (Miller 2001b: 227, 241). Miller critiques this perspective as inherently middle class, voiced by affluent academics comfortably distant from the experience of poverty, which is defined by a lack of material goods, such as housing, clothes, and food. Moreover, writings from this perspective, which tend to be speculative, ignore the many empirical studies of consumption that reveal most people do not value material objects more than their relationships with people but that objects play a fundamental role in those relationships (Miller 2001b: 226).

While this critique by Daniel Miller warns against viewing material consumption as intrinsically bad, Toby Miller (2007) reminds us that it should not be seen as intrinsically good either. He highlights how cultural studies has often viewed consumption in a less critical manner, particularly that undertaken by minorities, such as the "resistant" consumption of working-class subcultures. Cultural studies is renowned within other disciplines for its postmodern model of the consumer as the playful identity-maker (see Campbell 2005). This more positive and at times celebratory approach to consumption has led to criticisms not only from other disciplines but from left-wing journalists, who have accused cultural studies of being aligned with right-wing economics, suggesting that the discipline has become "the handservant of capital" (Miller 2007: 4).

Along with other scholars in material culture studies, such as Don Slater, I believe that the method of ethnography offers an effective means to avoid polarized views of consumption as purely positive or negative, for it encourages us to approach consumption as "a realm of everyday practice that has to be understood in its own terms, rather than from a moral high ground" (Slater, in Slater and Miller 2007: 8). Given the speculative nature of most scholarly work on consumption, it is of vital importance to conduct further empirical research into the complex nature of people's lived experience of consumption and its use in their self-formation. When dealing with actual consumers and their everyday experiences, the interpretation of consumption in postindustrial society becomes a lot less clear; it may be murky, messy, contradictory, or ambivalent. It may involve pleasure and anxiety, spending and thrift, inclusion and exclusion. It is almost always complex and is not easily reducible to categories such as materialism or consumerism (de Solier 2013).

GOOD TASTE: CONSUMPTION, DISTINCTION, AND THE SELF

Many scholars have suggested that the primary characteristic of postindustrial society is that it is a "consumer society" (Featherstone 1991; Lury 1996; Slater 1997; Baudrillard 1998). Jean Baudrillard, for example, has declared that "we are at the point where consumption is laying hold of the whole of life" (1998: 29). This has had a profound effect on how our selves and identities are formed. Rather than shaping selves through producing things, it is often argued that in postindustrial society, we now form our selves primarily through consuming things—in particular, through our taste for consuming certain kinds of things. Baudrillard argues that the notion of shaping a self through commodity choice is forced upon us by the capitalist system. Individuals self-consciously mobilize the "sign-value" of goods to communicate meanings about themselves, as commodities are "transformed into the substance of play and distinction" (1998: 28). Following the work of Mike Featherstone (1991), the notion of "lifestyle" has come to signify the centrality of consumption to this reflexive project of the self for many scholars (Lury 1996; Bell and Hollows 2005, 2006). Featherstone argues that the "modern individual within consumer culture is made conscious that he speaks not only with his clothes, but with his home, furnishings, decoration, car and other activities which are to be read and classified in terms of the presence and absence of taste" (1991: 86).

Yet it is Bourdieu's *Distinction* (1984), based on a large-scale survey in 1960s France, that remains the definitive study of taste. His work is concerned with the role taste plays in the formation of classed selves. Bourdieu argues that taste is not individual or natural but largely determined by class, particularly that of one's social origin, which is internalized in a set of dispositions he terms the "habitus." He argues that there is a socially agreed upon singular hierarchy of taste that can be neatly mapped onto the social structure in terms of the highbrow "good taste" of the dominant class (opera, for example), the "middlebrow taste" of the middle class (film, for example), and the lowbrow "popular taste" of the working class (football, for example) (1984: 16). "Good taste," then, is a form of cultural knowledge that confers class distinction, or what Bourdieu calls "cultural capital." It is acquired and deployed for purposes of status.

Bourdieu's theory has been critiqued in a number of ways by more recent work. Many scholars have argued that taste—and its class significations—has become more complex in late or postmodernity due to the blurring or collapse of aesthetic hierarchies of high and popular culture (Featherstone 1991), the democratization of "good taste" by the media and its adoption by the masses (Collins 2002), the convergence of taste between classes (Gans 1999), and the overwhelming level and variety of goods that "make it impossible to communicate refinement or distinction" (Warde et al. 1999: 106).

In the 1990s, Tony Bennett, Michael Emmison, and John Frow (1999) conducted a similar survey to Bourdieu's in Australia. In contrast to Bourdieu, they found that there is not a singular scale of cultural value that is universally binding (1999: 261). They argue that rather than "displaying a singular structure of value running from the legitimate and prestigious to the illegitimate and valueless," cultural practices in all their heterogeneity—from dining out to gardening to attending a football match—"are organised by different and often incommensurable scales" of value (1999: 263). They suggest that what may be generalized is the scale that runs from inclusive to restricted forms of involvement in cultural practices that cuts across the plurality of value systems.

In making this final claim, Bennett and his colleagues are drawing on the work of Richard Peterson and Roger Kern (1996), who suggest that there is a new hierarchy of taste that runs from more "omnivorous" taste at the top of the social structure to more "univorous" taste at the bottom. Peterson and Kern have empirically mapped the changing conceptions of what constitutes "good taste" in the United States from regimes based on exclusion (snobs) to ones based on inclusion (omnivores). They argue that there has been a shift in the taste of high-status people from a system of snobbery, based on the exclusive consumption of highbrow cultural products and practices, to one of omnivorousness, based on "eclecticism" and an openness to appreciating middlebrow and lowbrow as well as highbrow forms (1996: 901). It is such omnivorousness, they argue, that now stands as a sign of good taste and an expression of social distinction rather than an exclusive consumption of high culture. Where snobbish exclusion may have been effective as a marker of high status in a system with a singular aesthetic hierarchy, omnivorousness may be a more effective strategy in the contemporary context of numerous scales of value and an enormous variety of goods and practices in late modernity (Bennett et al. 1999; Warde et al. 1999).

CONSUMING MATERIAL OBJECTS: ARE FOODIES OMNIVORES OR SNOBS?

Food has long been used as a means of class distinction (Goody 1982; Bourdieu 1984; Mennell 1996). My previous work (de Solier 2005) has explored how food continues to operate as a source of status and distinction in late modernity, particularly among the middle class. This work examined the role of cultural capital in the field of food and distinguished between two forms of what I called "culinary capital": an "aesthetic culinary capital," which involves the accumulation of culturally legitimate systems of food taste, and a "practical culinary capital," which involves the accumulation of related cookery skills (de Solier 2005: 471). Peter Naccarato and Kathleen LeBesco (2012) have also explored the idea of culinary capital. They argue that omnivorous taste is a means to attaining culinary capital and status in contemporary food cultures. The question of the changing nature of good taste away from the exclusivity of the snob toward the inclusivity of the omnivore has become a growing concern in food studies since the turn of the century (Warde et al. 1999). In their study of foodie discourse, Johnston and Baumann (2010) link this shift to the taste formation and distinction practices of foodies. They develop a theory of the foodie as a particular "kind of cultural consumer—the omnivore" (2010: 205).

The foodies in my ethnographic research certainly imagined themselves to be omnivores and constructed themselves as such. Using adjectives such as "eclectic," "curious," and "adventurous," they employed a discourse of omnivorousness to describe their taste, suggesting that they like to eat all types of food. In a typical response, Sarah said:

> I'm a pretty adventurous eater, and I think you have to be if you're gonna be a foodie. I don't think you can be a foodie and be like, "Well I don't eat that, that,

or that, and I don't like that"...Personally I think to be a foodie you've got to be willing to try a lot of things, and I'll pretty much try anything.

In a similar manner, Nick said that "one of my rules for when I go out to eat is that I will try anything...because I sort of think—because it's food, I need to taste it all to appreciate what it is." Like Sarah, he believed that foodies should not be food snobs "because they're a bit too elitist about it, like 'I won't touch this restaurant,' 'I won't go to that restaurant,' you know, these kinds of things. And I don't like that particular type of thinking because I think, it's all food, and you've got to try all of it." This discourse reflects the openness to different forms of food that Peterson and Kern (1996) associate with the omnivore. Being an omnivore—or believing oneself to be one—was part of the morality of consumption for the foodies in my research; their disciplined moral code suggests that the right way to engage with this material object in self-formation is to try all its different varieties, to be inclusive, not reject this or that. The foodie self as an omnivore is considered a moral self because their love of food purportedly extends to all types of food and is not elitist. For these food enthusiasts, the highest priority they express in their taste is not politics (like vegetarians or vegans, for example) but flavor. They possess a taste for flavor, or more specifically, for a diversity of flavors. This is epitomized by the Slow Food movement's project to "Save the Universe of Flavours," to protect the diversity of flavors from homogenization by the global industrial food system (de Solier 2004). The Slow Food movement was founded in Italy in the 1980s to support the production and consumption of regional, traditional artisanal foods, which were believed to be threatened by the standardization processes of the modern food system. In 1989, it became The International Slow Food Movement for the Defense of and the Right to Pleasure and has since spread to more than 150 countries around the world (Petrini 2003; see also Leitch 2003; Parkins and Craig 2006; Wilk 2006). One of my informants, Jeff, expressed strong concerns about the homogenization of flavors: "I sort of bemoan this—what's the word?—'McDonaldization' of food, you know, where everything is pretty much the same." My informants used this declared omnivorousness and taste for diversity to strategically distinguish themselves from what they consider the more bourgeois and elite figure of the snob (the traditional highbrow), who is more selective and will only eat the best—epitomized for many by the gourmet.

CONSUMING COSMOPOLITANISM

When the foodies in my research described their taste in food as omnivorous, they were generally referring to the fact that they consumed a variety of different "ethnic" cuisines. Madeleine, for example, said her taste was "certainly wide ranging, taking in a lot of overseas cuisines"; while Eva described her taste as "broad, enjoying foods from a variety of different cultures." All of my informants enjoyed eating a variety of ethnic cuisines rather than simply that of their cultural heritage. They often found it difficult to name one particular cuisine they liked the most—and if they did, it was generally not their own ethnic cuisine. For example, for Surat, a Thai migrant, it was French and Japanese; for Madeleine, an Anglo-Australian, it was Moroccan, Italian, and Thai; for George, who was of Greek-Cypriot heritage, it was British cuisine; for Henri, a migrant with French heritage, it was Indian and Chinese; and for Nick, a Chinese-Australian, it was French and Italian. Amelia, who was Anglo-Australian, was particularly indecisive:

> I have said before that I could eat Asian meals every meal for the rest of my life. This of course allows me to eat Thai, Japanese, Indonesian, Chinese, Korean, Vietnamese, Malaysian, etcetera, so it's a bit of a cheat statement. I do tend to cook more Asian influenced food, but it's not to say I don't enjoy European styles just as much. In fact I've been very keen on traditional regional Italian in the past few months.

This constitutes a particular form of cultural omnivorousness based around ethnic diversity, which is commonly considered a cosmopolitan taste formation. In particular, it constitutes a form of the elite cosmopolitanism described by Ulf Hannerz, who defines it as "an intellectual and aesthetic stance of openness toward divergent cultural experiences, a search for contrasts rather than uniformity" (1990: 239). True cosmopolitans, according to Hannerz, seek out difference, such as culinary difference. This cosmopolitan taste distinguishes foodies from another type of enthusiast for this material object, the "food chauvinist" (Counihan 2004), whose passion for food is confined to his or her own ethnic cuisine. These enthusiasts are not omnivores but what Peterson calls "univores," those who have a restricted taste formation and "tend to be actively involved in just one" aesthetic tradition (1992: 254). Univores' love of food is commonly an expression of their ethnic or national identity, whereas foodies' love of food involves the reflexive cultivation of a cosmopolitan identity. Nick described the difference between his own taste formation as a foodie and that of his Chinese parents, who were univores:

> The foodie is all about all foods, rather than one particular style of food. And so, for me, I can get my Chinese type of cuisine at any time, and I want to go back to it eventually, but for the moment I want to get some ideas from every where else. Whereas for my parents who are not foodies, they're just very used to the food that they normally eat and they don't really think about it enough and are not interested enough to explore other flavours, so they stick with the same thing.

This cosmopolitan taste appears to be common among foodies in different countries, as Johnston and Baumann (2010) found evidence of a similar taste for ethnic cuisines in their research in the United States. Yet where they found this taste formation—and the foodie identity—to be predominantly limited to white people, my research found this was not the case in Australia, where this identity was determined more by class than race or ethnicity.

Indeed, this taste for culinary difference is not unique to foodies. Other scholars have shown it to be a more common taste formation among the middle class, particularly in multicultural societies, such as Australia, the United States, and the United Kingdom, for whom it functions as a form of "cosmo-multicultural capital" that fuses "notions of diversity with notions of classiness, sophistication and international distinction" (Hage 1997: 122). Alan Warde, Lydia Martens, and Wendy Olsen (1999) conducted research on omnivorousness in the United Kingdom in the 1990s that measured the variety of ethnic restaurants participants frequented. They found such omnivorousness was higher among the educated middle class; in particular, it was linked to higher incomes, degree-level qualifications, urbanity (living in London), and higher social class, more so than other forms of eating out (1999: 118). They concluded that in England, "experience of foreign cuisines is a mark of refinement, the possession of which is class-related" (1999: 124).

While Warde and his colleagues see the taste for ethnic culinary diversity as exclusive to the middle class in England (1999), in Australia, this taste is even more widespread and democratized among the general population. Various scholars have mapped the increasing cosmopolitanism of food tastes in Australia as a product of processes of globalization, migration, international travel, changes in the food industry, and the influence of the media (Hage 1997; Gallegos 2005; Symons 2007; Duruz 2011). While such taste may have once been exclusive to the middle class, it has spread beyond class boundaries because it is increasingly linked to national identity, not class identity. As Australian national identity has been made over as multicultural, it has become *Australian*—the duty of a good citizen—to eat a range of ethnic foods, whether through dining out, eating takeaways, or cooking at home. It has become a banal, everyday form of cosmopolitanism in which many Australians participate to some degree. This appears to be similar in the United States (Gabaccia 1998).

However, there are still class-based distinctions within such cosmopolitan culinary consumption in Australia. The educated middle class—including foodies—gain their distinction from the lower classes by the greater diversity of ethnic cuisines they consume, as well as by their pursuit of "authentic" ethnic cuisine (Hage 1997). For while the lower classes consume various ethnic foods, they are associated with the consumption of the more lowbrow and less authentic Westernized versions of such cuisine, such as Sweet and Sour

Pork or Lemon Chicken, which any foodie will tell you is not "real Chinese" (as Nick told me at length). But while the foodies in my research were ethnically omnivorous, does this mean they are true omnivores? To answer this question, we need to look more closely at their broader taste in this material object, at what they do and don't, or will and won't, eat.

CONSUMING CLASS?

To be a "perfect omnivore" in the domain of food does not come down to simply eating a variety of ethnic cuisines. Rather, it involves the taste for, and knowledge of, foods with a range of cultural values—the appreciation of highbrow, middlebrow, and lowbrow foods (Peterson and Kern 1996: 904). Are foodies, then, perfect omnivores? Do they truly like to eat all types of food?

Most of my informants constructed their taste as omnivorous in terms of the status hierarchy of foods, such as claiming to "enjoy dining out at both high-end and low-end restaurants." However, I argue here that the large majority were not perfect omnivores because they didn't, or wouldn't, eat lowbrow foods. The foods that attract such low cultural value are those associated with the "unsophisticated" and "uneducated" taste of the (white) lower classes, such as "inauthentic" Westernized ethnic food, industrialized mass-produced processed food, and most importantly, the bane of many a foodie's existence, fast food like McDonalds and KFC. The tension and slippage between the discourse of omnivorousness employed by foodies and their exclusion of, or snobbery toward, fast food is reflected in Henri's comment about his taste formation: "I'm definitely an omnivore, so I mean I'll eat almost anything, with the exception of McDonalds. I refuse to eat fast food, I think it's crap!...It's pretty snobbish, but yeah...I just don't like the taste, I don't like the quality." Almost all of the foodies in my research shared this distaste for fast food and refused to eat it. As Bette put it emphatically, "No. No. No. Never!" This also appears to be common to foodies more generally, as the large majority of the participants in Johnston and Baumann's research in the United States had a "strong aversion" to fast food, as such food was often disavowed and provoked disgust (2010: 198). The reason most of my informants gave for not eating fast food, such as McDonalds, was not one of politics, of personal health, or weight, but one of aesthetics—they disliked the flavor, and their descriptions ranged from "unappealing" to "disgusting." Interestingly, this differed from their stance against the lowbrow mass-produced processed food sold in supermarkets, which was voiced more politically in terms of a critique of the modern industrial food system (see Chapter 5). While foodies profess a taste for gustatory diversity and an appreciation of all types of food and flavors, this is tempered by their aesthetic judgment of quality. This relates to the high moral value foodies attach to consuming "good quality" food as "eating right," which I explore later. Flavor is only one, albeit highly important, part of these aesthetic judgments of quality, which also include other sensory dimensions, such as smell and appearance. As Fine argues, much of "what we mean by 'quality' has this sensory, or aesthetic, dimension; the object or performance transcends functional requirements" (1996: 194; see also Roe 2006a). In addition to perceiving the aesthetic limitations of fast food, some of my informants saw such food as not even meeting functional requirements. As Leah said, "I don't consider it real food." Fast food was perceived, then, as having low use-value, exchange-value, and sign-value, as Bette described: "The food is terrible—cheap and nasty." While Johnston and Baumann argue that it is reasonable for foodies to reject fast food because it is inauthentic and nonexotic (2010: 198), I would argue that these characteristics are symbolic of fast food's lowbrow status and association with the lower classes, which is the real reason why foodies reject such food. The refusal of fast food is epitomized by the taste formation promoted by the Slow Food movement— founded by elite intellectuals—which despite its discourse of gustatory diversity is radically opposed to fast food in favor of regional, traditional, artisanal foods. Yet, more generally, the distaste for fast food and industrialized mass-produced packaged food is shared by most members of the educated middle class; it is a class-based taste formation rather than one specific to foodies.

Only a few of the foodies in my research could be considered true omnivores: they ate low-, middle-, and highbrow foods and valued the flavor of food on its own terms, rather than—or as well as—in terms of its cultural value. As Surat said of fast food, "it's just another kind of food to me, and it can taste nice, I'll have a hamburger every so often." He regularly ate "anything from instant noodles and canned soup, to a degustation menu in fancy restaurants." Katarina, who had eaten at some of the world's top restaurants, said "McDonalds' French Fries are on a par with what you'd get in the best French bistro!" She disliked the snobbery toward such food among many foodies, saying "I'm not getting on my high horse over fast food; I'm not a food snob like that." These omnivorous foodies, however, were the exception rather than the norm.

When most of my informants said they dined out in "low-end" restaurants, they were generally referring to inexpensive authentic ethnic restaurants (like "a cheap and cheerful Vietnamese meal or authentic pizza," as Celina put it), not to fast food establishments. This was also common to the foodies in Johnston and Baumann's research. Like foodies themselves, Johnston and Baumann classify such ethnic food as lowbrow because of the inexpensive cost (2010: 194). However, while authentic ethnic restaurants may be low in economic value, as I have shown, they have a higher cultural or symbolic value associated with the middle class and can therefore be considered a middlebrow taste. The foodie's cosmopolitan taste for a range of authentic ethnic food, I argue, is middlebrow in status.

Many ethnic restaurants serve "peasant" cuisines, that is, cuisines that are, or have historically been, considered lowbrow in their place of origin, the food of peasants and the working class. Bourdieu refers to this as "the taste of necessity, which favours the most "filling" and most economical foods" (1984: 6). Yet cultural value is socially and historically specific, and when placed within the scales of value in contemporary Australian society— and similarly, Britain and the United States—such foods take on middle-brow distinctions, as they are appropriated into middle-class taste cultures and systems of social distinction. While the term middlebrow historically referred to the popularization (and commercialization) of highbrow taste cultures in the early to mid-twentieth century (Rubin 1992), this represents the reverse process: the usurpation of the tastes of the working class by the educated middle class. The appropriation of "authentic," "traditional," and "artisanal" peasant cuisines again reaches its pinnacle in the Slow Food movement for whom the figure of the peasant functions as a romanticized icon (Leitch 2003; see also Miele and Murdoch 2002; West and Domingos 2012). This appropriation of peasant cuisine represents a process of gentrification (Peterson and Kern 1996: 906; Gans 1999: 11) in which the tastes of the lower classes are usurped by the middle class. I found that most foodies, then, will eat the food considered lowbrow in other countries and cultures but not the food considered lowbrow in contemporary Australia. To put it another way, they will eat the food of the ethnic poor but not the white poor.

For foodies, part of the appeal of peasant cuisine lies in its preparation by a particular kind of expert—not credentialed chefs but cooks who have acquired their culinary knowledge, skills, and recipes as they have been passed down from generation to generation, via the traditional mode of acquisition within the family. These cooks possess what I call a *traditional expertise*, built up through generations of experience; as Leah described it, "the people who have been cooking for thirty years because their parents cooked, and their grandparents before them, and it's the family business." Foodies like this cuisine precisely for its lack of professional qualities, for being homemade, for the fact that it is, or they imagine it to be, the cook's "grandma's recipe" or "how their mum does it." This is cuisine as craft, not art (as in haute cuisine): it is rustic and simple rather than refined and complex. The assimilation of such peasant cuisine into middlebrow food cultures is symbolized by the culinary tastes promoted by more popular TV chefs, such as Jamie Oliver and Nigella Lawson, who present more rustic and simple styles of cooking compared to haute cuisine TV chefs, such as Australia's Neil Perry or the United Kingdom's Heston Blumenthal. However, Oliver and Lawson's middlebrow versions of peasant cuisine were perceived by some of my informants as less "authentic" because these hosts did not acquire such traditional expertise within the family and their recipes are not based on their own culinary traditions and heritage.

Finally, virtually all of the foodies in my research also possessed a taste for the highbrow haute cuisine served in fine dining restaurants. Haute cuisine generally refers to the elite cuisine prepared by qualified professional chefs in high-end restaurants (see Trubek 2000). Such restaurants are the focus of systems of evaluation and rankings through restaurant criticism in material media such as food newspaper supplements, food magazines, and restaurant guidebooks (e.g. *Michelin Guide* and *The Good Food Guide*) (see Floyd 2006; Warde 2009; Lane 2010). This represents the pinnacle of professional cuisine. It is the high professional standards and credentialed expertise that foodies find appealing about such cuisine in comparison to the traditional expertise of peasant cuisine. Foodies generally prefer each expertise to correspond to its designated cuisine: credentialed expertise to haute cuisine and traditional expertise to peasant cuisine. Haute cuisine represents cuisine as art, not craft. In Bourdieu's terms, haute cuisine is the "taste of luxury" that, in contrast to the taste of necessity, "shifts the emphasis to the manner (of presenting, serving, eating etc.) and tends to use stylized forms to deny function" (1984: 6).

The category of haute cuisine, as its name suggests, has traditionally been the domain of French cuisine. It first emerged in the stately homes of the French aristocracy in the medieval period before being commodified in restaurants patronized by the bourgeoisie in the late eighteenth century (Trubek 2000: 3; see also P. Ferguson 2004). Despite the continuing high cultural value of French cuisine as a sign of refinement, the new leading force in haute cuisine over the past decade has been the avant-garde scientific culinary style known as "molecular gastronomy," pioneered by chef Ferran Adrià in Spain, as well as Heston Blumenthal in the United Kingdom and Thomas Keller in the United States (see de Solier 2010). I explore fine dining in depth in the following chapter.

Thus, I found a similar taste for food as a material object among foodies in Australia as that possessed by foodies in the United States. Like Johnston and Baumann (2010), I argue that foodies are not snobs because their taste formation is not exclusive to highbrow food. However, unlike Johnston and Baumann, I argue that foodies are not omnivores either. Rather, I argue that foodies construct and imagine the self as an omnivore because they consider this to be a moral self form through the consumption of material objects in postindustrial society. The *idea* of omnivorousness, then, is central to how people reflexively shape moral selves through their taste in material culture, but this may differ from *practice*. For while foodies may employ a discourse of omnivorousness in their shaping of the self, in practice, most repudiate lowbrow mass-produced food such as that found in fast food restaurants and supermarkets. There is a discrepancy between what they say and what they actually do, between their discourse of omnivorousness and inclusion and their practice of snobbery toward and exclusion of lowbrow foods. I would argue, then, that most foodies can only be considered "partial omnivores" (Bennett et al. 1999: 190), as their taste formation crosses the boundary between middlebrow authentic ethnic cuisine and highbrow haute cuisine. This partial omnivorousness, however, is still located at the higher end of the taste spectrum.

CONSUMING MATERIAL MEDIA

If foodies are only partial omnivores of food, are they perfect omnivores of food media? Which particular texts do they consume and why? The specific material media foodies like, I argue, does not only depend on the formation of taste for the material object represented but also the level of material knowledge and expertise communicated about it. It thus reflects the importance of material education in foodies' self-formation through food and their morality of consuming media as a form of education, of productive leisure, rather than entertainment (see also de Solier 2008).

The informants in my research displayed a particular taste for highbrow material media in which the gastronome is (or has been) a fine dining chef. For example, the most favored cookbook among my informants was *The Cook's Companion* (1996) written by Stephanie Alexander, one of Melbourne's most famous nouvelle cuisine chefs and restaurateurs of the 1970s and an Australian culinary icon, akin to Alice Waters in the United States. This book is over 1,000 pages long and weighs 2.5 kilograms. For John, one of my informants, it was a favorite book: he described it as "a great resource...As a record of information it is fantastic, including what flavours go with what." I found that foodies mainly had a taste for cookbooks written by local Melbournian fine dining chefs whose restaurants they had visited (such as Shannon Bennett and Greg Malouf) as well as those by other award-winning Australian chefs (such as Tetsuya Wakuda and Neil Perry), although some also owned cookbooks by international fine dining chefs (such as Thomas Keller and Charlie Trotter). The taste for material media produced by fine dining chefs reflects the foodie's trust in professional expertise, which is central to their self-formation through objects in late modernity. Many of these cookbooks released by fine dining chefs—in contrast to their television programs—are intended more for a professional audience of fellow chefs and people working in the food industry rather than laypeople, and thus the level of material knowledge they impart is of the highest order. This is one of the reasons why the foodies in my research liked such media and found the cookbooks useful in their gastronomic education. In addition to such contemporary professional cookbooks, several of my informants owned more canonical historical books written by—and for—culinary professionals, such as French chef Auguste Escoffier's *Le Guide Culinaire* (1907), which he described as "a practical guide for future chefs of large restaurants" (Escoffier, quoted in Trubek 2000: 26), and the encyclopedia of French cuisine, *Larousse Gastronomique* (Montagné 1961), to which Escoffier also contributed. One of my informants, Nick, said, "I don't really have a favorite cookbook, but there's one book that I think everybody should have, who is a foodie and likes cooking, and that's *Larousse Gastronomique*."

My informants also displayed a strong taste for television cooking shows hosted by fine dining chefs. These programs generally represent highbrow culinary taste and are more instructional and informational. These include Australian programs, such as those hosted by Neil Perry and Stefano de Pieri, as well as international imports, such as the programs of British chefs Rick Stein, Gary Rhodes, and Nick Nairn, and America's Ming Tsai. Very few American food programs are imported onto Australian free-to-air television, which is where the large majority of my informants watched food programming, particularly on the public broadcasters (see de Solier 2008). Their taste for such highbrow food television was a result of both the culinary taste formations represented, as well as the high level of material information communicated. Sian described how she preferred programs with "more in-depth information," and similarly, Tim said, "I prefer programs that give me interesting information without the hype."

Where these more highbrow instructional programs appealed to all of my informants who watched food television, this was not the case for what we can consider more popular middlebrow cooking shows; these shows were a source of greater debate. In this category, we can place programs such as those of British TV chefs Jamie Oliver and Nigella Lawson and Australian TV chefs Kylie Kwong and Bill Granger. Despite some of these hosts being (or having been) professional fine dining chefs, their programs are categorized as middlebrow because of the increased emphasis placed on entertainment and the celebrity self, as well as their promotion of middle-class taste, as opposed to the greater focus on the material object of food in the more instructional highbrow programs. Some of these middlebrow programs, particularly the British ones, also represent cooking more as a form of casual leisure or fun rather than as serious and intellectual. As Jamie Oliver states in the opening credits of *The Naked Chef:* "Cooking's *gotta* be a laugh. It's gotta be *simple,* it's gotta be *tasty,* it's gotta be *fun*." The informants in my research also made distinctions between these categories of cooking shows. For example, Mary, who was in her mid-thirties, said, "there's no glamour or celebrity" in the programs of Rick Stein and Nick Nairn, unlike those of Jamie Oliver and Nigella Lawson. She enjoyed watching the more celebritized middlebrow programs but preferred the more highbrow instructional shows, which "for me are good because my primary interest is actually the food and the flavour." While many of my informants shared this taste for both kinds of programs, others disliked middlebrow shows because of their emphasis on entertainment and celebrity rather than knowledge about the material object of food. The most vocal of these critics was Leah, also in her thirties. She enjoyed highbrow programs, saying, "Rick Stein is great, he's passionate about what he cooks, and about tradition, and fresh food, and food being a part of so many people's lives." However, she believed that Nigella Lawson's programs were "for people with no idea on food, same with Jamie Oliver, and it's almost insulting to the intelligence." She was highly critical of such TV chefs as celebrity-commodities who "show off their kids on TV and sell their favourite songs on CDs because it's called diversifying and extracting an extra few dollars from people's pockets." Jeff was even harsher in his criticism, provocatively referring to Jamie Oliver and Nigella Lawson as "food sluts," highlighting the immorality he perceived in their approach to food. However, foodies such as Leah and Jeff were in the minority in my research. Jamie Oliver's various programs were watched by many of my participants who *did* find them informative, and he was the most popular of these middlebrow TV chefs. Bette, who was in her fifties, said she liked Jamie Oliver "because he's so enthusiastic and down-to-earth, and the list of ingredients is everyday and not normally long." A substantial number of my informants also owned and used cookbooks released by these middlebrow TV chefs, with Jamie Oliver's being the most popular, followed by those of Nigella Lawson. Interestingly, some foodies, who did not watch the television programs of such chefs because of their emphasis on entertainment and celebrity, cited these TV chefs' cookbooks as among their favorites. As Ruth, a passionate baker in her fifties, said of Nigella Lawson:

> You know, the lips and the plunging necklines and the "oohs" and the "aahs" doesn't do it for me. My foodies have got to be less sex, more, you know—Nigella sort of sells Nigella. But on the other hand, her cookbooks are really good. One of Nigella's books is really brilliant on baking...So I can probably take her in print but not on screen.

In the cookbooks released by such TV chefs, the focus is more on the material object of food and conveying knowledge about it as opposed to entertaining through the celebrity self.

As with food itself, the large majority of my informants did not consume lowbrow food media. Most of them avoided commercial broadcast food television, which was considered low in cultural value. In contrast to public food television, which foodies saw as high quality and informative, commercial food television was described as "cheap" and "entertainment-driven," which reflects the common "value-laden distinction between commercial and public broadcasters" (Bennett et al. 1999: 260). This included commercial cooking shows, such as Australia's *Huey's Cooking Adventures* (see de Solier 2005), as well as reality TV and game-show formats, which were described by some, such as Raymond, as "pathetic." Tess, for example, constructed herself as something of an omnivore of food programs, declaring that she loved them all, yet said, "I don't like things like *Ready Steady Cook.* They rarely put together interesting dishes—more for the masses than the foodies." Such lowbrow food television was disliked both for the less sophisticated culinary taste formation that it represented as well as the high emphasis placed on entertainment over information. Only a small number of my informants were perfect omnivores of food television and did watch such lowbrow programs; however, none of the informants consumed lowbrow print publications. Reality programs such as *Ramsay's Kitchen Nightmares, MasterChef,* and *Jamie's School Dinners* were not considered lowbrow because of the centrality of high-profile haute cuisine chefs or social justice themes. For example, Leah, who described *Ready Steady Cook* as "total rubbish," said she enjoyed *Ramsay's Kitchen Nightmares:* "I think he's great. He's got drive, vision and he doesn't muck around, even if he is a bit rude at times, but he works in high pressure situations."

As with their taste in food, then, most of the foodies in my research can only be considered partial omnivores of food media, as their taste crosses the boundary between highbrow and middlebrow media, but excludes lowbrow forms. However, they did not go to significant lengths to construct the self as an omnivore of material media, which suggests that this is considered less important in their moralities of self-making through material culture than being an omnivore of objects. The homologous nature of their taste in food and media in their self-formation stems from the fact that foodies acquire much of their taste in food from the media.

WHAT (NOT) TO EAT: MATERIAL MEDIA AND TASTE EDUCATION

In *Distinction* (1984), Bourdieu questions the essentialist ideology of natural taste. He argues that taste, like all forms of cultural knowledge and competence, is not innate; rather, it is learnt. He suggests there are two key ways in which taste is learnt: the main way is through the family, which is the taste of the class habitus or social origin, and the second, less "legitimate" way is through the education system. Bourdieu argues that the family has the strongest influence on culinary taste, that it is "in tastes in *food* that one would find the strongest and most indelible mark of infant learning" (1984: 79; original emphasis). Unlike art or music, it is "the ordinary choices of everyday existence, such as furniture, clothing or cooking, which are particularly revealing of deep-rooted and long-standing dispositions because, lying outside the scope of the educational system, they have to be confronted, as it were, by naked taste" (1984: 77). Bourdieu dismisses the role of the media in offering taste education in such ordinary choices, describing material media, such as home magazines, as "semi-legitimate legitimizing agencies" (1984: 77).

While the family obviously has the greatest influence on culinary taste at a young age, as Erickson argues, "family is not destiny" (1996: 223). Contra Bourdieu, recent scholarship has highlighted the crucial role the media now play in the acquisition of good taste, particularly now that even traditional forms of cultural education (such as that in art or literature) are not part of most university degrees. Jim Collins has argued that the media now function as a finishing school, particularly for the knowledge class: "The acquisition of taste, unlike money, is a matter of the right education...no-one receives those lessons in how to live tastefully from a secondary or university education anymore, but that knowledge has to be found *elsewhere,* specifically from various forms of popular culture" (2002: 17; original emphasis). While Collins examines the acquisition of high culture through literary adaptation films, it is material media that specialize in guiding the "ordinary choices of everyday existence" identified by Bourdieu, in material objects such as food, clothing, and furniture.

Earlier, I showed how recent literature on material lifestyle media has emphasized how it educates audiences in matters of consumption. In particular, it has highlighted how such media teach viewers to use consumption in the construction and improvement of the self through systems of taste (Bonner 2000; Palmer 2004; Bell and Hollows 2005, 2006). Material media not only teach their audiences to consume, then, but they also teach them *what* to consume in different domains of material objects, such as food (de Solier 2005), clothes (Sherman 2008), homes (Rosenberg 2011a), and gardens (Taylor 2008). In the United Kingdom, the power of TV chefs to influence the audience's taste in food has become known as the "Delia effect," since Delia Smith's use of cranberries in one of her programs sent sales of the fruit skyrocketing (Hastings 2008). Material lifestyle media, then, offer their audiences a taste education. More specifically, most media—particularly highbrow and middlebrow forms—offer them an education in culturally legitimate systems of taste that can be used in self-improvement and social distinction. I have explored these questions of how cooking shows and TV chefs teach classed systems of taste and how to acquire and deploy culinary capital elsewhere (de Solier 2005; see also Powell and Prasad 2010; Naccarato and LeBesco 2012).

While existing textual analysis of material lifestyle media emphasizes how they teach their audiences good taste, there has been very little empirical research conducted into whether people do in fact learn or put into practice the sophisticated taste formations such media promote. The research that has been conducted to date suggests that, contra such arguments, the majority of people do not put into practice such taste regimes. For example, Dover and Hill found that although material lifestyle programs show viewers "patterns of living, and templates for self-improvement" based on consumption and taste, the viewers in their research were not "placing greater emphasis on using these patterns in their everyday lives"; rather, Dover and Hill argue that lifestyle television "teaches us how other people live their lives, and how television transforms the lives of other people" (2007: 37). Similarly, Lisa Taylor's research among middle- and working-class gardening enthusiasts found that they resisted the interpellations into consumption within material lifestyle media as they "tended to reject the idea of gardening as a consumer activity" (2008: 167). She argues that these gardeners were unreceptive to the advice offered by lifestyle experts, as the gardeners were "too firmly rooted to their traditional 'way of life' to be interested in the pursuit of new, consumer-driven lifestyle garden projects" (2008: 172).

In contrast to these earlier studies, my ethnographic research confirmed the speculations of textual analysis, as I found that foodies do learn and put into practice the "good taste" promoted by material lifestyle media. It was through food media rather than the family or the education system that most of my informants acquired their sophisticated taste in food. This is demonstrated by the homology between their culinary taste and that promoted by the media they consume and its difference to that of their family. The large majority of my informants did not grow up in families that ate a variety of different ethnic cuisines or haute cuisine. While the family obviously had the greatest impact on foodies' culinary taste in their early years, foodies gradually acquired their taste for such ethnic and haute cuisine through material media. For some, this mediated taste education started quite young. For example, George, who was in his thirties, had grown up watching TV cooking shows, which sparked a taste for other ethnic cuisines—and for more diversity—than what his Cypriot-Australian mother cooked at home:

> George: I grew up watching things like Gabriel Gaté and Bernard King [French-Australian and Anglo-Australian TV chefs]. I think it was probably Gabriel Gaté that sort of sparked my interest—along with the fact that I used to watch mum cook—in more of a variety than just what we used to do at home. And I'm probably talking about being eight, nine, ten years old.

> Isabelle: So you were watching them then?

George: Yeah! And I know that because we moved out of a house when I was twelve, and I was cooking in that house, and I remember that and I've discussed it with mum since. And I actually did dishes myself, when I was twelve at the latest, because you know, that's when we moved out of there...So I was doing things like spaghetti bolognaise and lasagna from go to whoa [beginning to end].

Isabelle: And so are these things that you picked up off the TV?

George: Yeah, TV, more than mum doing them, yeah.

Like George, Maureen not only acquired new tastes through media but also put those tastes into practice in her cooking. Now in her mid-sixties, Maureen reminisced about how she had discovered new tastes in lifestyle magazines in the 1950s while growing up in the country:

I'm a self-taught cook. My mother and grandmother were good old-fashioned cooks, and I was baking cakes etcetera from an early age. Where I was different was that by the time I was fourteen or so, I was making pizzas and spaghetti bolognaise, which were very avant-garde dishes in those days...I think there may have been an article in the *Women's Weekly* with recipes and I had to have a go. It was like discovering the Holy Grail.

In addition to the cosmopolitan taste for ethnic diversity, my informants also acquired more general notions of classiness and good taste from material lifestyle media. As members of the knowledge class, most of my informants had achieved upward social mobility through their tertiary education, rising in the social structure above their lower-middle or working-class origins. Their sophisticated taste in food, then, was frequently not the taste of their class habitus, learnt within the family, but a more elite taste, learnt through the media as part of their broader material education. This was reflected in comments foodies made about their parents' reaction to their taste in food. For example, Anne liked to cook recipes from a food magazine or cookbook most nights of the week, partly because it helped her to plan her cooking around her partner's shift-work and her stepdaughter's visits. While she took great pleasure in planning and preparing such recipes, she said "my mother thinks that I cook too fancy, she says 'Everything you cook is so fancy'!" This led Anne to play down the sophistication of her cooking around her mother, as she described, "we might be having, you know, crusted lamb with a bulgur and parsley salad, and I say that to my mother and she says 'Oh you cook too fancy!' but if I say we're having lamb on the barbie with a salad on the side, that's ok!"

The acquisition of notions of classiness and sophistication from material lifestyle media was demonstrated most clearly in a story told by Sarah, who was in her twenties, and spoke more openly and explicitly about class than my other informants. In this story, she compared the Australian television programs *Neil Perry: Rockpool Sessions* and *Huey's Cooking Adventures,* both of which she watched. The former was a highbrow cable cooking show hosted by Neil Perry, one of the country's top haute cuisine chefs, and set in his award-winning Sydney restaurant Rockpool. The program sought to educate viewers in a taste for haute cuisine, as Perry prepared dishes such as a "Warm Salad of King Prawn, Veal Sweetbread and Tea Smoked Oyster with Harissa" from his restaurant menu. This taste education was evident in Sarah's comments, as when she watched the program, she said she often thought "Wow! That looks amazing; I'd love to eat that one day." In contrast, *Huey's Cooking Adventures,* which screens on commercial broadcast television, is the most lowbrow Australian television cooking show. While its host, Iain Hewitson (Huey), is a professional chef, he is not represented as such but rather as a figure of parental masculinity within the home, as his program targets budget-minded lower-middle-class housewives with simple family recipes. The show promotes an ideology of thrift with segment titles such as "budget beaters," in contrast to *Rockpool Sessions*'s ideology of luxury. It is sponsored by Bi-Lo, a cut-price supermarket chain, and many recipes are based around Bi-Lo's generic brand ingredients, including preprepared and processed foods. Huey's recipes, such as "Pork and Noodle Balls," are always Westernized, as he emphasizes that they are "his take" on an ethnic dish, which reflects a lower-middle-class Anglo-Australian attitude toward ethnic food rather than the middle-class and foodie desire for authenticity (de Solier 2005). Thus, the taste formation represented on *Huey's Cooking Adventures* is not commensurate with foodie taste because of the predominance of cheap supermarket products, processed food, and the lack of authenticity. Most of my informants, as I showed earlier, did not watch such lowbrow food television; however, Sarah, who was somewhat of an omnivore of food television, said she enjoyed watching the show:

Sarah: Huey! *Huey's Cooking Adventures!* I really like watching that! I think he's *so* not a foodie at all! [*laughs*] He's not really the foodie, sort of—you know, people would probably identify more with Neil Perry, or something like that, if they identify as a foodie.

Isabelle: So you like watching his show though?

Sarah: Yeah! He's really funny, he always makes mistakes...He's got this white plastic ladle—and I think "Neil Perry would never be seen dead with a white plastic ladle on his cooking show"—and this white plastic ladle is stained, like he must have used saffron or turmeric or something in a previous episode, and he's got this stained orange-white plastic ladle, and I just think "That is *so* not classy!" I guess he's a guilty pleasure to watch, because he's certainly *not* someone that I think a foodie would normally identify with, but it's just a bit of fun!

Sarah learns class-based notions of good taste comparatively through these two television cooking shows. In her story, classiness—or rather the lack thereof—is symbolized by a particular material object, the plastic ladle used by Huey. While Sarah watches such lowbrow food television, she watches it more as a form of entertainment than as a form of gastronomic education. Yet she does learn from the program. Unlike Neil Perry's program, from which she learns good taste, Sarah learns what *not* to eat, or what not to do, if you want to look classy from Huey's show. In the case of foodies, then, we see that material media play a key role in how people shape and improve the self through the consumption of material objects in postindustrial society, as these media provide the primary source of education in good taste.

THE (IM)MORALITY OF DISTINCTION

There was a strong moral belief shared by most of the foodies in my research that it is wrong to be elitist, that this is not the right kind of self to form. Many of my informants expressed a strong opinion that they did not want to appear "pretentious," "snobbish," or as many put it, "wanky"; displaying distinction in this way was considered immoral. Their rhetoric of antielitism may have been a strategy of moral presentation of the self to the social researcher, constructing the self as a "good person," yet my perception was that in most cases it was genuinely felt. It may be explained in part by the strong history of antielitism in Australia (Bennett et al. 1999; Turner and Edmunds 2002), as well as by the upwardly mobile class trajectory of many of my informants as members of the knowledge class. One of my informants, Ruth, was particularly reflexive about this process, as she said, "my education was what enabled me to have the lifestyle I have...which is probably why I'm sensitive to sounding wanky or pretentious." It was important for most of my informants not to think of themselves in these terms, or for others to think of them in such a way. So how did they negotiate this in their self-formation?

One way, as I have shown, is through omnivorousness—the omnivore is considered a moral self to form through the consumption of material objects, as opposed to the elitism of the food snob. While I have argued that foodies are not in fact true omnivores because they repudiate lowbrow processed and fast food, foodies can still imagine themselves as such by rejecting these goods from the category of food altogether—it's not "real" food. The immorality of distinction was also reflected in the terminology foodies used to define their identity. The majority of my informants preferred to use the English term foodie over terms with French origins like "gourmet," "gourmand," or "connoisseur," which they thought sounded more "elitist," "wanky," or "snobbish." As Henri, who was himself of French heritage, put it: "I think 'foodie' is less pretentious...Yeah, anything that makes you sound like—'gourmet' or 'gourmand'—it's a bit up yourself basically." Thus, while acquiring good taste through the media may make one a better person in the foodie's eyes, displaying it conspicuously certainly does not. While material lifestyle media often promote such displays of distinction, particularly in the language of its experts, this is a point of moral difference between food experts, such as TV chefs and restaurant critics, and amateur foodies. In some cases, foodies do slip into sounding wanky, but they are quick to acknowledge they have crossed into dangerous territory and engage in moral regimes of self-governance and self-discipline. For example, Sarah, when watching Neil Perry's high-end cooking show, commented that "he sounds like such a wanker" in his description of food. She went on to say that "I probably get a bit like that sometimes, but I stop myself when I realize I'm being an idiot! Sometimes I say to my friends, 'Oh yeah, I know, I'm a foodie wanker,' like I do realize that it's bad that I present myself that way." Foodies like Sarah acknowledge that such behavior is immoral; they are engaged in a moral project that requires that they monitor and discipline how they present themselves to others. For some of my informants, this meant rejecting the term foodie altogether because it was considered too elite and wanky.

I have argued that the foodie's sophisticated taste and the status it confers is not especially unique to this identity, but is shared by much of the educated middle class. Yet it is crucial to note that there are different factors at play here. Some members of the middle class pursue food knowledge and taste instrumentally as a form of culinary capital to gain social distinction. Erickson found this to be the case among some professional and managerial workers in Canada, as they admitted to having no interest in food, yet still displayed a high level of knowledge of, and capacity to talk about, food and restaurants (1991). For such individuals, I would argue, food knowledge is accumulated solely as a form of cultural capital; it functions as a form of conspicuous knowledge—its primary purpose is display.

This stands in stark contrast to the foodies in my research, who as I have shown, are seriously committed to this material object as a central life interest, and whose knowledge is not accumulated primarily for the purpose of display for others as culinary capital but rather as a form of care of the self and productive leisure. If individuals recount their food knowledge purely for purposes of status, it is important that their audience is listening for this to be effective; whereas for foodies, like many enthusiasts with central life interests, it is often not essential that others are listening when they speak—their discussion of food is part of the uncontrollability of their enthusiasm (Dubin 1992; Stebbins 2007). The foodie's approach to food as an amateur, then, is another way in which he or she negotiates the immorality of distinction. Where using food instrumentally in self-formation, simply to gain distinction, may be considered immoral, shaping the self as an amateur, with a deep and serious commitment to this material object that is developed through practices of productive leisure, is not.

The theories of taste and distinction discussed here are the main means by which scholars have understood the role of consumption in making selves in general, and foodie selves in particular. However, I argue that the foodie's self-formation through food cannot be reduced to the superficial pursuit of cultural capital and status. Rather, it involves a more substantial process of negotiating moralities of both the consumption *and* production of material culture in postindustrial self-formation in which distinction is just one (problematic) part. Moreover, production holds a higher moral value in this process and comes to shape consumption in foodies' self-formation. For it is not so much *what* foodies consume but *how* they consume it—their serious and productive approach to consumption—that differentiates them from other members of the middle class. In the following chapters, I explore this in relation to the two social practices of consumption that are central to the foodie lifestyle: dining out and food shopping.

4

Dining Out: Restaurants, Serious Consumption, and Molecular Gastronomy

Eating out can take a variety of forms, from eating a packed lunch at work to grabbing some fast food on the go, to having dinner at a friend's house, or going to an exclusive restaurant (Warde and Martens 2000; Beriss and Sutton 2007). We may eat out as a means of necessity or as a form of leisure, pleasure, and sociability; eating out may involve different modes of food provision, by friends or family, the state, or the market. My focus here is on the more specific practice of dining out in restaurants. Yet as Toby Miller has observed, this is commonly represented not as a form of eating out, but as different from it: the food media "draw fairly rigorous distinctions between *dining* out—costly, occasioned, planned, and dressed for—and *eating* out—easy, standardized, and requiring minimal presentational effort" (2007: 118, original emphasis).

The modern restaurant has a long history. The first restaurant was opened in Paris in 1766 by Mathurin Roze de Chantoiseu. Originally, the word restaurant referred to the restorative meat broths such establishments served, which were believed to return sick or tired individuals back to health (Spang 2000: 1). In contrast to the restaurants of today, then, these early restaurants were designed for people who could *not* eat a meal because they were too weak or ill. But as the rules governing guilds changed, these establishments began to serve solid foods. Indeed, with the French Revolution and the decline of the *ancien régime,* restaurants became the new home of haute cuisine, as this refined cuisine shifted from the private sphere of noble homes to the public sphere of the restaurant, from patronage to market (Trubek 2000: 38). Paris was home to a restaurant boom at the turn of the nineteenth century, with the number of restaurants growing from around 100 in the late 1700s to over 3,000 in the 1820s (Pitte, cited in P. Ferguson 1998: 604–5). This led to a novel leisure practice of dining out, particularly among the bourgeoisie, as restaurants democratized the consumption of haute cuisine from the aristocracy to the middle class. The profession of restaurant criticism was also pioneered at this time in the journalism of Grimod de la Reynière (1803; see MacDonogh 1987; Garval 2001; Gigante 2005), while the audience of his *Almanach des Gourmands* followed his lifestyle advice and pioneered dining out as a leisure practice.

In the early twenty-first century, we are in the midst of a similar boom in restaurants and dining out in countries like Australia, the United Kingdom, and the United States. This boom began in the 1970s but has taken on greater cultural significance over the past decade, as dining out has become affordable to more people due to a growing middle class and has become the focus of an ever growing variety of material media. Television programs such as *MasterChef, Ramsay's Kitchen Nightmares,* and *Heston's Feasts* have raised public awareness of haute cuisine, its restaurants and chefs, while an array of *Good Food Guide*'s and restaurant reviews have continued to advise people on where and what to eat (see de Solier 2005, 2008; Floyd 2006; Hollows and Jones 2010). The popularity of dining out has been linked to the overall gratification it provides for most people, which stems from a combination of factors including the food, service, sociability, and value for money (Warde and Martens 2000: 170). So dining out is a popular practice of consuming things today, but does everyone consume things in the same way?

SERIOUS CONSUMPTION

Much contemporary research on consumption focuses on *what* people consume, exploring both the material objects themselves and questions of taste and cultural preferences. But it is equally important, I would argue, to consider the question of *how* people consume. One perspective that is particularly productive in this respect is theories of social practice, whose merits for the study of consumption have been highlighted by Warde (2005). He argues that consumption is not a social practice in itself but "a moment in almost every practice"; it is "partitioned through its boundedness within practices" (Warde 2005: 137, 146–47). This suggests that rather than trying to understand consumption as an abstract whole, we need to examine how people consume within certain social practices and consider how modes of consumption differ between practices and even within the same practice.

Approaching the study of consumption from this perspective involves asking different kinds of questions, including how particular practices are internally differentiated and where individuals or groups are positioned within them (Warde 2005: 149). Social practices involving consumption are internally differentiated on many dimensions, not only in terms of taste, class, or other demographic factors, such as gender, race, ethnicity, or age. From this perspective, social differentiation is explored in new ways, such as differences in levels of knowledge, skill, and competence in a practice, the degree of commitment toward and involvement in it, and the stage of a person's career in it, including participation as a professional or amateur (2005: 138, 147, 149). These modes of differentiation are more useful in distinguishing the way foodies consume food within the practice of dining out, for example, than factors such as race or gender, or even taste, where foodies share much in common with the educated middle class.

The modes of differentiation identified by theories of social practice share many similarities with those used in theories of leisure to determine how practices are internally differentiated into professional work, unpaid work, serious or productive leisure, and casual leisure. In terms of dining out, for example, Stebbins (2002) has observed how this practice is internally differentiated into casual and serious leisure, and his distinction between the two is largely based on the different approach taken to the consumption of the material object. He suggests that as casual leisure, people "more or less uncritically consume restaurant fare" as "pure entertainment and sensory stimulation." In contrast, those who dine out as serious leisure—such as foodies—adopt an intellectual approach to the consumption of cuisine based on knowledge, reflection, and analysis, as they participate as "more or less knowledgeable experts" (2002: 70). While Stebbins refers to casual leisure diners as "consumers" and serious leisure diners as "buffs" (2002: 70), it is important to recognize that buffs are consumers too. What distinguishes these categories of practitioner is not that one is a consumer and the other is not; rather, both are consumers, but they are different types of consumers. They are distinguished by different approaches to consumption in terms of their level of interest, attention, commitment, knowledge, and skill.

While Stebbins's distinction between these different modes of consumption in restaurants is speculative, Warde and Martens (2000: 199) make a similar distinction in their empirical research. They suggest that diners can be differentiated in terms of their degree of contemplation or intellectual engagement in the practice. This ranges from diners whose experience is primarily one of entertainment and involves low levels of concentration in their consumption of food (casual leisure) to diners who pay high levels of attention to the practice, particularly to its moments of food consumption that involve aesthetic appreciation and intellectual reflection (serious leisure). Where Stebbins associates the latter type of engagement with buffs, Warde and Martens similarly associate it with "enthusiasts" such as "gourmets and connoisseurs" (2000: 200), or foodies.

What becomes clear from combining these perspectives is that people consume material objects differently within the same social practice, and that modes of consumption can be differentiated in terms of levels of attention, knowledge, and skill. Warde and Martens found that most people take the more casual approach to consumption in restaurants, where it constitutes a form of entertainment and relaxation. The most common reason their participants gave for enjoying dining out was socializing (2000: 204), which disputes Finkelstein's argument that dining out is "a rich source of incivility" (1989: 5). In such casual dining, the primary focus is on one's companions, while the food provides more of a backdrop for the social experience. In contrast, for enthusiasts such as foodies, the food moves into the foreground alongside one's companions—partners, friends, or family. This form of dining involves both material and social relationships; indeed, the two are intertwined: Conversation with companions about the food consumed is one of the pleasures of dining out for foodies. As Umesh explained to me, "it's about the taste and the quality of the food, as well as the companions with whom it is shared." He dined out fortnightly with friends and monthly with his extended Sri Lankan-Australian family.

My ethnographic research with foodies investigated this latter mode of consumption in depth. I theorize it here as what I call *serious consumption,* which refers to a knowledge-based approach to consumption as a form of productive leisure. This is considered a moral approach to the consumption of material objects in self-formation because it is productive and work-like. It encapsulates how the morality of knowledge as the new productive force in postindustrial society comes to shape consumption in self-making in the context of anxieties over materialism and consumerism. Serious consumption is a form of knowledge-based leisure that involves acquiring a material education in the object consumed and deploying such knowledge in acts of consumption. Material media thus play a key role in the serious consumption of objects, as they often provide much of the knowledge required. This mode of consumption is also characterized by a strong interest in and commitment to the material object being consumed. For some people, including foodies, serious consumption takes on even more work-like characteristics as it involves the emulation of the approach of professionals to consuming material objects, a kind of expert consumption. For example, the serious manner in which foodies approach consumption in dining out—based on aesthetic judgment and intellectual reflection—emulates the approach taken to such consumption by professional restaurant critics. The contemplation of ingredients, composition, sensual qualities, culinary style, and presentation are the very things considered by restaurant critics, who make their living from consuming, judging, and writing about food. Here, I examine how foodie selves are made through serious consumption in the practice of dining out, concentrating on the experiences of those informants for whom this practice was central to their self-formation. However, serious consumption is not specific to dining out or to foodies; it is common to productive leisure practices and material enthusiasms, such as those based around cars, bikes, or clothes, where it is used to shape different sorts of selves.

MORALITIES OF MATERIAL CULTURES AND FINE DINING

Like other scholars of material culture, I am interested in the moral cosmologies that shape people's consumption and the role consumption plays in their self-formation (D. Miller 2001b; Wilk 2001; Slater 2010). As Slater has observed, consumption "is a space in which people formulate and per-form fundamental questions concerning their most substantial values and ends, their sense of who they are and who they should be" (2010: 282). The importance of examining people's moral cosmologies becomes even more significant in the current context in which the morality of making a self through consumption has been called into question not only within academia but within postindustrial society more broadly, with the growth of anticon-sumerism. Scholarly critiques of consumerism and materialism have been popularized—particularly among the educated middle class—through books such as *The Overspent American: Why We Want What We Don't Need* (Schor 1999) and *Affluenza: When Too Much Is Never Enough* (Hamilton and Denniss 2005). Kim Humphery has shown how anticonsumerist sentiment has be-come more intense in the West in recent years, to the point where excessive consumption is not only condemned by social commentators and challenged by social movements, but also "popularly understood by the western public as socially undesirable" (2010: 3; see also Binkley and Littler 2008).

This anxiety over consumerism and the moral status of consumption was common among the foodies in my research. Many possessed a distrust of consumption—particularly, excessive consumption—as morally suspect. In-deed, their attitude toward both consumption and production shares many similarities with that of the middle-class Protestants described by Weber (1930), to whom this ideology may be traced. So how do foodies negotiate these anxieties in the formation of their identities?

The problematic status held by consumption in general within the foodie's moral cosmology is negotiated by choices over what categories of material ob-jects are deemed appropriate for making selves. Many foodies believe that the consumption of food, in which their self-formation is invested, is of a higher moral value than the consumption of other material objects, such as clothes. Some of my informants, particularly the baby-boomer generation, found the consumption of clothing superficial. This distinction between clothes and food in self-formation has a symbolic dimension. While clothing sits on the surface of the self, food travels deep within the self and shapes it from the inside out. There is a rich body of work from scholars in material culture studies that shows why clothing is anything but superficial (Woodward, S. 2007; Miller, D. 2010). But its consumption, like all material things, is invested in moral re-gimes and is more central to making some selves than others.

The foodies in my research did not reflexively think of themselves as "consumers"—like people who shape their selves through stylish clothes—because they believe food is a necessity not a luxury, a need not a want. Their perspective is similar to the "worldly asceticism" of Protestants, which only "approved the rational and utilitarian uses of wealth which were willed by God for the needs of the individual"—that is, spending on "necessary and practical things"—whereas spending on fashionable clothes was considered "the idolatry of the flesh" (Weber 1930: 115). Some foodies went to great lengths to distance themselves from that type of consumption, which was invested in "fashion" and "style" and the associated endless replacement of goods. For example, when their favored weekly food supplement in the city's broadsheet was moved to the style section alongside fashion, several of my informants reacted vehemently. This included John and Elena, who immediately cancelled their subscription to the newspaper in protest. As John described: "We were deeply offended, because it's just the wrong attitude to food, like food is *not* a fashion item ... It's meeting a basic need first and foremost, and you've got to never lose sight of that, and when you start turning it into fashion, you lose touch with the bedrock purpose of it. I resent that." This moral sentiment was echoed by other foodies. As Jeff put it, "I guess it's not food as a fashion accessory for me ... I guess if you're interested in the food, that just detracts from it." Ruth was also incensed: "Suddenly in *Epicure* there was all this advertising and style, they included the style section in it ... It was about clothes, fashion, that sort of stuff—*way* not what we want in our *Epicure.*" She responded by writing an email complaining to the editor, saying, "this is *not* appropriate; this is *not* what we value about *Epicure.*" Ruth was not alone in this endeavor; Pippa responded similarly: "I wrote the most scorching email about opening up my *Epicure* and finding fishnet stockings! I went right off ... I was outraged! It's such an insult to the industry, you know, and to the reader, just assuming that you'd be into fishnet stockings because of your food interest." Pippa stresses that food and fashion are used to shape different kinds of people, different sorts of selves. Representing food as simply a fashion item provoked such outrage in these foodies because it was felt to undermine and demean the serious and substantial relationship they have with food in their postindustrial self-making—it is not just an accessory, but is fundamental to the self. As Ruth put it, her relationship with food was a "way of being"; it was this way of being that was felt to be under threat. The overwhelmingly negative response by their audience led the newspaper to remove the food supplement from the style section, thus restoring the distance—within the Melbourne foodie community—between food and fashion.

Like many people with high levels of education, most foodies see themselves as culturalists rather than materialists, people whose self-making is bound up in the pursuit of cultural experiences and knowledge rather than the accumulation of material things. What is unique about food, I argue, is that it offers culturalists an opportunity to partake in the pleasures of material culture without the evidence—or guilt—of accumulation. For food consumption differs from most other forms of material consumption in significant ways, and these differences are central to the foodie's preference for food and its use in their self-formation. The key difference lays in the longer lifecycle of most other material things—such as a house, a car, jeans, or shoes—that are not used up instantaneously, as is food. These material objects generally have a much longer social life after the commodity phase (Appadurai 1986) in which they are acquired. Unlike clothes or shoes, food *must* be endlessly replaced, yet it doesn't accumulate: the goods are completely used up in the process of consumption. There is little or no physical evidence of an immoral act of consumption. While it may accumulate on the body, there are moral dimensions to this too: over-consumption and obesity are associated with the lower class, not with middle-class discipline and refinement (see Kwan 2009). Food, then, is a material object with a culturalist status, and this is one of the reasons for its popularity as a site of self-making in postindustrial society, particularly among the educated middle class. It allows people to retain a sense of moral propriety, a sense of themselves as culturalists, and a sense that they are not materialistic consumers (de Solier 2013).

Where the ascribed moral value of food consumption becomes problematic in the foodie's cosmology is that while food itself may be a necessity, foodies possess a particular taste for luxury (and fashionable) foods. This is epitomized by the expensive haute cuisine many consume in fine dining restaurants. For example, Amelia said, "I love eating out at all sorts of places, but the fancy places always impress me." Sarah described how she too was impressed by the cuisine in such restaurants, saying, "you can have something that is so standout there that you wouldn't get just anywhere—like the pasta is cooked to absolute perfection, or the meat is cooked to perfection." Haute cuisine has long been an object of conspicuous consumption, used in the display of wealth and status competitions. According to Veblen (1934), this is the most wasteful and morally suspect form of consumption. The consumption of expensive luxury restaurants can thus cause anxiety for some foodies, as they are concerned about being viewed as materialistic conspicuous consumers. In order to reconcile this anxiety with their taste for such restaurants, many foodies implement a type of asceticism that restricts the frequency of their consumption and thus the overall level of consumption. The large majority of my informants did not dine in expensive restaurants weekly or fortnightly but around once every few months. For example, John and Elena said, "we don't spend that kind of money," in reference to just throwing money at restaurants. They are careful about when they dine out and how much they spend on it. Like many foodies in my study, they limited their expensive fine dining by concentrating on cooking quality meals at home. Raymond also focused more on cooking and saved fine dining for special occasions, when "a couple of times a year," he and his wife would "spend 300 to 400 dollars at a top flight restaurant in the city." Another informant, George, preferred to focus more on cooking haute cuisine meals at home by following recipes from the cookbooks released by professional chefs rather than consuming the same meals in restaurants.

Indeed, the large majority of my informants placed more significance on cooking than dining out in their self-formation. They were much more interested in talking about what they had cooked than what they had consumed in restaurants. For most of my informants, cooking played a larger role in how they shaped their self as a foodie than fine dining; it was only those who were serious restaurant enthusiasts for whom dining also played a central role. This is tied to the higher moral value foodies place on food production over its consumption. For most, morality is based on what you do and make as a foodie, not what you consume in designated consumption spaces, such as the restaurant, which needs to be restricted.

In contrast to the ascetic taste of Protestants, who favored "sober utility as against any artistic tendencies" (Weber 1930: 114), foodies possess a taste for luxury, but this taste is tempered—even disciplined—by asceticism in terms of frequency. The key difference between the asceticism of foodies and that of Weber's Protestants, however, is the fundamentally opposite relation to pleasure in whose name this asceticism is deployed. For Protestants, this asceticism—manifest in the abstention from consumption, particularly of luxury goods—was deployed in order to *deny* pleasure. As Weber describes it, "this asceticism turned with all its force against one thing: the spontaneous enjoyment of life and all it had to offer" (1930: 111). Pleasure, and leisure, was to come in heaven, as a reward for the work done on earth (1930: 104). In contrast, foodies deploy their mode of lite-asceticism—the restriction of consumption of luxury foods—not only to allay anxieties about consumerism but also as a strategy to *maximize* pleasure. The new secular moralities of consumption in self-formation do not seek to diminish the enjoyment of life but to enhance it. The foodie's strategy of moral asceticism constitutes a form of what Kate Soper calls "alternative hedonism," whereby changes in consumption in response to consumerism lead to new or increased pleasures. These pleasures can only be secured through restricting consumption and therefore are "conditional on 'alternative hedonist' commitments to self-policing" (2008: 572). This is illustrated by the case of Surat, one of the most serious restaurant enthusiasts in my research. He had migrated to Australia from Thailand as a teenager. Now in his early thirties, he was undertaking a doctorate in computer engineering and working in information technology. He described how he limited his consumption of fine dining restaurants in order to maximize the satisfaction he gained from it:

Even French and Japanese [his favourite cuisines], sometimes when you have them up to a certain point you can over-do it. You don't appreciate them as much. One of my eating buddies is doing a PhD in economics. He describes it as "diminishing utility." It's like some food, if you have too much, you don't appreciate its value anymore.

Researchers in material culture studies have drawn attention to the "different discourses on which people draw as they relate to particular types of goods in particular kinds of places" (D. Miller et al. 1998: 24). Here, Surat employs an economic discourse of consumer satisfaction to describe his approach to dining out, representing himself as a *homo economicus* involved in a rational calculation of value, cost, and saving. He went on to demonstrate this theory with an example of how he had gone on a foodie holiday a few years earlier with his then girlfriend and had planned a range of restaurants to eat in for lunch and dinner over the four-day trip. He said: "After a few meals, I don't appreciate them as much. I think towards the end it was more like a waste of money. You don't feel its value as much as in the beginning." Valuing the food consumed is central to foodies' moral approach to luxury restaurant consumption, and it comes through restriction. This theory of diminishing utility, while not explicitly named, was implicit in many foodies' responses. For example, Sarah, another restaurant buff, limited her visits to haute cuisine restaurants to a couple of times a year. As she described:

> I would never want to be in a position where I could just say, "Oh, let's go to Rockpool, just for Friday night dinner," you know? I like the fact that—"Wow," it's such a big event and I'm so excited to be going ... I feel like that makes it so much more special than someone who can just go and it's no big deal at all.

Thus, even serious restaurant enthusiasts like Surat and Sarah restricted the practice of dining out at haute cuisine restaurants, saving themselves for these experiences in order to fully appreciate such luxury consumption. There is a sense in which foodies have to earn their pleasure in restaurants. As Weber observes, "even the wealthy shall not eat without working" (1930: 106); you have to earn your food, particularly morally suspect luxury food. Most foodies earn it through cooking—being productive—most of the time. Through such strategies, fine dining takes on the status of the treat for many foodies. As Daniel Miller has argued, the treat is often perceived as a reward for work done, as something that is earned. The notion of the treat brackets off excessive expenditure within clear boundaries, marking it as the opposite of everyday consumption, and in doing so, tames such "transgressive" purchases and resolves moral anxieties (D. Miller 1998: 40–41, 100).

There were only a few foodies in my research who did not restrict their consumption of haute cuisine restaurants, and they expressed a sense of guilt and shame about it. For example, Maria (a housewife) and Katarina (an accountant), who dined out regularly, both said they spent "too much" money on restaurants. There was a sense that such excessive spending was wrong and that they *should* be restricting it. Katarina was the most frequent fine diner in my research. But she talked about the number of restaurants she had visited in a negative way, as something bad rather than something of which she was proud. She expressed the belief that this level of spending wasn't right, and she kept referring to it as "scary"—not just scary that she had spent so much, because she could afford it financially, but perhaps scary that she had become a conspicuous consumer. The fear appeared to be not only that others may perceive her this way but also that she herself did not see this—conspicuously consuming—as a moral way of forming the self. Such foodies avoided adding up how much money they had spent on restaurants. As Maria put it, "I don't know that I am ready to know just how much I spend," while Katarina said, "I don't even want to put a dollar value to it, and I'm not going to." They did not want others to think of them as consumerist or to face this vision of themselves. Thus, even among those foodies who did not restrict their fine dining, there was a similar moral judgment of excessive spending as wrong (de Solier 2013).

In addition to limiting fine dining and being productive cooks most of the time, the other way most foodies earned their luxury cuisine was through their work-like mode of consumption. For foodies negotiate the morally suspect status of consumption not only through what things they consume, and what level they consume, but also how they consume. Their mode of serious consumption, which involves the acquisition and deployment of knowledge and emulates the approach of professionals, is a way of bringing consumption back into the realm of work and production, thereby allaying the moral anxieties it induces in postindustrial self-formation.

FROM RESTAURANT GUIDES TO *IRON CHEF*: MATERIAL MEDIA AND SERIOUS CONSUMPTION

In dining out, serious consumption does not simply involve the deployment of knowledge and skill in the restaurant; it also involves the acquisition of knowledge and skill before visiting the restaurant. This is part of the work of serious consumption. Foodies acquire knowledge relating to restaurants as part of their broader gastronomic education. This includes not only taste knowledge but also knowledge about the local and global restaurant industry, chefs and their careers, culinary styles and ingredients, and so on. Like most of a foodie's knowledge about food, this restaurant knowledge is acquired from material media. This education constitutes a fundamental part of foodies' serious consumption, as it functions as a means of preparation that assists them in their appropriation—and maximizes their appreciation—of food in restaurants.

One of the main ways that foodies try to maximize their appreciation is by researching restaurants before they dine out, particularly by acquiring recommendations to assist their consumption choices. In their research on eating out, Warde and Martens found that only a minority of consumers looked to the food media for restaurant recommendations (13% used newspapers, 5% food guides, and 4% television programs) (2000: 203). The majority of people relied much more heavily on recommendations from friends or relatives, on "trustworthy personal informants" (2000: 204). While the foodies in my research use these personal sources too, most consult restaurant reviews from the media when making their decisions, from annual restaurant guides, to more up-to-date reviews in newspapers or food magazines. The comparatively high use of restaurant reviews among foodies reflects their respect for, and trust in, professional experts as guides in their self-formation through material culture.

For foodies, the reviews written by professional critics function as simplifying and ordering mechanisms that help guide them through the abundance of restaurants. For example, Madeleine used the reviews in annual restaurant guides and the weekly food newspaper supplement. As she put it, "there's so many places in Melbourne to choose from it's good to have some tips from a source I trust, to help decide on new places to try." Sian, who used a range of local and national restaurant guides, said, "these guides are also reasonably reliable. All the information is to hand, for example, telephone numbers, times and prices." Thus, these reviews make the process of selecting a restaurant to dine at easier by offering a description of the type of dishes served, the food prices, and the restaurant location. The annual guides also made it easy to research particular styles of restaurants or cuisine; as Amelia said, "I find *The Good Food Guide* very useful because it can help you find what you are looking for—if you want a Korean restaurant, if you want a good place for breakfasts, if you want BYO, etcetera."

Foodies use expert reviews to maximize their dining experience through the selection of a good restaurant. Therefore, these reviews also function as risk-minimization mechanisms. As Giddens observes, expert systems are integral filters in the situations of multiple choice in which individuals negotiate their lifestyles in late modernity: these individuals use experts to filter risk to help construct their self-identity amidst a diversity of options (1991: 5). This use of expert restaurant reviews as a risk-minimization mechanism was made clear by Sarah. She emphasized how these expert systems were particularly useful in negotiating consumption choices within moral systems of limiting spending and maximizing appreciation: "It's just all the research into finding the good ones rather than the dud ones that cost the same amount of money but aren't good. And that's why I guess I read *Epicure* and stuff all the time, and then find the ones that are—'Oh, that sounds affordable *and* good.'" However, the risk-minimization mechanisms of expert systems do not always work. Sarah went on to discuss this in relation to the reviews of one of the city's major critics, saying: "I've gone to restaurants that he's recommended, and I haven't liked them ... And I think, 'I don't know why he wrote that because I didn't find it that good.' So I definitely like to make up my own mind."

Toby Miller has highlighted the shifting focus of print food media, from an emphasis on production—home cooking and recipes—in the 1960s to an emphasis on consumption—dining out and restaurants—in the 1970s. By the 1980s, he observes, "food writers assumed the title 'critics.' They offered instruction on enjoyment rather than production" (2007: 119). Despite this discourse of consumption voiced by restaurant critics, knowledge of material production remains central to foodies' appreciation of cuisine in restaurants and is often sought through other forms of food media. For most of my informants, this production knowledge was linked to their own practical culinary skills, as many liked to figure out how the dishes they consumed in restaurants were made, often so they could attempt to replicate them at home. Yet the centrality of material production knowledge to dining is demonstrated most clearly by the case of Surat, who didn't acquire such knowledge for practical purposes but solely for serious consumption. He was one of only two of my informants for whom cooking did not play a central role in self-formation as a foodie; like Mathew, his identity was formed through the consumption of food and through the production of food media. Yet knowledge of food production was nevertheless central to his self-formation, which he acquired largely from cookbooks. Surat possessed a small but significant collection of cookbooks, mostly written by professional haute cuisine chefs. He did not just look at the photographs, but he examined the recipes, saying, "so that I can understand when I go and dine out, understand how certain things are made," in order to maximize his appreciation of the cuisine. In addition to owning books by Australian chefs whose restaurants he had visited (e.g., Tetsuya Wakuda and Neil Perry), Surat also owned books by international chefs (e.g., America's Thomas Keller) and canonical professional texts like Escoffier's *Le Guide Culinaire* (1907) and the encyclopedia of French cuisine, *Larousse Gastronomique* (Montagné 1961). Of the latter two, Surat said: "They are good reference books. They have some recipes but they also explain about ingredients." Thus the acquisition of knowledge of the production of material objects was central to Surat's serious consumption of them. This education equips Surat with a particular form of expertise in professional culinary production—what Harry Collins and Robert Evans call "interactional expertise": the possession of the theoretical knowledge of how something is done, without the practical skills and ability to do it oneself (2007: 14). In addition to cookbooks, Surat used food television to acquire this theoretical culinary knowledge. He discussed this in relation to the Japanese program *Iron Chef*:

I watch it to see how they would make certain things and do certain things, what is the reason or what are the skills or what is the knowledge behind the things they do, and then watch the review when the judge tries the food afterwards, and what they have to say with certain dishes. It's something that I can probably think about when I go out and dine out myself, I can probably think about something similar. I can probably analyze—a little bit, not in the stressful sense—but, you know, "Okay, why did they do this? And how have they done this?"

Surat watches *Iron Chef* to acquire knowledge related to both the production and consumption of restaurant cuisine. Just as he acquires the production knowledge from professional chefs, so he acquires the consumption knowledge from professional critics. It is this professional and knowledge-based approach to the consumption of cuisine that many foodies deploy when dining out.

SERIOUS DINING: MOLECULAR GASTRONOMY RESTAURANTS

Bourdieu suggests that there are two contrasting aesthetic approaches to consumption. The first is the more intellectual approach that he calls the "taste of reflection." This, he argues, is the culturally legitimate mode of aesthetic appreciation associated with the dominant class, which values "the stylization of life, that is, the primacy of forms over function, of manner over matter" (1984: 5). He contrasts this to the "taste of sense," which he associates with the working class, who value substance over style. In their research on eating out, Warde and Martens (2000) found that substance rather than form was more important to most people in this practice. Most of their informants preferred quantity over quality and did not want to be left hungry; physical sufficiency was the primary standard of evaluation. They expressed a dislike for the small servings of haute cuisine, as one person put it, "where there's one little thing in a little bit of sauce over here on a big plate" (2000: 192). The approach to consumption of these more casual diners is thus close to Bourdieu's notion of the taste of sense. Their appreciation of food was based more on sensual gratification—on sensations of taste, sight, and smell—than it was on intellectual reflection. Yet these sensations were not described by diners in their accounts of meals out, which Warde and Martens suggest was a result of both the immediacy of such gratifications and the lack of a vocabulary among most diners to describe such sensual dimensions of food. Most would report the menu rather than describe the taste or smell of a dish, as they found such sensations difficult to express (2000: 194). As Fine demonstrates, this difficulty in describing flavors and smells is not restricted to diners but is also common to many lower-level professional chefs (1996: 206). Such vocabulary generally belongs to the head chef in haute cuisine restaurants, and more specifically, to gastronomes, such as restaurant critics.

Many foodies, however, have learnt or co-opted such expert vocabulary from gastronomes, which they use to describe the sensual dimensions of their dining experiences. This vocabulary is another form of knowledge such amateurs acquire that emulates the approach of professionals in their interactions with, and self-formation through, material objects. For example, Sarah discussed how her descriptions of the sensual dimensions of restaurant fare were perceived as professional-like by her friends:

> My friends laugh and say, "You should be a food writer, or something like that," because I will describe things, I'll go that extra step to describe them. They'll say "Oh what was it like?" and I'll say "Oh well they had a really good balance, like, there was a hint of chili but it wasn't too much, and it was really nice, it had coriander," and I'll be able to identify things that were in it.

Foodies like Sarah gain intense sensual gratification from restaurant meals, are able to recall such sensations long after eating the dish, and describe them in similar language to professional critics. While such gratification is associated with Bourdieu's taste of sense, the aesthetic judgments that professional critics—and foodies following them—make of restaurant cuisine consider not only such sensual properties but also the stylistic properties of food, properties that are associated with the alternate taste of reflection. Thus, their judgments consider not only the flavors but the balance of flavors, the combination of textures, the visual presentation, the methods of preparation, the style of cuisine, the cultural and historical references, and the culinary skill of the chef. Foodies, unlike most diners in Warde and Martens's research, are concerned with quality over quantity, with questions of form and style, with the composition of a dish, and the skill of its execution. It is these things that foodies learn to think about and analyze in their serious consumption of food when dining out. Thus, while most diners approach the consumption of food in restaurants with the taste of sense, foodies' aesthetic approach in their serious consumption falls somewhere in between Bourdieu's contrasting taste of sense and taste of reflection. What is most important is that the foodie's mode of appropriation emulates the culturally legitimate aesthetic approach of professional critics.

This reaches its pinnacle in restaurants associated with molecular gastronomy, which has become the leading force in haute cuisine over the past decade. Most commonly associated with Ferran Adrià at elBulli in Spain, it has also been made famous by Heston Blumenthal at The Fat Duck in England and Thomas Keller at The French Laundry in the United States, yet its effects have been felt in fine dining restaurants all over the world, including Australia. As its name suggests, molecular gastronomy is a scientific culinary style. It is renowned for importing ingredients, tools, and methods from the laboratory into the kitchen, such as hypodermic syringes, test tubes, liquid nitrogen, and synthetic molecular solutions. It was invented in the late 1980s by the scientists Nicholas Kurti and Hervé This to apply physics and chemistry to restaurant and home cooking. It entered the domain of haute cuisine restaurants, starting with elBulli, in the mid-1990s. I have examined the development of molecular gastronomy in detail elsewhere, from its origin in the laboratory, to its expansion into fine dining restaurants, and its more recent adoption by foodies within the home. I argue that in the laboratory, molecular gastronomy is harnessed to the professional scientist's project of "culinary enlightenment", which involves both universalizing objectives, such as establishing culinary truths and recipe-formulas, and the pursuit of culinary progress through new ingredients, methods, tools, and dishes. In the restaurant, it is tied to the professional chef's pursuit of "culinary creativity"; for Adrià, this is based on developing new techniques, such as siphoning and spherification, that lead to new culinary concepts, such as elBulli's now famous foams and liquid ravioli (see de Solier 2010).

At elBulli and other molecular gastronomy restaurants, the cuisine is designed to provoke intellectual as well as sensual appreciation in the diner. elBulli highlights the importance of "the intellectual stimulation that can be derived from appreciating irony, a sense of humour, decontextualization or cultural references in a dish. This is referred to at elBulli as the 'sixth sense'" (Adrià et al. 2008: 318). In addition to providing pleasure, much molecular cuisine aims to challenge the expectations of both the senses and the mind and the integral relationship between them. This is done by combining ingredients or techniques that do not conventionally go together, such as using savory ingredients in desserts like elBulli's Bacon Croquant Flute with Pine Nut Ice Cream, or "deconstructing" traditional dishes such as paella and reconstructing them as "Kellogg's paella, which consists of Rice Krispies with an intense seafood reduction, alongside flash-fried shrimps, a piece of shrimp sashimi and an ampoule that contains a thick brown extract of shrimp heads" (Jeffries 2006).

Many of the foodies in my research had eaten in restaurants that served molecular cuisine. They appreciated its sensually and intellectually challenging nature. Jeff, for example, recalled eating a dish of venison carpaccio with chocolate, olive oil, and strawberry ice cream, of which he said:

> Those sorts of foods, they play with your head and with your tongue. They're clever. And they work on the texture and flavor and—yeah, putting aside what they are, and concentrating on the textures and the flavors ... It's not about that purity of food, it's about here's some textures, here's some flavors, try them out, see what you think, and it's like, "Oh right, that really worked, that's good."

Another informant, Adam, highlighted how the notion of challenging yourself through the consumption of material goods—characteristic of the taste of reflection—is integral to the mode of serious dining pursued by foodies and distinguishes them from other diners in haute cuisine restaurants when faced with such challenging food. This occurred in his description of his visit to Tetsuya's in Sydney in 2005, the year it was voted the world's fourth leading restaurant (World's 50 Best Restaurants 2010):

> Every now and then you get given something in a degustation that's a little bit different, a little bit challenging, and at Tetsuya's it was the blue cheese ice cream. And—it's just a combination that doesn't quite click. But then we tried it, and you know, we both absolutely loved it, we thought it was just fantastic. But then we noticed that people at other tables were sending them back, because they couldn't get their heads around the fact that it was blue cheese, they couldn't understand that it was done as ice cream. They just didn't want to take that sort of risk in trying something different. And it would get replaced with something like a chocolate tart. You know, it would have been extraordinary, but it's like—"Well, why are you here? Are you here because of the restaurant's name? Or are you here to try new food? Or are you here to challenge yourself?"

Adam makes a moral distinction between foodies like himself who go to fine dining restaurants to participate in the serious consumption of food and other diners who may be there purely for more instrumental purposes of social status. Part of the foodie's moral approach to consuming this material object in self-making is a belief that one should challenge oneself and ones preconceptions of this material object—this is central to the relationship developed between the object and the self. Yet Adam's comparison is not only based on a different willingness to challenge oneself by consuming such avant-garde food, it is also based on one's knowledge and ability to understand such food. Some diners, for example, may have gone to Tetsuya's because of its status, and, while surprised by the blue cheese ice cream, they may have risen to the challenge of trying it, and even liked it, yet may have left none-the-wiser that what they ate was molecular cuisine. For foodies, on the other hand, serious consumption is not only about rising to the challenge but also about understanding the cultural and culinary references of the food they consume: It is about knowing, as Adam does, that the blue cheese ice cream is not just a weird whim of a chef, but that it belongs to the culinary style of molecular gastronomy, and that this style was pioneered by Adrià at elBulli. This was illustrated even more clearly in a story told by Mary. She spoke about the first time she ate another elBulli innovation, culinary foam, at a fine dining restaurant. Describing a dish, she said:

> It had the most amazing thing in the world; it had a citrus foam, which is part of this wonderful molecular gastronomy that everyone is going on about. And it looked like cappuccino froth—but it's a citrus one! And earlier on in the night I had a parsnip one, which was on one of the little appetizers! Oh, it was just amazing! … It got started by Ferran Adrià, that Spanish chef, the world leader of all of this.

The foam, for Mary, is not just froth; she understands that it is part of molecular gastronomy and that it was pioneered by Adrià in Spain, just as Adam understood the context of the blue cheese ice cream. The reason these foodies, unlike more casual diners, can understand or get their head around such cuisine is because, as we saw with Surat, they have spent time and effort acquiring food knowledge as part of their serious consumption as productive leisure. They possess the knowledge of culinary styles that allows them to shift from the primary stratum of meaning—the sensible properties of food—to the secondary level of meaning—the stylistic properties, which is characteristic of the taste of reflection. Foodies seek such understanding in order to maximize their appreciation of the food they consume in haute cuisine restaurants. In the moralities of consumption that govern foodie self-making, then, if one is going to consume luxury restaurant cuisine, one should restrict it, rise to the challenges posed by it, and do the work required to understand it.

AMATEURS, PROFESSIONALS, AND CONSUMER EXPERTISE

Through the experience of dining out in restaurants and the knowledge acquired from various material media, foodies develop a level of expertise in the consumption of this material object. They express and share this expertise in a variety of ways, particularly in their mediated and face-to-face engagement with professionals—both restaurant critics and chefs. One way they do this is by constructing their own reviews of restaurants they have visited. Sarah described how she annotated her copy of *The Good Food Guide* with her own judgments of restaurants, both for her own future reference and to recommend restaurants to her friends:

> I kind of—oh, this is really bad, my friends always give me crap for this, even my foodie friends—because I tick off the restaurants I've been to, and I write little comments—like "bit too expensive," or "very nice," or then stars next to some and "THE BEST!" And then people—I've never thought there's anything wrong with it, I thought "Oh well, I'm keeping a record of what I'm doing"—but then I lent the book to a friend, and she came back pissing herself, like "What are these little comments? 'THE BEST!' Oh, I want to go *there* Sarah!" And I was *so* embarrassed! For a while after that I couldn't bring myself to annotate my book anymore, because I thought "they're gonna laugh at me!" But now I'm like, "stuff 'em."

Sarah described how she judged restaurants in terms of criteria such as the quality of the food, the service, the atmosphere, and price. Her annotation of the restaurant guide adds a further layer of meaning to the mass media text—a layer of personal meaning, as she records her own ideas, opinions, and experiences of consumption—that in some cases may contradict the original meaning in the professional critic's review. Yet it also documents her career in the practice of dining out and forms part of her reflexive self-formation through food and food media. As we saw earlier, she approaches the consumption of food in restaurants in the manner of a professional critic and makes aesthetic judgments based on the same properties. In writing these judgments down, she takes on a further task of the professional reviewer and makes her serious consumption even more work-like. But while Sarah occasionally harbored the desire to be a professional critic, she believed she didn't have the necessary writing skills: "I think it's a pipe dream, sometimes I just think about it but I would never act on it." I explore how foodies express their expertise in this form of material consumption through writing reviews further in Chapter 8, where I examine how amateur bloggers communicate their restaurant knowledge publicly and the power struggles this leads to with professional critics.

In addition to this mediated engagement with the professional consumers of restaurant cuisine, foodies engage in face-to-face interaction with the professional producers of such cuisine, as they share their expertise with haute cuisine chefs. While Sarah's amateur foodie friends made fun of her display of expertise, many professional chefs respect the expertise that foodies have acquired in the consumption of this material object. For example, Beth described how she liked to share her knowledge of restaurant cuisine with local chefs with whom she had cultivated relationships throughout her career dining out. She liked to think of herself as a "professional patron," which meant that she took her dining seriously, like a work role, but moreover, it meant that she wanted to share the expertise she had acquired with culinary professionals in order to help them provide diners with the best possible experience. This marginal role highlights how "amateurs in pursuit of their leisure goals help professionals reach their work goals" (Stebbins 2001: 17). In adopting the role of professional patron, Beth cements her status as an insider in the foodie social world, demonstrating her commitment to advancing the local restaurant industry. Her professional patronage is a form of community involvement, as she attempts to contribute to the cultural enrichment of the local restaurant scene through the knowledge and experience she has acquired from other places.

As well as offering their consumer expertise to chefs, some foodies are approached by chefs who are interested in foodies' opinions. Adam described how he was elated at being approached online, via the website *eGullet,* by a local molecular gastronomy chef who sought his expert consumer opinion:

> He actually asked me and my friend to do his twenty-five course tour menu with wine, just because he wanted to know what we thought about it! ... We had a few

discussions with him on the website and then—yeah, we'd been there a couple of times for dinner and he'd treated us really well ... It was just really flattering to be asked. Yeah, and so he came out to talk about what we thought of it.

Adam had gained the respect of this chef through his postings on the forums on *eGullet,* a key site in which professionals and amateurs interact in the foodie social world. While for the price of a degustation menu, the chef gained valuable market research with members of his target audience, this nevertheless demonstrates how some professional chefs respect the knowledge and opinions of amateur foodies and the expertise they have acquired in the consumption of this material object through their serious dining. But it is not just in restaurants that foodies take such a serious approach to consumption in their self-formation: their consumption of food in shopping, too, is shaped by this moral approach.

5

Shopping: Slow Food, Ethical Consumption, and the Morality of Quality

Shopping is commonly understood as the main practice of consuming things through which we make the self in postindustrial society. Through the purchase of material objects, such as clothes, cars, or food, we shape our sense of who we are and who we want to be. But shopping as a social practice cannot be reduced to this act of buying. Rather, it should be understood as "a network of activity of which the actual point of purchase of a commodity is but a small part" (D. Miller et al. 1998: 14).

The social practice of shopping is internally differentiated into forms of labor and leisure. Both these forms are associated predominantly with women, as shopping has historically been culturally coded as a feminine practice (Friedberg 1993; Rappaport 2000). The distinction between shopping as leisure or labor is often based on the types of material goods consumed: while shopping for fashionable clothes is commonly understood as women's leisure (Friedberg 1993; Campbell 1997), shopping for food is considered women's (unpaid) work (Charles and Kerr 1988; DeVault 1991; Koch 2012; Naccarato and LeBesco 2012).

Food shopping is the most common form of shopping, something that needs to be done regularly as a necessary maintenance activity. Because it has to be done, and has to be done frequently, this obligatory form of shopping is experienced by most as a chore (Oakley 1990; Bowlby 1997). For this reason, food shopping has been absent from scholarly understandings of shopping as leisure, positioned in most cases as the opposite experience. It has also been absent from accounts of shopping and self-making, which tend to focus on more traditionally leisured and stylized forms—on the more glamorous realms of shopping for clothes and shoes rather than the everyday, routinized realm of buying bread and milk. But shopping for food, I argue, has become an increasingly popular practice of self-fashioning today—particularly among those who are not so interested in clothes shopping—where one of the distinctions is that it is undertaken as a form of leisure. This is epitomized by foodies.

SERIOUS SHOPPING

While scholars suggest that the categories of shopping as labor and leisure are not mutually exclusive, food shopping as a leisure practice is a particularly complex and ambiguous phenomenon, a hybrid of the characteristics associated with these contrasting categories. For example, Lehtonen and Mäenpää distinguish between shopping as a "pleasurable social form" and a "necessary maintenance activity" (1997: 144). For the foodies in my research, food shopping is both: it involves spending long amounts of time, the experience of pleasure, and an emphasis on experience, but it's also a means to an end, involving planning, making purchases, and seriousness. This was the case for both my female and male informants, who were generally responsible for the food shopping in their households, yet nevertheless experienced it as leisure. While food shopping may be more obscure as a form of leisure because of its obligatory nature, the presence of such obligatory foundations does not mean it cannot be experienced as leisure. As Stebbins argues, "the line between obligation and leisure is not always clear and depends to a large extent on one's attitude to the activity" (1992: 4).

Moreover, while food shopping as a way of meeting basic needs may be an obligation, the serious and professional manner in which the foodies in my research approach this practice, and the significant time and effort they invest in it, certainly are not. What distinguishes foodies from other food shoppers is not just that they experience this practice as leisure but that they participate in it as productive leisure. Food shopping as a consumption practice is crucially connected to cooking as a production practice in the making of foodie selves. While both these activities are undertaken as leisure, their pursuit as productive leisure means that foodies do adopt a work-like approach to them. This is not the approach of unpaid labor but rather that of paid labor: amateur foodies take the approach of professional chefs to both their cooking and their shopping. They take their shopping seriously because they take their cooking seriously, and shopping is the means by which they acquire the raw materials for their culinary production. Thus, the foodie's approach to consumption within the practice of shopping—like that of dining out—can be conceptualized as serious consumption, as it involves a work-like approach to consumption as productive leisure, based on significant knowledge, effort, commitment, and a professional stance. The moralities of productive leisure come to shape shopping, too, as a moral practice of consuming material objects in postindustrial self-making. This morality influences what foodies buy, where they buy it, and how they appreciate it.

Foodies spend a lot of time and effort seeking out quality ingredients for their home cooking, as do chefs for their restaurant cooking. Like chefs, foodies believe one should cook from scratch, which involves buying a range of fresh ingredients. Many of my informants had adopted professional terminology (popularized by TV chefs) to describe their serious shopping in work-like terms, such as "sourcing produce" from "suppliers." Like chefs, foodies tend to have multiple suppliers, sourcing different ingredients from each one, and they go to significant lengths to acquire the best quality produce they can. For example, John and Elena had a range of different suppliers from whom they sourced various ingredients: pork from an organic produce shop, red meat from a small butcher, quail from a stall at the market, duck from a specialist poultry shop, seafood from a small fishmonger, and olive oil and balsamic vinegar from specialist gourmet food stores. Other informants described the lengths they went to in order to "hunt down" obscure ethnic ingredients in different suburbs across the city: a Middle Eastern ingredient here, a Vietnamese ingredient there. There is now a body of material media dedicated to assisting this serious shopping, most notably the annual *Foodies' Guide* (Campion and Curtis 2009), detailing over 400 specialty food stores in Melbourne alone, from bakers and butchers to chocolatiers. The emergence of new forms of self-making through food shopping is due in part to the growth of this alternative food retail sector in postindustrial society, as these more aestheticized and romanticized shopping spaces offer greater opportunities for self-fashioning than the space where most people shop: the supermarket.

The retail innovation of the supermarket originated in the United States in the 1930s (Bowlby 1997) and took hold in Australia in the 1960s (Humphery 1998), tied to processes of suburbanization and increases in car ownership. It was built on the idea of convenience: "self-service and everything under one roof, meaning no need to stand in line at innumerable counters in a succession of different food stores" (Bowlby 1997: 104). The convenience of supermarket shopping also includes its extended opening hours (many supermarkets are open twenty-four hours a day or at least from six o'clock in the morning until midnight). Supermarkets dominate food retailing in Australia, as they do in the United States and the United Kingdom. Indeed, Australia has one of the most concentrated grocery markets in the world, where the two main supermarket chains (Coles and Woolworths) account for almost 80 percent of the grocery market and 60 percent of the fruit and vegetable market (Fyfe and Millar 2012a,b). Thus, the mainstream practice of food shopping is based around the single space of the supermarket and the idea of convenience.

In contrast, the serious shopping of foodies is based around the idea of effort and multiple alternative shopping spaces, such as greengrocers, butchers, bakers, delicatessens, ethnic grocers, specialty shops, markets, and farmers' markets. It is a mode of shopping that is time-intensive. In addition to the extra time spent visiting multiple suppliers, this serious shopping involves greater organization of time, as unlike supermarkets, these alternative suppliers are open limited hours (most local greengrocers and butchers close at six o'clock in the evening and may not open on Sunday; markets are only open until early afternoon and are generally closed on at least two weekdays, and farmers' markets only operate on Saturday mornings). Thus, if one works full-time, it is a significant effort to shop anywhere but the supermarket.

Lehtonen and Mäenpää use the term "trippism" to describe the experience of going to a single destination, such as a mall or supermarket, to do one's shopping. But the serious shopping of the foodies in my research conforms more to the opposing notion of "tourism," as it involves travelling around visiting a number of places in a circuitous journey (Lehtonen and Mäenpää 1997: 148–49). Like tourists, foodies possess maps of the places they visit, yet they take the form of a mental cartography of place. This mental food cartography was described by Pippa, an academic in her early fifties. She used the term "food lines" to describe the paths she travelled on this map to source produce:

> I'm aware that I've got these, what I call "food lines." You know, I spend a lot of my Saturday morning out on my food lines around Melbourne. I've got this kind of mental map of where I'll go to buy all my organic produce...Yeah I've got shops everywhere. I just kind of have the maps in my head, and I'll know what's needed in the house. So it's like a real lifestyle, sort of, fun thing.

Pippa's description of her food lines highlights a particular geographic knowledge of the city related to her landscapes of food shopping. Of all my informants, George had the longest food lines, which extended beyond the city across country and regional Victoria. He said, "I love cooking at home, and therefore I visit every corner of the state to source what I consider quality produce." George's food lines extended from local greengrocers in his suburb to farmers' markets across the city, to butchers in regional towns, and to rural farms. This serious shopping is, by definition, slow shopping, as it takes a lot more time and effort than visiting the supermarket. This effort is made in pursuit of "good quality" ingredients, which is central to the foodie's morality of shopping as a practice of material consumption.

THE MORALITY OF QUALITY

Shopping has become an "increasingly moral activity," argues Daniel Miller (2001a: 133; see also Littler 2009). This observation developed out of his ethnography of shopping in London. In contrast to the foodies in my study, Miller's informants—mostly working-class and middle-class housewives—did their food shopping, as most people do, in the mainstream space of the supermarket. Miller argues that his informants' shopping was governed by a morality of thrift (2001a: 134) in which "saving money" rather than spending money was central to ideas about the "right" way to shop. Such savings were commonly made by seeking out different types of "bargains," such as the supermarkets' generic or home-brand goods that cost considerably less than brand-name products or sale items that were marked down from their regular price (Miller 1998: 51–52). Miller describes how the notion of saving was constantly foregrounded in his informants' discussions of shopping: "The conversation would not be of the form, 'I spent three pounds on beef'...but of the form, 'look I saved fifty pence on ice cream'" (1998: 56).

In contrast, this notion of thrift was not foregrounded by my foodie informants in their discussions of shopping. Rather than save money, the large majority of foodies emphasized that they were willing or prepared to spend more money in order to acquire "good quality" food for the home. For example, Nick said, "I'm willing to pay more for fresh, good quality ingredients." Sian, too, thought that quality was "very important" when it came to shopping, while Tess declared that "price is not important. Quality is everything." Foodies' shopping, then, is governed by what I term a "morality of quality" (de Solier 2013) because it is quality that is of the highest importance in foodies' ideas about what constitutes "good shopping." The moral value these amateurs attach to quality stems from both their work-like emulation of the values of professional chefs—who always emphasize the importance of quality ingredients—and their middle-class taste. Indeed, this morality of quality appears to be governing the shopping of a growing number of people today, in what has been called the quality "turn" (Goodman 2003).

The question of the morality of food shopping has been of particular concern in geography and agro-food studies. Michael K. Goodman, Damian Maye, and Lewis Holloway have highlighted the need for scholars to examine "questions about what we should and should not eat, what becomes regarded as 'good' and 'bad' food, and how these constructions are intimately situated and contextualised, what sets of criteria define the 'good' and 'bad' meanings embedded in particular foods, [and] who decides on how these criteria are defined" (2010: 1782). As Lewis Holloway and Moya Kneafsey observe, this involves exploring the "ambiguities and subtleties" of ideas of "quality" in people's food shopping (2000: 296). My research found that foodies have a complex set of criteria through which they judge the quality of this material object in their shopping. Central to their judgments are sensory properties, such as flavor, smell, and appearance, yet these judgments are influenced and sometimes short-circuited by other factors such as the mode of production and distribution through which additional values are placed on properties such as fresh, local, seasonal, traditional, small-scale, and artisanal—properties associated with what Rachel Laudan terms "culinary luddism" (2001: 36).

It is some, or all, of these various properties that are invoked when foodies refer to food as "good quality." As Laudan points out, while culinary luddites see this as a return to traditional preindustrial food values, the idea that food should be fresh, natural, and local is actually a modern moral belief. For our ancestors, natural food often tasted bad, was unreliable, and usually indigestible: "Eating fresh, natural food was regarded with suspicion verging on horror, something to which only the uncivilized, the poor, and the starving resorted...Local foods were the lot of the poor who could neither escape the tyranny of local climate and biology nor the monotonous, often precarious, diet it afforded" (Laudan 2001: 38).

It is somewhat easier to identify what foodies consider to be "bad quality" food than it is good quality. These are the foods that are the result of industrialized and globalized systems of mass production and distribution and are sold in supermarkets; that is, the products of "culinary modernism" (Laudan 2001). This includes the fresh produce sold in supermarkets, but it is epitomized by the highly processed foods and preprepared convenience meals they sell. As Celina put it:

> I never buy things like frozen meals or even frozen vegetables or fish fillets, or partly prepared ingredients like a pizza base or already marinated meats...I am continuously appalled by what people consider to be an adequate meal— something that has been processed, frozen, packaged and sitting in a freezer in a supermarket for who knows how long and then microwaved.

These lowbrow processed foods, as I argued earlier, are associated with the consumption practices of the lower classes. The foodie's morality of quality, then, cannot be separated from matters of class. These issues of class taste are implicit in the moral discourse voiced by many foodies about what people should buy and eat. For example, Beth said emphatically: "How can there be people who say they can't afford to eat right? There is an oversupply of great food, but people buy processed food, and become addicted to that. There are affordable alternatives, it is so accessible...And it's very affordable. I mean, it's *very* affordable." As Bourdieu argues, such perspectives transform the taste of necessity of the poor into a "taste of freedom," reducing it to a "pathological and morbid preference" for such foods, "a sort of congenital coarseness, the pretext for a class racism which associates the populace with everything heavy, thick and fat" (1984: 178). In this neoliberal discourse, the choice to eat wrong symbolizes the irresponsibility of the lower class; their lack of personal responsibility denies them the status of being good self-governing citizens. As Toby Miller has argued, in neoliberal society "ethico-aesthetic exercises are necessary to develop the responsible individual...'Good taste' becomes a sign of, and a means toward, better citizenship" (2007: 11). He argues that the consumption of industrialized processed foods by the poor cannot be reduced to matters of taste; it is also, fundamentally, a question of economic resources: "Despite clear correlations between youth obesity and local prices of fresh fruit and vegetables—nothing to do with consumer choice—the high moralism so prevalent in the U.S. media has led to a doctrine of personal responsibility, militating against both collective identification and action" (2007: 120). Likewise, despite the claims about the affordability and accessibility of great food by this high-income earning foodie, research has shown that many Australians on low incomes and welfare payments are suffering "food stress" (Burns et al. 2008). The cost of fresh foods has risen at a higher rate than processed foods in recent years, and the consumption of the latter by those on lower incomes is not necessarily a result of issues of taste or nutritional knowledge, but importantly, of price: they simply cannot afford to "eat right". In addition, the artisanal foods that foodies consider good quality are also more expensive than mass-produced processed foods. Thus, unlike foodies, not everyone is prepared to, or can afford to, spend more money for good quality food.

How, then, does this morality of quality that governs foodie shopping—which involves a willingness or preparedness to "spend more" for good quality food—connect with the moral asceticism foodies displayed toward excessive expenditure and its connotations of consumerism in fine dining? Why do they find it morally legitimate to spend more on food in shops and markets, but not in restaurants? The difference is that while fine dining restaurants are considered by foodies to be luxury consumption—which is particularly morally suspect and in need of restriction—buying good quality food for the home is not. Thus, they can legitimize spending more on shopping because the food is regarded as a necessity required for life maintenance. While foodies recognize that the taste for and practice of fine dining is elite and not affordable for everyone, most do not consider purchasing costly quality foods from alternative suppliers for the home to be elite; it's just "right" (Beth). Spending more on food for the home is also legitimated by the close connection between this form of consumption and the material production practice of cooking, and the higher moral value cooking holds in foodies' self-formation. Nevertheless, while they are willing to spend more on quality ingredients, some foodies still construct their overall levels of spending as somewhat thrifty: By knowing where to buy "good quality food for a fair price" (Celina) and "buying produce that is in season" (Sian), these foodies suggest that they "don't actually spend heaps on food" (Pippa). This qualification is used, once again, to allay their anxieties about appearing to be materialistic conspicuous consumers and to defend their shopping choices in the face of suggestions of consumerism or elitism—to construct what they feel is a moral self through their consumption of material objects (de Solier 2013).

SLOW FOOD AND THE POLITICS OF CONSUMPTION

The serious shopping of foodies and their associated morality of quality is also invested in a politics of consumption. Their postindustrial self-formation through food involves a critique of the industrial food system and its global modes of production and distribution. As I argued earlier, the food that my informants judged to be bad quality is that which is a product of what is variously termed the "industrial food chain," "modern food system," or "culinary modernism" (Pollan 2006; Beardsworth and Keil 1997; Laudan 2001); that is, food of large-scale, industrialized, and global production and distribution. In contrast, the food they consider to be good quality is a product of the residual "pastoral food chain," "traditional food system," or "culinary luddism" (Pollan 2006; Beardsworth and Keil 1997; Laudan 2001); that is, food of small-scale, traditional, artisanal, and local production and distribution in "alternative food networks" (Goodman et al. 2012). Foodies' shopping is invested in a critique of, and resistance to, the dominant mode of global industrial food production and distribution. This highlights an intriguing point of difference between their consumption of food in the practices of shopping and eating out. For whilst foodies avoided "bad quality" lowbrow foods in both shopping (supermarket food) and eating out (fast food), it was only in relation to shopping that their reasons for doing so took a more explicitly politicized form. In contrast, the reason most of my informants gave for avoiding fast food, such as McDonalds, was aesthetic—they did not like the flavor—rather than a political stance against global capitalism or the modes of production and distribution of multinational corporations. Most foodies were more politically opposed to supermarkets than they were to fast food chains in the modern food system.

The global industrial food system is what Giddens calls an "abstract system," a type of disembedding mechanism that lifts social relations out of local contexts and face-to-face relations and recombines them across wide time–space distances (1991: 2). The foods for sale on the supermarket shelf are disembedded from time through their lack of seasonality and disembedded from place, as their producers may be on the other side of the world. In postindustrial societies, it is not just the production of material artifacts in manufacturing that has declined but also the production of food in agriculture. As Toby Miller observes, since the late 1980s, more countries have imported food from around the world, to the point where the "consumption of food became radically disaffiliated from its conditions of production and circulation" (2007: 117). It is this disembedding of food production from local contexts and social relations to which most foodies are opposed, and some expressed a sense of loss as a result of this process in global modernity. As Sam put it:

You know, people in the old days used to have their own vegetable plots or vegetable gardens, and now everything's mechanized, and it's transported, and it's refrigerated, and it's often grown a very very long way away from home. And particularly where we import food from all over the world, we also lose the seasonality; we get stuff that's out of sync with the world.

Foodies' alternative consumption practices, then, are also a means of re-embedding food. Re-embedding is the "reappropriation or recasting of dis-embedded social relations so as to pin them down (however partially or transitorily) to local conditions of time and place" (Giddens 1990: 79–80). Food is re-embedded into local time and place through consumption practices, such as eating locally produced, seasonal foods, and even more so, by purchasing these foods directly from their producers at farmers' markets, thus reinstating face-to-face relations between producers and consumers. This process of re-embedding food is part of the reflexivity of late modernity, as some people return to what they see as traditional or preindustrial ways of life in their self-formation in response to the risks of postindustrial global modernity. The foodie's self-making thus also involves supporting *other* people to produce material things in postindustrial society, and the way they do this is by supporting local production through their consumption.

The philosophy and politics of re-embedding food has been encapsulated by the international Slow Food movement, the key culinary luddite institution (Laudan 1999), which advocates the consumption of local, seasonal, traditional, artisanal foods, and is opposed to the global industrial food system. The Slow Food movement originated out of Arcigola, a league for food and wine started by communist intellectuals in 1986 to support regional foods in Italy. In 1989, in opposition to the opening of a McDonalds at the Spanish Steps in Rome, it became the International Slow Food Movement for the Defense of and the Right to Pleasure. It seeks to protect traditional regional foods from the standardization processes of mass-produced fast food, and the modern food system more generally, by assisting artisan producers and encouraging the consumption of local traditional foods (Petrini 2003; see also Miele and Murdoch 2002; de Solier 2004; Gaytán 2004; Wilk 2006; Sassatelli and Davolio 2010). The international not-for-profit organization, whose headquarters are in the village of Bra in northern Italy, now has over 100,000 paying members—both producers and consumers—across 153 countries.

Slow Food is an example of the trend toward what has been termed "lifestyle politics." In contrast to the collective forms of civic engagement traditionally associated with politics, this refers to a more individualized mode of politics in late modernity organized around specific lifestyle-related issues (Bennett 1998). In neoliberal societies, such lifestyle politics often involve modes of activism through consumption choices. The Slow Food movement's lifestyle politics is particularly rooted in commodity consumption; as Alison Leitch argues, it operates through a "promotional politics, where consumers are envisaged as international political activists by virtue of market choice" (2003: 457). Slow Food's politics of consumption envisages consumers not only as political activists but as coproducers: "We consider ourselves *co-producers, not consumers*, because by being informed about how our food is produced and actively supporting those who produce it, we become a part of and a partner in the production process" (Slow Food 2010, original emphasis; see also Labelle 2004). As this suggests, knowledge of food production—of how food is produced, by whom, and where—is central to this politics of consumption. Indeed, David Goodman, E. Melanie DuPuis, and Michael K. Goodman argue that shared knowledges of food production are fundamental to alternative food networks, as producers and consumers share "ways of 'knowing and growing food'" (2012: 53). They suggest that "the knowledge practices of reflexive consumers are expressions of agency and so constitute a politics of food" (2012: 47).

This was echoed by the foodies in my research who were members of the Slow Food movement. Ruth, for example, said: "Food *is* politics. And so being a member of Slow Food is important to me because it's about the politics of food, how it's grown, who owns it, and how food is used as a political weapon as much as anything." While only a few of my informants were paying members like Ruth, all of their serious shopping practices were in keeping with the philosophy of Slow Food, whether they directly associated these practices with the movement or not. This is because the philosophy of culinary luddism that Slow Food promotes has become the dominant ideology among the experts to whom foodies turn for their lifestyle guidance, advocated by chefs and food writers alike. Many television cooking shows promote the alternative consumption practices advocated by Slow Food, as TV chefs extol the benefits of buying fresh, local, seasonal produce. Indeed, Lewis argues that "a variety of food shows today present audiences with models of production, preparation and consumption that offer themselves up as an apparent alternative to the massified, supermarketized world of industrial food" (2008b: 232). The scenes depicting such alternative material consumption were one of the appeals these programs held for some foodies, as Mary said:

> Actually, one of the things I like most about those sorts of shows is seeing the chefs actually source the produce. So, seeing them go to the delis or the markets, and all the stuff that's there—which may or may not be available here, if it's an overseas show—and how they prepare it and what they do, all that sort of thing. I love that moment.

Such material media, as I argued earlier, promote a logic of consumption, yet the programs preferred by foodies promote alternative models of consumption and are one of the ways in which foodies acquire knowledge about the politics of food production that they deploy in their serious consumption. However, the version of food politics such programs represent is a soft-politics designed for lifestyle television. While the programs may focus on alternative foods and their producers, the promotion of alternative food networks on such programs is not couched within a political discourse but in a softer moral discourse of quality: you should buy fresh food from the markets because it is "better quality", it "tastes better". The stories the shows tell are about the benefits of local, small-scale, organic farms, rather than exposés on the environmental or labor politics of large-scale industrial farming. It is lifestyle television, not current affairs; its discourse remains firmly within middle-class romanticized ideas of "the good life." It also neglects to show the significant effort, and often financial cost, involved in this type of alternative consumption.

While the experts of food media inform the politics of consumption of foodies through the philosophy of Slow Food they espouse, it is not these mediated experts who constitute the main professionals with whom food-ies interact and from whom they acquire material knowledge in their serious shopping. Rather, their practices of re-embedding shopping in local contexts involve developing strong face-to-face relationships with suppliers and produc-ers. As John said:

> Personal contact is certainly very important to me, and I think that's part of—I'd say, to me, one of the characteristics of a foodie would be that you value that interaction with the producers or the suppliers. I think that's part of the enthusi-asm. It's not just the ingredients, it's where it's come from and it's who's selling it.

Research in material culture studies has emphasized the investment in social relationships that occurs through the practice of shopping (D. Miller 1998; Miller et al. 1998). For many foodies, shopping is a particularly social experi-ence in which they develop relationships and networks with people through the material object of food. John's shopping does not involve simply picking out some tomatoes and taking them to the cash register to pay; it involves talking to the supplier about the produce on offer and learning where it's from. For foodies, the establishment of relationships with suppliers is part of both the politics of re-embedding shopping in face-to-face relations, as well as part of their serious shopping, as they emulate the practices of professional chefs. It is both the social interaction and the knowledge that suppliers im-part about the produce that foodies value in their shopping experiences. As Mary says:

> I go to the markets every Saturday, and every market stall that I go to the owners know me because I've been going there for years. And they'll all chat to me, they'll say "Okay, so Mary, what's on the menu this weekend? Who's coming over? Is it

formal or casual? What are you doing?" And so it's great fun! It means you learn about the food, and it's interactive.

Many foodies are interested in acquiring as much knowledge as they can about produce as part of their material education in food. Thus, it is important for them to have knowledgeable suppliers who are experts on the produce they sell. John described how his suppliers were particularly helpful in passing on information about things such as "what is best at the moment, which ingredients work well for a particular dish, and how to prepare a specific ingredient."

One of the most important forms of knowledge that foodies seek from their suppliers is the history of the produce, or as some termed it, its "provenance." They are interested in learning about the "social life" or "cultural biography" (Appadurai 1986) of the material objects they consume. In particular, they want to know where produce comes from and whether or not it is local. For local produce—as well as face-to-face relationships—is central to foodies' politics of re-embedding shopping. Local produce is understood as embedded in both place and time, as it is associated with seasonality and freshness. However, as Holloway and Kneafsey point out, it is important to explore the ambiguities of ideas of localness in people's food shopping, just as we do those of quality (2000: 296)—and, I would add, to explore the connections between the two. Indeed, the category of "local" was quite nebulous among my informants and ranged from produce that came from farms on the outskirts of the city to that from anywhere in Australia; the main distinction connoted by the term was that the produce was Australian, not imported. As well as talking to suppliers about the origins of produce, some foodies favored suppliers that labeled produce by place of origin. For example, Anne said:

> The greengrocer I go to—I don't buy my fruit and veg at a supermarket, the stock at the supermarket is so bad—the thing I like about my greengrocer is that everything's Australian grown, and if it's not, they label it, so you know for example if the oranges are coming from California, or if the garlic's coming from China. It's really important for me, because I prefer to eat Australian garlic and not Chinese garlic, not just because it's Australian, but because it tastes better.

Here, we can begin to see the complex relationship that exists between local food and quality food in the foodie imaginary. In part, Anne wants to buy Australian garlic because it is local and related to the politics of re-embedding food. In part, Australian garlic is believed to taste better *because* it is local, and therefore fresh and seasonal, not having been picked too early and transported across the world. Yet while these ideas of locality and freshness impact on ideas of flavor, ultimately the deciding factor is quality, not locality: she buys it "not just because it's Australian, but because it tastes better." In this case, the food that is local is also judged as the best quality, so it is easy to reconcile the politics of consumption with the morality of quality. Where decisions become more of a dilemma for some foodies is when an imported product is judged to be of better quality than a local product, and the politics of local consumption and the morality of quality cannot be reconciled, a problem I return to later.

Another way in which foodies seek out quality local produce is by purchasing it directly from producers at farmers' markets. As Tess put it, "the reason I shop at farmers' markets is that I know the product was picked the day before and is only transported for a couple of hours, rather than across the world." Farmers' markets constitute the most embedded form of shopping in which consumers engage face-to-face with the producer who has grown their apples, reared their pork, milked the cows, or made the artisanal cheese by hand. As a result, these markets are the mode of shopping favored by the Slow Food movement, and they have grown rapidly in Australia, the United Kingdom, and the United States over the past decade (Holloway and Kneafsey 2000; Ashley et al. 2004; Banwell et al. 2006; Slocum 2008; Vileisis 2008).

One of the appeals of shopping at farmers' markets is the aesthetics of authenticity and tradition that are on offer to consumers; they are "predominantly middle-class spaces, trading not simply in produce, but also in culturally rich values of authenticity, simplicity and 'heritage'" (Ashley et al. 2004: 117). Sharon Zukin (2008) highlights how the location of urban farmers' markets in "authentic spaces" within cities such as New York is central to the authenticity on offer. This is also particularly true in Melbourne, where farmers' markets are held in such places as children's farms and community vegetable gardens, as well as in heritage spaces such as former convents and gasworks. The latter examples symbolize the expansion of historical culture into shopping, not only through the traditional foods on offer but also through the heritage spaces in which they are located: they combine the consumption of architectural and gastronomic heritage. But there is also a "discipline of time and space that shopping at the farmers' market requires" (Zukin 2008: 737), as these various markets in Melbourne each operate on one Saturday of every month, alternating weekly between the different urban locations. I argue that the inconvenience and effort of such slow shopping—of waiting for market days, of waiting for produce to come into season—is a way in which foodies control and order time in their creation of a self in the "runaway world" of late modernity (Giddens 2002); this stands in contrast to the seamless time of supermarkets, which may be open and brightly lit for twenty-four hours a day and filled with seasonless produce. Slow shopping is a way of reversing the process of time–space distantiation.

While the return to these more traditional modes of shopping is seen as a way of combating the risks involved in the modern food system, the embedded face-to-face relations of such alternative shopping—like the disembedded relations of abstract systems—are also based on trust. Most of my informants, like Tess, trusted that the food on offer at farmers' markets was what it claimed to be; however, George was more skeptical, saying:

> Even with farmers' markets, if you go to enough of them you see which people sell at more than one farmers' market and they're not actually the producer, you know, you can tell that they buy things from the wholesale market and then come along there and sell it, because it's packaged just the same as anywhere else that gets stuff from the wholesale market.

In late modernity, then, it is not only abstract systems, such as the modern food system, that are based on relations of trust. Rather, trust is also central to the face-to-face relations of the alternative food system: trust that those selling the produce at farmers' markets are in fact farmers and that the produce is from their farm. Even if this is the case, there is still an element of trust that the produce is local and "only transported for a couple of hours," for as I discuss shortly, some produce at farmers' markets has been transported much further.

ETHICAL CONSUMPTION AND THE MORALITY OF QUALITY

The ethics of consumption are also of concern in the serious shopping that foodies undertake, and these ethics intersect in complex ways with the moralities and politics of consumption in foodie self-formation. The question of ethical consumption has been of growing concern for scholars across the social sciences and humanities in recent years (D. Miller 2001a; Barnett et al. 2005, 2010; Littler 2009; Lewis and Potter 2011; Carrier and Luetchford 2012). In comparison to moral or political consumption, ethical consumption refers more specifically to altruistic consumption decisions that place the interests of others before those of the self. It concerns issues of citizenship and civic responsibility, of how one's consumption impacts upon others. As Toby Miller argues, the "selfless, active citizen" and the "selfish, active consumer" are ideal types that are problematized by "cross-pollinating subjectivities" such as the "consumer who purchases products to favor the environment and labor" (2007: 32). Such ethical consumption is increasingly seen as a responsibility of good consumer-citizens in neoliberal societies (Barnett et al. 2010). Lewis suggests that in late modernity consumption has become, to a certain extent, deprivatized and "tied increasingly to questions of care and responsibility to the community" (2008b: 238). She traces this development in relation to lifestyle media and notes that food media, such as those used by foodies, have demonstrated a growing concern with questions of civic responsibility and citizenship—such as the impact of food consumption on the environment—that gestures toward a kind of "communitarian ethics of care-based consumption" (2008b: 231). Ethical concerns, then, and their relationship to consumption, are gaining wider currency within society in late modernity.

Daniel Miller differentiates between two main concerns in ethical consumption: Green shopping, which involves environmental concerns, and Red shopping, which involves labor concerns. He argues that ethical consumption "is a means by which the immediate interests of the household are subsumed in the larger concern for others" (2001a: 134). Whether it's the social welfare of producers or the global environment, ethical consumption involves putting the interests of others before those of the self. In its purest form, it is a selfless kind of consumption, but one that may be used in making a moral self (see Barnett et al. 2005). Miller highlights the complex nature of ethical dialogues in late modernity in which different ethical concerns for others as well as concerns for the self are intertwined: "Ethics have become extremely diffused across many different issues. As a result, the various strands of altruism, taste, self-interest, and so forth are so deeply interwoven within the same sentence" (2001a: 123). Take, for example, this statement by one of my informants, Leah: "People should buy local food, and learn to make things themselves. Not buy the cheapest, imported canned food, or takeaways. It's bad for your body, the economy, and the global environment." Here, the defense of the moral superiority of buying local, fresh ingredients and cooking them from scratch shifts easily between ethical concerns about local producers and the global environment, as well as self-interest in the health and appearance of one's own body.

Green concerns have become increasingly mainstream in recent years, particularly following Al Gore's 2006 documentary on climate change, *An Inconvenient Truth*. The display of knowledge of, and concern for, environmental problems has become particularly popular among, and an expectation of, the (neoliberal) middle class (Rosenberg 2012). As Daniel Miller argues, "both the ability to clearly articulate the logic of Green as discourse and to give an account of oneself in those terms, as also the ability to actually afford the practice of Green shopping, are differentiated along lines of class. The claims to morality they assert tend to become the claim to the moral superiority of the middle class" (2001a: 139). His research found that although many shoppers voiced a Green discourse, they did not actually put it into practice. This, he suggests, is because ethical shopping is incompatible with the morality of thrift that governs their shopping practices because Green goods are often more expensive. He argues that if "moral shopping is almost entirely defined by the act of thrift and saving money, then the expense of ethical shopping can make it regarded as a form of extravagance that betrays the underlying morality of shopping" (D. Miller 2001a: 134).

Food has become one of the key sites of ethical consumption today. As Michael K. Goodman and his colleagues observe in their discussion of "ethical foodscapes," "while all food has ethical implications and import, *some* food has taken on the connotation of being, in particular ways, more ethical in its specific location in the foodscape," such as local, organic, and fair trade food (2010: 1783, original emphasis; see also Lockie et al. 2002; Guthman 2003; Whatmore and Clark 2006; Luetchford 2008). For the foodies in my research, ethical concerns—both Green and Red—related to their politics of consumption in terms of resistance to the global food system. Their preference for buying local produce expressed both their main Green concern—food miles—and their main Red concern—supporting the welfare of local producers. In terms of Green issues, the impact of carbon emissions on the environment from transporting food long distances was of greater concern to foodies than the use of pesticides and genetically modified crops. Thus, buying local produce was more important to them than buying organic produce: While all my informants preferred to buy local, not all bought organic. Buying local was also understood as a form of Australian cultural citizenship, as foodies displayed a sense of responsibility to support the local economy and producers. Most only expressed concern for the welfare of Australian farmers, not overseas farmers. While their Green ethics were global, their Red ethics were local. Thus, it is the ethical concerns that align most closely with their politics of re-embedding shopping in local contexts that are of the highest importance for foodies. Their shopping, then, is not purely self-interested but displays a degree of care for the global environment and local producers.

Yet while foodies' consumption of local produce is couched within—and legitimated by—a Green discourse in terms of food miles, it may not be as environmentally ethical as this discourse suggests. Cathy Banwell and her colleagues (2006) have questioned the Green ethics of slow food shopping due to its reliance on cars and the subsequent food miles accrued in the automobiles of both producers and consumers. In their study of a farmers' market in Sydney, they found that the "local" produce on offer had often been transported hundreds of kilometers by road, with some driven from as far as 750 kilometers away. They also found that most consumers drove their cars to urban farmers' markets—although they were embarrassed to admit it—as well as to other alternative suppliers (2006: 224).

This car reliance was certainly common among the foodies in my research, almost all of whom drove their cars along their food lines in their shopping trips to farmers' markets and other suppliers. Moreover, a car was necessary to source produce from multiple suppliers around the city in one touristic shopping trip, as many did each Saturday, or to venture outside the city to source produce from regional suppliers and farms. Thus, while research on supermarket shopping has criticized its dependence on cars (Bowlby 1997: 93), slow shopping, from markets and other alternative suppliers, may actually be more car reliant than fast shopping from supermarkets (Banwell et al. 2006: 235). Indeed, by driving to multiple suppliers around the city, foodies ultimately drive more food miles to source their produce than an average shopper's single destination trip to the supermarket. This driving of significant food miles by slow food consumers and producers occurs in a context in which 74 percent of global carbon emissions from the transport sector are produced by cars (Intergovernmental Panel on Climate Change 1999). While my informants did not demonstrate an awareness of these contradictions in their shopping practices, a study of alternative food schemes in the United Kingdom found that their consumers—who similarly possessed a strong concern over food miles—did recognize the greater distances driven by consumers or producers in some forms of alternative consumption, such as buying from farm shops, farmers' markets, and box schemes, and found them ethically problematic as a result (Kneafsey et al. 2008: 115).

But it is not only the fresh produce that foodies consume that has often travelled long distances; the traditional, artisanal, handcrafted foods they buy, such as cheese and cured meats, have often travelled much further, by air or sea, from other countries. For the foodie's taste for "local" foods includes locally distinctive traditional foods from all around the world—particularly Europe. Imported food, then, is fine as long as it is regional, traditional, and artisanal—the taste of *terroir*—and not homogeneous and mass produced. Despite Slow Food's political discourse of opposition to the globalization of food, "the distribution of slow food products is as much about global, as well as local, production and distribution networks" (Banwell et al. 2006: 233). Banwell and her colleagues argue that the "considerable distances traveled by some artisan products from overseas to Australia may be as great or greater than those traveled by mass-produced supermarket products" (2006: 235). Considering that most of the food imported into Australia comes from neighboring New Zealand (Commonwealth of Australia 2008: 13), consuming Grana Padano from Italy or Jamón Ibérico from Spain is going to leave a significantly larger carbon footprint. If foodies were seriously concerned about food miles and carbon emissions, they would avoid imported artisanal foods in favor of local versions made within a 160 kilometer (100 mile) radius from where they live, as in the Locavore movement (see Stanton et al. 2012), and they would avoid using their cars to source produce.

Thus, while there is an expression of care for the global environment and local producers, for most of my informants, these functioned more as "convenience ethics" that "give the shopper the feeling that they have done their bit, but in practice at no cost to themselves" (D. Miller 2001a: 132, 131). Foodies could claim these ethics and feel good about their shopping practices because in most cases these ethics conveniently corresponded to what foodies considered to be good quality food. Feeling ethical, in such cases, was an added bonus for buying what they would anyway; it did not involve any self-sacrifice or putting the interests of others before those of the self, as self-interest and altruistic concerns coalesced. However, in cases where such ethical concerns—and the politics of consumption in which they were embedded—were in conflict with the foodie's morality of quality, it was this governing morality—quality—that ultimately won out. For first and foremost, foodies are enthusiast shoppers—or what I have termed serious shoppers—rather than ethical shoppers, and it is the pursuit of quality food that is central to their enthusiasm that is of paramount importance.

I found that food ethics and politics, while intertwined with conceptions of quality, are ultimately subordinated to the latter, both for those foodies for whom such ethics were a matter of convenience and for those who were more seriously concerned with ethical issues. For the latter, the decision to privilege quality over ethics in consumption choices was never easy. Sam, for example, spoke at length about the politics and ethics of food production, dis-tribution, and consumption, and displayed concerns about issues such as the global environment, local farmers, free trade agreements, and government subsidies. When I asked him how this affected his own consumption, he said that he always tried to buy Australian products but that some decisions were particularly difficult when he knew that a foreign product was "better" than the local equivalent. He gave the example of buying tinned tomatoes—one of the few canned foods of which foodies approve—which posed a particular dilemma. This was because he had met local tomato growers as part of his tertiary studies and understood their financial struggles, yet he thought that Italian tinned tomatoes were of a better quality. For Sam, this dilemma was partly a matter of Australian cultural citizenship, as he felt a sense of respon-sibility to support his fellow citizens. As he put it, "What right have I got to buy a tin of Italian tomatoes?" He described how buying the Italian tomatoes may have been justified in terms of thrift, as they were sometimes less expensive than the Australian product, yet this was not his main concern:

> The overriding factor for me at the end of the day is—whether I got them for more or less—often the Italian tomatoes are actually a better product, because they're riper, there is often more tomato in the actual tin—even though their weight might be similar, there's more tomato content—and the liquid that the tomato's in is actually tomato juice, whereas the ones here in Australia are very often either a brine or very light watery tomato stuff…But it's not to say that even though I chose to go and buy that tin of Italian tomatoes that I don't think about the implications—and there's a number of times I'll stand there and I've got the two tins in my hand, and I'm thinking—so sometimes I'll buy both! One of each! Just to make myself feel okay. Or sometimes I'll grab one off the shelf and then walk

away with it and I'm thinking "What about those people up in the bush?" It makes you feel uncomfortable! Because it would be easy to disregard them and just simply consume on the basis of, "Well I think this is a better product," you know.

For Sam, the decision to buy Italian tomatoes is particularly problematic because of his previous face-to-face relations with local producers, as he tries to reconcile his concern for their situation with his own self-interest in quality. Such consumption does pose an ethical dilemma for him in his self-making through food, yet he ultimately buys either Italian tomatoes, or both Italian and Australian, but not just Australian, which would involve putting ethics before quality. Buying both types constitutes a compromise, whereby he is getting both quality and ethics, in separate cans. Ultimately, even for such ethically anxious foodies, the morality of quality is sovereign.

Shopping, then, is an important social practice to examine, for in it we see the intersection of moralities, politics, and ethics in the new forms of self-making through material objects in postindustrial society. Where much scholarly debate focuses on the explicitly political and ethical dimensions of shopping and of consumption in general—on what we think matters, or should matter—by undertaking ethnographic research, we find what actually matters to people, and my research shows that morality is most powerful in the contemporary self; while it connects with politics and ethics, morality is ultimately of utmost importance for modern self-making through the consumption of material objects. This is tied to the broader moralities of productive leisure that govern self-formation through material culture in postindustrial society. The foodie's shopping is worthy of study not just because it is political or ethical, then, but because it is serious and moral.

So consumption is still one of the ways in which we make the self through material culture in postindustrial society. But that does not mean it is about developing consumerist and materialistic forms of selfhood. And it's not simply a matter of mobilizing systems of taste and the sign-value of objects, of saying "I wear Nike so I am sporty," or "I wear black so I'm a goth/emo." Rather, the new forms of self-making through material objects that we see exemplified in the foodie are reflexively developed in response to anxieties about materialism and consumerism in postindustrial society, anxieties about the moral status of making a self through consuming material things. It is not a playful postmodern process of identity making. It involves more work than simply saying "I eat haute cuisine so I'm a foodie." When taste *doesn't* say enough about you—because you may share that taste with many members of the middle class, but not share the same morals regarding that taste, especially in terms of distinction—that self-formation has to come through the *way* you consume the material object. It is the way foodies consume haute cuisine and the way they shop for quality food that makes them a foodie. And that, in their eyes, is a moral way because it involves work and a productive approach in leisure as amateurs. But while this issue of consumption has dominated discussions of how we make the self in postindustrial society, through the example of the foodie, we see that it is not only through consuming material culture that we create a late modern self but also through producing it in forms of productive leisure.

6

Producing Things: Material Media and Moralities of Production

Production has historically held a higher moral value than consumption, and it continues to do so in the new forms of self-making through material culture in postindustrial society. But today, it is both the old or industrial sense of production—material—and the new or postindustrial sense of production—knowledge—that carry a high moral value in self-formation. These combine in forms of productive leisure that relate to both material production and knowledge—that is, in acquiring the knowledge and skills required to produce things (such as a culinary education) and deploying these skills in forms of material production (such as cooking). Material media play a central role in the former process in postindustrial society because we no longer acquire such skills in work (or increasingly, the family). It is through such popular media that many of us learn how to produce material objects and incorporate this production into our self-making. But it is not just the practice of productive leisure in which material media guide us today but also the morality of this endeavor in our self-formation.

MATERIAL MEDIA, PRODUCTIVE LEISURE, AND SELF-IMPROVEMENT

The media have a long history of educating in productive leisure that stretches back to the early nineteenth century (Bailey 1978; Gelber 1999). They have played a key role in the history of leisure education, which has sought to teach people to use their free time constructively by encouraging them to engage in self-improving and work-like activities that involve making material things. This extends from the quilting and woodwork promoted by the media in the earlier stages of industrial modernity to the productive skills, such as craft and DIY, taught by the postwar hobby media (Gelber 1999). In postindustrial society, I argue, this education in the production of objects as a form of productive leisure is continued by certain forms of material media, particularly those focused on cooking, gardening, and DIY. Most research on contemporary lifestyle media has overlooked—or rejected—this education in production, concentrating instead on how such media teach commodity consumption. The promotion of consumption—and the education in "good taste" and how to deploy it in self-formation and self-improvement—is crucial to the lifestyle guidance offered by material media, as I have shown. Yet the forms of material media under investigation here, I argue, also teach people to construct and improve the self by *producing* material objects in forms of productive leisure. The two are linked in the models of self-formation these media advance: one needs to buy the (right) raw materials (ingredients, tools, seeds), but these should provide the foundation for productive engagements with material culture rather than simply consumerist modes. For it is material production, I argue, that is represented as having the highest moral value in self-making by these media: producing something oneself—be it a meal, a bookshelf, or a rose—and acquiring the productive skills to do so, is represented as better than simply purchasing such objects—as leading to a better self, a better you, in a postindustrial world. Thus, these material media educate audiences in the moralities of productive leisure that guide the new modes of self-making in the late modern world.

Where in industrial modernity, the working class was the object of the media's education in productive leisure, today the middle class is the subject of material media's curriculum. It is the (aspirational) middle class who are seen as having room for improvement through productive leisure pursuits, such as cooking, gardening, or DIY. This can be seen as part of the overall project of self-maximization that is central to processes of individualization and forms of middle-class personhood in neoliberal societies (T. Miller 2007). These neoliberal technologies of the self—material lifestyle media—suggest that it is not enough to simply consume in leisure; one is also expected to learn and produce things, to acquire and deploy manual skills. Productive leisure becomes the site for different types of self-actualization than those offered by white-collar knowledge work: to be a cook, gardener, or DIY renovator rather than a public servant, business manager, or teacher. These forms of material lifestyle media suggest that good neoliberal citizens are productive both at work and in leisure. Yet they also teach that these extracurricular productive activities should be thought of as leisure rather than domestic labor.

So is material media's pedagogy in productive leisure being used by postindustrial audiences in self-fashioning and self-improvement? Are they acquiring such productive skills and engaging in material production? There seems to be some agreement that DIY and gardening television programs are connected to an increase in these practices (Allon 2008; Rosenberg 2008b, 2011a; Taylor 2008). In contrast, it is commonly assumed that culinary television programs are linked to a decline in cooking. The cliché circulating widely in academia, the press, and popular culture nowadays is that people watch others cook on television but no longer actually cook themselves; they eat TV dinners or takeaways while watching celebrity chefs on the box. This is summed up in the title of Pollan's (2009) article in the *New York Times,* "Out of the Kitchen,

Onto the Couch." He argues that food television has transformed "cooking from something you do into something you watch." This echoes arguments made earlier by scholars that food television has transformed cooking into a spectator sport (Chao 1998: 23) and a vicarious activity that offers "pleasure for the arm chair cook and the couch potato alike" (Adema 2000: 114). This perspective suggests that cooking shows are a form of "food porn" (Chan 2003; Rousseau 2012b) where pleasure is gained from watching others perform the practice, but viewers do not partake themselves, being branded instead as "food voyeurs" (Adema 2000: 116). Rather than teaching viewers productive skills in how to cook, then, television cooking shows—combined with ready-made meals—are held responsible for culinary deskilling and are linked to the decline or even the "end of cooking" (Pollan 2009).

This idea that people watch television cooking shows but never cook may describe the experience of some people. However, such arguments are usually anecdotal, and while there is very little empirical research on culinary skills and practices, that which does exist suggests that it is not the typical experience. Tim Lang and Martin Caraher (2001) have conducted quantitative research into culinary practices and skills in the United Kingdom, which they suggest is similar to the experience in Australia (although the United States may prove to be a different case). They found that while there has been a decline in cooking—due to a rise in eating out, takeaways, and ready-made meals—this does not mean that no one is cooking: The majority of people still eat home cooked main meals seven times a week. Around 7 percent of main meals were ready-made, and 5 percent were takeaways (Lang and Caraher 2001: 8). In contrast to the deskilling theory, Lang and Caraher found that most people did not lack culinary skills: the large majority of women (94%) and men (80%) were very or fairly confident in their ability to cook from scratch (2001: 9). Rather than a loss of skills, Lang and Caraher argue that a key culinary transition occurring is the transformation of cooking from a domestic chore into a form of leisure (2001: 4). Elsewhere, they link this transformation to the popularity of food television programs (Caraher et al. 2000: 29) that promote this philosophy. This suggests that while television cooking shows may not be linked to an overall increase in cooking (unlike DIY and gardening programs), they *are* connected to an increase in cooking as a form of productive leisure.

MATERIAL LIFESTYLE TELEVISION AND PRACTICAL LEARNING

The common argument in lifestyle television studies—that such programs no longer teach material production like their hobbyist predecessors—often involves the assertion that audiences no longer acquire practical knowledge or skills from such programs, nor do they want this education. However, such arguments are generally based on textual analysis or anecdotes, with no detailed empirical research to support them. Very few scholars have conducted research among audiences of material lifestyle television to examine whether or not they gain a practical education from such programs. One scholar is Annette Hill, whose research involved a large-scale questionnaire, semi-structured focus groups, and in-depth interviews with families (2005: 194–5). Hill argues that contemporary lifestyle programs—while often more entertaining than those in the past—contain informative elements that offer "'learning opportunities,' as viewers have the opportunity to learn from the advice given in the programmes, but may choose not to take up or act on such advice" (2005: 79). She suggests that audiences are "likely to talk about information as learning, and learning as practical tips and advice...The term 'learning' suggests an informal, personal relationship with facts in popular factual television" (2005: 89).

Hill's research on practical learning from material lifestyle television focuses on the genres of DIY and garden programs. She found that there was a difference between the type of learning viewers described from watching instructional DIY and/or garden programs and from watching entertaining makeover programs. In relation to instructional programs, with their more didactic address and direct advice to viewers, Hill found that viewers spoke confidently about the practical advice and productive skills they had acquired, such as tips on how to plant shrubs (2005: 100). In contrast, she found that while viewers associated makeover programs with practical learning, they were hesitant to give concrete examples of things they had learnt. They spoke more ambivalently about learning ideas (such as painting a blue feature wall) rather than practical advice from makeover programs. These ideas were stored for potential use in the future, yet they were generally only applied in the imagination (2005: 97). However, Hill suggests that her informants' reluctance to give examples of practical learning from makeover television was at least partly a result of their perception of the genre as entertainment and their awareness of the stigmatization of reality TV as "trash TV" within the press and society more generally: they "attempt to manage the impressions of other people (including academic researchers) by making light of the idea of learning from reality programming" (2005: 85–86). Talking about makeover programming as entertaining is the main public discourse, and the "respectable" discourse of the educated cultural elite. Thus, Hill suggests that the issue of practical learning needs to be understood in the context of audience genre expectations as well as the social stigmatization of genres. She concludes that the notion of learning from television shows explicitly aimed at entertaining is problematic for viewers and that they are only open to this idea of learning if there are clear didactic elements to the program (2005: 99–101). Thus, while her informants were comfortable talking about the practical education in material production they had acquired from instructional DIY and gardening programs, they were less comfortable discussing this in relation to makeover programs. However, this does not necessarily mean that viewers did not acquire such an education from these programs, only that they were potentially embarrassed to admit it.

Lisa Taylor (2008) found similar results in her research into material lifestyle television viewing among gardening enthusiasts. She found that the stigmatization of television led middle-class gardeners to distance themselves from the act of consciously selecting to watch garden makeover programs, as they commented that they would only watch such programs "if they are on" or "because they are always on" (Taylor 2008: 159). The enthusiasts in her research were not invested in relationships or concerned with emulating professional experts but rather with continuing their own traditional, ordinary knowledge and practices. Like Hill, Taylor found that these gardeners said they tended to learn ideas rather than practical advice from makeover television and that these ideas were generally not practically applied: "lifestyle ideas captured the head rather than the hand or arm; the idea of transformation tended to exist in the imagination and at the level of conversation rather than in practice" (2008: 174). Nevertheless, some gardeners did learn practical production knowledge from material lifestyle television, again, generally from more instructional programs such as *Gardener's World*. As one of Taylor's informants said, "You get ideas, but you also get good advice. I mean I've learnt quite a lot from them. How to take cuttings, what to do and what not to do and what to put them in" (2008: 172). Others had also acquired what they considered to be valuable information (e.g., which plants grow in certain conditions). For these gardeners, material lifestyle television did serve "an educational role by providing information, tips and advice" (2008: 172). Thus, postindustrial audiences do acquire a practical education in material production from contemporary gardening and DIY television—in particular, the more instructional programs—which is used in their self-formation through material objects in these productive leisure practices. But what about television cooking shows?

FOOD TELEVISION, CELEBRITY CHEFS, AND CULINARY EDUCATION

Critics have claimed that in postindustrial society, "the audience watches cook shows for entertainment" and that learning "how to cook specific dishes, honing one's own culinary abilities, or becoming an accomplished cook no longer seem of primary importance to many cook-show viewers" (Chao 1998: 27, 23). In contrast, my research found that learning to cook—to produce—was of utmost importance for postindustrial audiences of culinary television, such as foodies. For my informants, watching food television was a form of productive leisure in which they sought and acquired new knowledge and skills as part of their culinary education. This was considered a moral approach to consuming food television. As a result, my informants tended to only watch forms of food television that they found informative. As I showed earlier, while all of my informants who watched food television liked the more instructional (and highbrow) cooking shows—such as those of Rick Stein—there was greater debate about more entertainment-oriented (and middlebrow) cooking shows—such as those of Jamie Oliver—which some foodies liked and watched and others didn't. Nevertheless, most spoke confidently about having acquired productive knowledge and advice (as well as ideas) from the former type of program, and for those who watched the more entertaining shows, from the latter. Although these programs may be more entertainment-oriented than their instructional counterparts, foodies still learned practical things from such cooking shows and were comfortable discussing what they had learned. This stands in contrast to Hill's (2005) research on DIY and garden makeovers, where viewers *only* gave examples of learning ideas and were hesitant to give examples of practical learning. However, even entertainment-oriented cooking shows, such as those of Nigella Lawson, are more didactic and instructional than reality house and garden makeovers, as they still deliver more direct advice to viewers, which may explain why foodies are more comfortable with the notion of learning from such programs.

While most of my informants expressed more practical learning, they also spoke more broadly about learning ideas from culinary television, such as ideas for dishes or flavor combinations to use in their cooking. For example, Henri—a professor—watched a lot of culinary television, including both instructional programs, such as those of Rick Stein and Australia's Stefano de Pieri, and more entertainment-oriented programs, such as those of Ainsley Harriott and Nigella Lawson. When I asked him why he watched such programs, he said: "Usually I like to actually watch and get some ideas. So I like to look at it, and think, 'That's a good idea, I could cook that, that looks great,' you know, and learn a few things. Yeah, so it's educational." Madeleine also said she watched television programs, including Jamie Oliver's shows, to learn new ideas for her cooking. As she put it, television cooking shows "give you ideas, which you can then embellish yourself." However, in contrast to the ideas learnt by the makeover television viewers studied by Hill (2005) and Taylor (2008), which were only applied in viewers' imaginations, the foodies in my research *did* practically apply ideas they learned from television in their home cooking. This is because, as amateurs, they are more involved in emulating the practices of professional experts, but also because the tasks involved in applying such lifestyle ideas are much smaller, less expensive, and less risky in self-formation. Following Rick Stein's suggestion to cook fish pie for dinner is easier, cheaper, and safer than following Laurence Llewelyn-Bowen's suggestion to paint pictures on a feature wall.

Beyond ideas, many of my informants described learning how to cook specific dishes from television shows, but they generally committed the key elements to memory rather than writing them down. Ruth, for example, was a dedicated amateur cook, and she spent much of her spare time acquiring new culinary knowledge and skills. She watched a range of television cooking shows but preferred the more instructional programs featuring professional chefs. She described how she had recently replicated a recipe demonstrated by the Australian fine dining chef George Calombaris, most famous for his role as a judge on Australia's *MasterChef:* "He made this fantastic boneless lamb neck, baked with yoghurt and fennel and white wine, and then after that's been cooked he slices it and barbeques it." Ruth reproduced the recipe "by memory" a couple of weeks later; as she put it, she "forgot a few things, but it *did* work." It is in this fashion that foodies generally learn recipes from the informal curriculum of culinary television rather than making exact reproductions of the dishes prepared by TV chefs. They often take what they like from the recipes they see demonstrated and alter them as they see fit. As Bette described, "a lot of recipes can be condensed to something simpler, or use different ingredients to suit what's available." Another of my informants, George, also discussed watching Calombaris's lamb recipe episode. Having Greek-Cypriot parents, George found the recipe interesting because it put a "twist" on Greek cooking, something for which Calombaris—one of Australia's earliest molecular gastronomy chefs—is famous. For George, this episode did not inspire him to prepare the recipe, like it did Ruth, but to learn more about "what yoghurt does" and how it "turns cheesy and curdy" and to experiment with how he could use this technique in other dishes.

For some of my informants, the education in material production offered by culinary television was not necessarily about learning how to cook particular recipes or dishes but more specifically about learning the practical skill of improvisation, of how to come up with and prepare a meal from the ingredients one has available. This was the case for Katarina, a food television fan. She subscribed to the cable food channel and watched cooking shows every day; her favorite programs included those of Rick Stein and Nigella Lawson. When I asked her whether she had learnt anything from watching these shows, she said:

> Oh, definitely! Totally! Like I can come home now, and cook a pretty good meal out of a bare pantry, you know. Like the other day I came home and I thought we had nothing to eat and I cooked a pumpkin and chickpea curry, which I thought was pretty cool, given that there was bloody nothing except the piece of pumpkin in the fridge! So yeah, I've learnt heaps...How to improvise is the main thing it's taught me—and skills, yeah, how to cook I suppose...How to look at a cupboard and make a meal out of something, and lately I've been doing stuff off my own recipes rather

than looking at a cookbook, and I find that really gratifying actually, especially when somebody says "Oh this is fantastic!" you know, and I know that I created that.

Here, the culinary education offered by television gives Katarina a different kind of confidence than cookbooks, as it is not necessarily about learning or reproducing recipes but acquiring the skill of improvisation that enables one to develop one's own dishes or recipes to reproduce in the future. Katarina's education in improvisation comes from the accumulation of a variety of practical advice and knowledge from different television programs. As she states, this improvisation provides greater scope for her own creativity to come through and leads to a sense of personal accomplishment. Thus, contemporary cooking shows *do* play a significant role in people becoming accomplished cooks. This was also evident in the case of Maria, another food television fan. She did not subscribe to the cable channel, but she tried to watch all of the programs on broadcast television; she was one of the few omnivores of food television among my informants. Her favorite TV chef was Rick Stein, but she liked many others, including Giorgio Locatelli, Delia Smith, Antonio Carluccio, and Ainsley Harriott. Like Katarina, Maria described how she enjoyed experimenting with the ingredients she found in her refrigerator and pantry to come up with a meal and how the recipes for such dishes came from somewhere in "the filing cabinets of my mind," often from something she had "seen on a cooking show," which sometimes led her to come up with a "wonderful new recipe." The sense of accomplishment in possessing this skill of improvisation is not confined to amateur foodies; Fine (1996) also found it among the professional chefs in his research. As one chef described:

> It's interesting that guys come home, and there's nothing to eat in the house, and I come home, and I look around and throw all this stuff together, and I can make a really nice dinner. They don't even realize that it's possible to do that...It's really an accomplishment thing. You feel like you've accomplished something when you're a cook. (quoted in Fine 1996: 44)

Other forms of practical knowledge and culinary advice that foodies acquire from TV chefs include tips on which utensils to use for particular tasks and how to prepare specific ingredients. For example, Caroline described how she found even TV chefs' simple tips helpful, such as the recommendation to use a serrated knife to cut eggplants. She said, "this sounds trivial but it is a really useful tip for me, as we use them at least twice a week." Ashley said she had learned a range of productive knowledge from television programs such as those of Jamie Oliver: "from big things like how easy it is to make your own fresh pasta, to little things like boil the lemon before stuffing it inside the chook to speed up the cooking process."

Finally, one of the main forms of practical knowledge my informants described learning from television cooking shows was technique, which helped them to hone their culinary abilities. Amelia, for example, was an omnivore of food television, watching anything from *Ready Steady Cook* to Jamie Oliver to Rick Stein. She said she had "learnt quite a lot from TV shows"—in particular, how to perform different cooking techniques. As Amelia put it, "television is great for learning about new techniques, or seeing a technique you may have only read about demonstrated visually for you." Henri, too, emphasized the benefits of television in learning technical skills: "Sometimes it's techniques, actually, just looking at techniques—you know, just looking at how they do it, how they mix things together, how they blend, how they cut." Some of my informants were very specific about the techniques they had learnt from television. For example, Sian said she preferred watching instructional cooking shows that "go into more detail and talk a bit more about techniques." She said she had learnt "how to segment an orange correctly, and how to remove the black skin from a squid," whereas for Bette, it was how to caramelize different fruits, among other things. For some of my informants, though, watching culinary television was not only about acquiring new knowledge of material production but also about confirming the knowledge they had already acquired in their gastronomic education. Sam, for example, was a passionate cook who had been pursuing this craft in his spare time for four decades. As he put it, "for me, it's not always the fact that I've learnt something new [from food programs]. For me, more often than not, it actually consolidates what I already knew, so it's very validating."

But it is not only foodies that acquire practical knowledge in culinary production from television cooking shows. In a large-scale quantitative study in the United Kingdom, Martin Caraher and his colleagues (2000) found that television was the second leading source of culinary education among adults, following cookbooks. It was also the second main source adults said they would turn to for further culinary education in the future (2000: 36–37). The study found that while most viewers considered cooking shows to be entertainment, they also wanted to, and did, learn to cook from them (2000: 38). Indeed, the study found a "thirst for learning about food and cooking" among participants (2000: 43) and that they had learnt new ideas, as well as practical advice, such as quick and easy ways to cook from scratch (2000: 39). In postindustrial society, then, television cooking shows are not merely entertainment texts but significant sources of education in the material production of food—both in their instructional and more entertaining forms.

FOOD PORN? COOKBOOKS AND CULINARY EDUCATION

Cookbooks have suffered the same criticisms as culinary television in recent years, being likewise labeled as forms of food porn whose function is to stimulate rather than educate. For example, Douglas Brownlie and his colleagues argue that the "pleasures of consuming cookbooks are related only secondarily to the act of cooking, what appears to be far more important is their role in seducing the eye" (2005: 16). Some of my informants were aware of such arguments and rejected them for not describing their use of these material media in their self-formation. As Ruth declared adamantly, "my cookbook collection is more than food porn." She was a devoted cook with a particular passion for baking. Her collection of cookbooks, which numbered in the hundreds, filled a door space in the "library" in her home. From these books, Ruth had learned to bake all the different flatbreads of the silk route, an accomplishment of which she was particularly proud. When I asked her about her use of cookbooks, she said:

> A collection of food books to me is not about just gorgeous books that just sit on the desk or the coffee table or are opened on the shelf. I mean I can do open books as well with beautiful photographs, but mine will have splashes all over them, you know! I know I should—I've got one of those things where you put a little cover on—I've got all that, but I'm into cooking, so I splash it a bit...So that to me means I've got the right attitude about my books. They're not about, you know, just the look of them, or the pretty pictures, or the gorgeous way you do food and present it. I love a beautiful book, but I love it to invite me to cook with it. And then if it gets splashed, it gets splashed.

Ruth emphasizes the moral superiority of this practical use of cookbooks in her self-formation; it is not about just consuming cookbooks visually or displaying them for distinction but about using them to productive ends, to learn and to make things. The splashes on her cookbooks record her culinary history on their pages; they document her career as an amateur cook, the recipes she has learnt and reproduced. These literally material traces add new layers to the cultural biography of each of her cookbooks, to the social lives of these material things.

Cookbooks play a vital role in culinary education in late modernity, not only among foodies but among the broader population. Caraher and his colleagues' quantitative research found cookbooks to be the leading source of culinary education among adults, more important than television or magazines, mothers or friends (2000: 35). Cookbooks were also the first source people said they would turn to in order to acquire further culinary knowledge and skills (2000: 37). Thus, cookbooks and television cooking shows, rather than being pure entertainment or food porn are the main source of culinary education for adults in postindustrial society, both for foodies and non-foodies alike. The acquisition of knowledge in the production of food from the experts of material media is a modern mode of culinary education that stands in contrast to the traditional mode of education within the family, where culinary knowledge is traditionally passed down from mother to daughter. This mediated culinary education is reflective of ways of learning, and of leisure, in postindustrial modernity.

Despite the immense significance of cookbooks as a source of culinary education, there has not been any qualitative research that focuses on this role. Indeed, while cookbooks have become an increasingly fashionable topic within academia in recent decades, most research takes the form of textual or historical analysis, with a particular focus on concerns of gender and nation (Appadurai 1988; Schofield 1989; Bower 1992; Floyd and Forster 2003a). Caraher and his colleagues highlight the limitations of their own quantitative research: it did not explore "what sort of learning people do from cookbooks" (2000: 35). They hypothesized that cookbooks may be used more in "reinforcing and expanding messages once people have basic skills" (Caraher et al. 2000: 35). However, my research with foodies suggests that this is more the function of the culinary education offered by television. Cookbooks, on the other hand, were used in more formal learning practices, by both novice and expert amateur cooks, to acquire basic or advanced culinary skills.

In contrast to culinary television, cookbooks offer a more formal curriculum based on rules and precise instruction, epitomized by the literary genre of the recipe (see Leonardi 1989; Floyd and Forster 2003a). Indeed, culinary learning from cookbooks is much more concerned with specific recipes than is learning from television. For my informants, cookbooks were used both to learn new recipes as well as to learn recipes through which they could acquire new productive skills. Celina, for example, was a keen cook and owned around forty cookbooks. She used them a lot in her everyday cooking as well as for dinner parties for friends and family, when she generally prepared a three-course meal. In regards to buying new cookbooks, she said, "they need to contain recipes that I believe will teach me new concepts and skills, as I want to keep improving." This demonstrates how the acquisition of skills in material production is understood as a moral process of self-improvement in foodie self-formation. Cookbooks, for foodies, are not just commodities; they are material technologies for improving competence (on competence, see Watson and Shove 2008). Here, I focus on how two foodies at different stages of their careers as amateur cooks—the first a novice, the second an expert—use cookbooks in their projects of culinary education.

Nick, a foodie in his early twenties, had migrated to Australia from China as a child. He grew up in the suburbs of Melbourne, eating his mother's Chinese cooking, alongside occasional visits to the local Chinese restaurant. He first developed an enthusiasm for food while working in London after finishing his degree, when he began eating out at a variety of different restaurants. Living away from home for the first time, he realized he couldn't cook. When he returned to Melbourne, he embarked on what he spoke about reflexively as a project of culinary self-education. He didn't just want to consume food; he felt he should be able to produce it too, and he set out to acquire the skills to do so. This culinary education wasn't bound up with his ethnicity, with learning to cook Chinese cuisine from his mother. It was about learning to cook a range of different ethnic cuisines, and this knowledge needed to be acquired from material media.

This reflexive project of culinary education may be more specific to foodies than to the general populace. In her research on cooking in the United Kingdom, Frances Short found that most people "do not purposefully set out to learn to cook or become 'a cook'"; rather, learning to cook is "an arbitrary process; people pick up cookery tips, ideas and inspiration 'by chance' as they go about their daily food and cooking business" (2006: 37). She describes one of her informants, Stacey, as a "learner cook," as she would like to be an amateur cook and recreate the dishes of professional chefs. However, Short observes that "there is no particular plan or structure to her learning," and "despite the fact that she often looks at food articles in magazines and cuts out things that appeal to her 'for one day in the future' she hasn't used any as yet" (2006: 76). While Stacey wants to learn to cook, she doesn't want to devote too much time to doing so. She is more what Stebbins (1979) would categorize as a "dabbler" rather than an amateur.

In contrast, Nick, as an amateur, is highly committed to his culinary education and regularly devotes time to it. He also has a particular plan that structures his educational project, a plan in which cookbooks and recipes play a central role. As he described it, this plan involves choosing a particular cuisine (for example, Italian) or a specific dish (for example, risotto) that he wants to learn to cook, finding a recipe for it in a cookbook and then practicing it over the course of a few weeks: "Once a week I try to pull out a recipe book and learn the recipe, and practice it a few times, and then start playing around with different flavors." He uses cookbooks to teach himself the basic skills, techniques, methods, and ingredients required of a dish. Once he has gained a degree of confidence in reproducing the recipe, he then experiments with his own personal inflections, or "perfects" the recipe through experimentation. He described this process of revision in relation to making sushi:

> I've sort of worked it out, how long to leave the rice for, how much water to put in, how much of the vinegar solution to put into the rice, and all sorts of little odds and ends and stuff. So I took the base recipe, and then kept playing with it, and at first, maybe the rice was too soggy or it didn't stick enough, and I thought "Oh, why *is* that?" and I'd play around with it a few more times and go "Ah! That's it! I've found it, the ideal."

While some recipes are better than others, many require a degree of personalization and revision because of the large number of variables that influence their reproduction. Nick described how once he thinks he has sufficiently mastered a dish, he'll "move on to a different style of cuisine. And when I get that inspiration, then I'll go off and find a book on it and try to work out exactly what it is that I want to learn and practice." As Giddens has observed, "the reflexive project of the self generates programmes of actualisation and mastery" (1991: 9). The successful mastery of each recipe functions as a step in Nick's career as an amateur cook, as part of his formation of a foodie self.

But it was not only foodies in the earlier stages of their career as amateur cooks who used cookbooks in their culinary education; more advanced amateur cooks also used books to learn new recipes and skills. They tended to use the professional cookbooks released by haute cuisine chefs. As practical guides, these cookbooks are often targeted at an audience of fellow professional chefs, not laypeople, as the recipes they contain are often very technical and require high levels of culinary skill. Foodies use these professional cookbooks to learn more advanced culinary skills and technical recipes because most television shows—even those hosted by haute cuisine chefs—simplify the knowledge represented for a less culinary-educated audience.

George was at a relatively advanced stage of his career as an amateur cook. As I showed earlier, he began his culinary education via food media as a young boy, when he used television cooking shows to learn how to cook different ethnic dishes beyond his mother's Cypriot cuisine. Like Nick, his culinary education was not focused on his own ethnic cuisine. He had learned to make many of his mother's dishes, such as pork sausages, because his two sisters were not serious cooks, and the recipes had not been documented, but this was not his main concern. "There are probably a few dishes that mum would make that I still have never tried," he said, "but most of them I know how to do. Not that I regularly do them, because there's too many other things to try!" Now in his thirties, George uses professional cookbooks to learn different cuisines and more advanced and technical culinary skills. As Stebbins has shown, amateurs are often oriented by standards of excellence set and communicated by professionals (1979: 25). George saw it as a challenge to attempt to reproduce haute cuisine recipes from professional cookbooks. In one story, he described a conversation he'd had with the British-born Melbourne chef Donovan Cooke regarding his cookbook:

> He said that you're never going to try the exact recipe at home, because it was all exactly like they did it at the restaurant, you know, it was too time consuming and very technical, but it gives you a background of all the dishes, and there's no harm in trying to incorporate some of it into the food you cook at home. So I took him up on that challenge and I reproduced things exactly like it's described. And it's been well worth it. Some of the best stuff that we've done at home has been from that particular cookbook. Yeah, you can do it, but you have got to go to a lot of effort.

In contrast to Surat, who, as I discussed earlier, uses professional cookbooks to gain interactional expertise in haute cuisine—that is, the ability to talk about how such food is produced—George uses them to gain what Collins and Evans (2007) term "contributory expertise," which involves not only the theoretical knowledge of how something is done but also the practical skills and ability to do it oneself. It refers to the "ability to perform a skilled practice . . . contributory experts have the ability to *do* things within the domain of expertise" (2007: 24, original emphasis). As George's comments show, the acquisition of such contributory expertise and the successful reproduction of professional dishes generate feelings of accomplishment for amateurs, something that we are familiar with today from *MasterChef*. Gelber argues:

> Achievement-generated pleasure from worklike leisure reinforces the participants' beliefs they are doing something that is good. In leisure, as in work, a difficult task done well is a source of pride . . . Such leisure is socially valorized precisely because it produces feelings of satisfaction with something that looks very much like work but that is done for its own sake. (1999: 12)

As well as this sense of achievement and morality in productive leisure, the replication of the recipes of professional chefs creates a sense of connection with them for amateurs. Janet Floyd and Laurel Forster suggest that through the "discovery, reading and even putting into practice of other women's recipes an imagined community is built" among women (2003b: 5). Similarly, amateur foodies construct imagined communities with professional chefs by putting their recipes into practice as another way of connecting with professionals in their self-formation through productive leisure.

Material media, then, are central to how we use the production of objects in our self-formation in postindustrial societies. They educate audiences in the moral value of production that is fundamental to productive leisure—that is, the morality of both producing material things and acquiring the knowledge and skills to do so. But beyond this moral education, many forms of material media continue to provide a practical education in how to make things. They provide the main way many of us acquire skills in material production to use to craft the self in a postindustrial world. Food media, such as television cooking shows and cookbooks, are not just entertainment spectacles or food porn, as many have suggested, but they are practical educational texts used by audiences, such as foodies, to acquire productive skills. Foodies consider this acquiring of productive skills to be a moral approach to consuming these material media in self-formation. However, it is not just acquiring productive skills from the media but also expressing these skills in practices of material production, such as cooking, that is central to the moralities of productive leisure shaping our use of material culture in self-making today.

7

Cooking: Manual Leisure and Material Production

As a social practice of production, cooking is commonly experienced, and theorized, as a form of labor. Historically, it has been internally differentiated into forms of paid and unpaid labor along gender lines. As unpaid domestic labor, cooking is feminized; along with shopping, it constitutes part of the socially expected "women's work" of food provisioning within the home, an unequal division of labor that has been the focus of feminist critique (Charles and Kerr 1984; Oakley 1990; DeVault 1991; Counihan 2004). As paid professional labor, on the other hand, cooking is masculinized, as the culinary profession—particularly high-end cooking—has historically been dominated by men (Fine 1996; Ferguson and Zukin 1998).

HOME COOKING: LABOR AND LEISURE

Despite moral panics about the death of cooking, empirical evidence shows that most people still eat home cooked meals most of the time (Lang and Caraher 2001; see also Short 2006). The responsibility for preparing these meals still falls largely on women. In the wake of second-wave feminism and the rhetoric of the "new man," women continue to undertake most cooking within the home. Caraher and his colleagues found that 80 percent of the women in their research cooked on most or every day. Nevertheless, they also found that a quarter of men cook equally as often (1999: 590), which may be a significant increase in responsibility for everyday cooking compared to previous generations.

But home cooking is also experienced, by some, as a form of leisure, and this trend appears to be increasing (Caraher et al. 2000). Short suggests that "cooking means both different things to different people and different things on different occasions" (2006: 116). Her research found that some people experienced cooking to be a chore, a form of domestic labor, while others described it as a source of great pleasure, a form of domestic leisure. Yet it was often not exclusively experienced as one or the other. The experience of cooking as domestic work or leisure was often shaped by time: both by the day of the week—the codified leisure time of the weekend was associated more with cooking for pleasure—and the amount of time one had to spend cooking, with longer periods associated with leisure. In this sense, there was a distinction or opposition between everyday cooking, which was more chore-like and obligatory, and cooking as leisure. Short found that while some women experienced cooking as leisure some of the time, none saw it purely as leisure because of their responsibility for everyday cooking and their lack of a real choice of whether or not to cook. She argues that only men who were freed from the responsibilities of everyday cooking could experience "cooking purely as a hobby," as they cooked on weekends or special occasions (2006: 78). Short sets up an opposition between the identifications of the family cook, who is "responsible for the weekly shopping, everyday meals, packed lunches, the washing-up and so on"—and is generally a woman—and the hobby cook, who cooks for leisure on weekends—and is generally a man (2006: 86). This suggests that in order for cooking to be a hobby, it has to be divorced from the responsibility of everyday cooking.

However, as I discussed in relation to shopping, Stebbins argues that the distinction between obligation and leisure may depend largely on a person's attitude toward the activity (1992: 4). He distinguishes between a "disagreeable obligation," which people experience as laborious, and an "agreeable obligation," which is experienced as leisure because it involves value commitment and is associated with pleasant memories and expectations (2007: 72–3). Luce Giard captures the sense of cooking as an agreeable obligation in her ethnographic research on women "doing-cooking" in France. She describes how for the women in her study, culinary activities are a daily responsibility, yet for many they are "a place of happiness, pleasure, and discovery" and a significant site of self-making (Giard 1998: 151). Thus, the disposition towards cooking as leisure is not only available to men, or more specifically, to those without culinary responsibilities.

It was this more complex experience of cooking that I found among foodies. Most female *and* male foodies in my study were responsible for the everyday cooking in their household. The majority of them fuse Short's (2006) polarized categories of the family cook and the hobby cook, as they are responsible for everyday cooking, but they nevertheless claim to experience most, if not all, of their cooking as leisure, whether it is undertaken on weeknights or at the weekend. It is not so surprising that my male informants could relatively easily categorize most or all of their cooking as leisure despite their responsibility for everyday cooking, because while cooking may be a household obligation for these men, it is not a social obligation. What is more surprising is the ease with which most of my female informants categorized cooking predominantly, or even exclusively, as leisure, despite both their household and social obligations to perform this everyday task. For example, Madeleine, who cooked most nights for her partner, described this practice purely as leisure, saying, "it's an absolute pleasure to be in the kitchen." Maureen, too, who cooked daily for her husband, said she experienced it exclusively as leisure and that she had always felt that way. This sentiment was echoed by Caroline, a semiretired teacher, who said that "even when I was teaching full-time, I regarded cooking the evening meal as a break between teaching and the inevitable pile of correction each night." She continued to enjoy cooking daily for her husband and for family and friends on the weekend.

In contrast to the female cooks in Short's (2006) study, most of my female informants did not feel that they lacked a real choice over whether or not to cook; if they didn't feel like cooking, they generally wouldn't. They thus set up boundaries in order to isolate cooking as leisure in their self-formation. The various foods made available by the market mean that women no longer *have* to cook meals as they did in the past—they can eat out, eat takeaway, or (for non-foodies) eat a ready-made supermarket meal. The "industrialisation of the kitchen" with factory-made preprepared meals in the 1950s (Symons 2007: 330), combined with the rise of dine in and takeaway restaurants in postindustrial society, has liberated women from the absolute necessity of cooking. These technological and industrial changes have provided the foundations for women to reflexively experience cooking as a form of leisure in their self-making. It is not producing food, then, but *buying* food—whether fresh ingredients or ready-made meals, takeaways or meals out—over which women have no real choice in postindustrial society (unless they are one of the select few who have a self-sufficient farm). They are liberated from the production of food—at least technologically, if not socially—but not its consumption. Ruth, who identified strongly as a feminist, described how this sense of choice over whether or not to cook enabled her to experience it as leisure in her self-making: "Because it's choice, I own how I do it and what I do and when I do it and things like that ... So I don't see it as a chore."

Thus, in the formation of foodie selves, cooking—the material production of food—is both discursively constructed and reflexively experienced as a form of leisure. Indeed, as with shopping, it is the delineation of the practice as leisure rather than labor that is central to this self-fashioning. But while the freedom from having to cook offered by the market allows foodies to own it as a choice and experience it as leisure, all of my informants shared a strong moral belief that people—and especially foodies—*should* cook and should *enjoy* it—that is, a belief in the morality of cooking as productive leisure. Like the philosophy advocated by TV chefs, such as Jamie Oliver and Hugh Fearnley-Whittingstall, foodies believe this is the right relationship to have to food as a material object in postindustrial society; rather than just consuming food prepared by others, people should develop a relationship with the food they eat and get to know it through producing it oneself.

In their own self-making, while foodies engage in cooking as leisure, they are again distinguished by the particularly productive and work-like approach they take to it, as they emulate professional chefs. We are all now familiar with such dedicated amateur cooks from the blockbuster reality TV program *MasterChef,* which has popularized the discourse of cooking as leisure and the serious approach of such enthusiasts. While some, like the contestants on the program, want to develop their passion for cooking into a profession, many others, like the foodies in my study, are keen to keep it as leisure.

FROM SLOW FOOD TO MOLECULAR GASTRONOMY: COOKING LIKE A PRO

In an era when it is no longer necessary to cook—hence the fears about the death of cooking—if one does cook, it is certainly no longer necessary to cook from scratch, using raw, fresh ingredients, as there is a wide array of preprepared ingredients available. Yet it is precisely this approach—cooking from scratch—that foodies take. These amateurs approach both shopping and cooking in the manner of professional chefs. Their shopping is governed by a morality of quality similar to that of chefs, as they source good quality, local, seasonal produce for their home cooking. Just as their serious shopping as productive leisure is characterized by work and effort—in terms of learning about produce and sourcing it from multiple suppliers—so too is their cooking—in terms of preparing dishes from scratch. It is an approach to cooking based on constantly acquiring new culinary knowledge and skills, which are learned from professionals via material media. Thus, it is not only their experience of everyday cooking as leisure that distinguishes foodies from other home cooks but also the effort and commitment, the constant acquisition and deployment of knowledge and skill, and the emulation of the attitudes, values, and practices of professional chefs that distinguishes their home cooking as the serious and productive leisure of amateurs.

The foodie's everyday approach to home cooking from scratch appears to be a marginal one. In her research among ordinary home cooks, Short found that these cooks did not use the term "'cook' in the way that many food writers and experts do, to mean the preparation of food 'from scratch,' from fresh, raw ingredients only" (2006: 28). Rather, most home cooking involved the use of preprepared ingredients, generally in combination with fresh ingredients. Even what her informants termed "proper cooking" or "real cooking"—which was highly valued cooking, such as for leisure or special occasions—was not necessarily from scratch but often included preprepared ingredients, although there was frequently a higher proportion of fresh ingredients (2006: 28, 34). Short highlights the acceptability of preprepared ingredients among ordinary cooks: "Unlike many food experts and scholars, cooks themselves, I found, do not necessarily start from the position that cooking with convenience or pre-prepared foods is less acceptable than cooking with fresh, raw foods. They are just 'part of cooking'" (2006: 31).

In contrast, preprepared ingredients and convenience foods *were* considered unacceptable by foodies, for as I have shown, these ingredients were incompatible with foodies' morality of quality. Foodies share the opinion of chefs and food writers—and that of the Slow Food movement—that cooking ought to be done from scratch using fresh seasonal produce, that this is the right way to cook. The morality of quality that governs their consumption of food in shopping is thus linked to a morality of cooking from scratch that governs their food production. Adopting such an approach to cooking was the main way that many of my informants said they "practiced" slow food in their everyday lives. As Leah described it, "We buy fresh local produce. I take time to cook things with no shortcuts. We very seldom buy pre-made things. The only thing would be canned tomatoes or beans." Madeleine, too, described how she tried to "adhere to the principles" of Slow Food in her home cooking:

> There's very little packaged food in our house. All our fruit and veg come from a local market, and our meat from a locally sourcing butcher. I take quite a bit of time preparing various foods from scratch, for example my own stock, which also helps me to use as much of any piece of food as possible, minimizing wastage.

Like alternative shopping practices, cooking from scratch formed part of foodies' opposition to the modern industrial food system, and their embrace of craft modes of production—their culinary luddism (Laudan 2001). My informants described making a variety of foods from scratch that other people often buy premade, such as sauces, stocks, salad dressings, curry pastes, pizza bases, pasta, bread, cakes, and biscuits. However, they did not make everything from scratch—their cooking did involve preprepared ingredients, such as olive oil, butter, milk, cheese, cream, ham, salami, and so on. These were not considered to be preprepared ingredients, though, because "preprepared" has the connotation of products that are highly processed, mass-produced, and distributed in supermarkets. The preprepared products foodies use are either considered to be less processed or differently processed, using artisanal craft techniques and small-scale production. A mass-produced brand-name salami from the supermarket is far more likely to be categorized as a preprepared ingredient than a handcrafted chorizo from the local Spanish delicatessen. This highlights the way in which the categorization of foods as preprepared is shaped by hierarchies of taste and cultural value (see also Short 2006: 31).

The ubiquity of haute cuisine chefs in the media over the past decade has had a significant effect on understandings of home cooking and conceptions of what constitutes a good home cook in postindustrial society. In previous times, a good cook might have been Aunty Shirley, who was famous for baking her lemon meringue pies, or Nanna Kathy, for her tasty Ukrainian cooking— these were figures whose culinary expertise was based on traditional, domestic, feminine culinary knowledge. However, Short shows that among ordinary cooks, the understanding of what constitutes a good home cook has taken on a far greater sense of an amateur proper, someone who pursues professional values and standards in their home cooking. Her informants thought that good home cooks were people "who can cook 'professionally' and make food like 'everyone on the telly'" (2006: 44). Thus, the general public's idea of what constitutes a good home cook is becoming more professionalized. Foodies, on the other hand, value both the professional model of the amateur home cook—to which they themselves aspire—as well as the traditional, feminine, familial model of the good cook, which is more romanticized in their imaginary and embodied by famous cooks like Australia's Maggie Beer, Britain's Claudia Roden, or America's Marcella Hazan.

While both ordinary cooks and amateur foodies place a high value on professionalism in domestic cookery, it is only the latter who specifically seek to emulate chefs in their own cooking. Short found that very few of her informants attempted to professionalize their home cooking, and those who did so were all men; they conformed to her category of the occasional hobby cook (2006: 78). In contrast, both the male and female foodies in my research emulated professional chefs through using quality produce to cook gourmet dishes from scratch. For John and Elena, cooking was a form of productive leisure in which they participated together:

John: We do enjoy cooking.

Elena: We have a lot of fun cooking together.

John: But the produce means that we can get close to a restaurant quality result. We can't do tricks that people like [Australian haute cuisine chefs] Tetsuya Wakuda and Shannon Bennett and so on can do, we don't aspire to that. But we can have quite a feast taking the good quality produce and applying—you know, we've both learnt a lot over the years, without formal training.

While John and Elena emulate restaurant quality in their cooking, they do not aspire to perform the culinary tricks of molecular gastronomy chefs; but other foodies do. Earlier, I discussed Mary's story of the first time she dined in a molecular gastronomy restaurant. She described her amazement and delight at the culinary foam that formed part of several dishes. She went on to describe how she wanted to learn the tricks involved in making such foam in her own home cooking:

> Mary: So I did all this research on how to make culinary foam. It got started by Ferran Adrià, that Spanish chef, the world leader of all of this. So I did all the research on him, and worked out how to do it. You use— you know those old fashioned cream whippers? So instead of getting whipped cream in a can, you can get these cool canisters, you put nitrous oxide in, and then you go "*shhhhh*" and it does it! So you do that. That's how you make it. But you do it like with skim milk and gelatin and all this sort of stuff.
>
> Isabelle: So have you tried it?
>
> Mary: I've had one attempt, and it wasn't too bad! Because there's no quantities, and it is science basically. So I've then had to go to all these food science sites on the Internet and work out, you know, the properties of food and how they react with stuff and all the rest—which is kind of bizarre, but it's interesting!

As Mary's story demonstrates, some foodies are cooking (or attempting to cook) the haute cuisine style of molecular gastronomy within the home. Elsewhere, I have examined how this is being undertaken by foodies in North America and documented on their food blogs (see de Solier 2010). In this style of cooking, foodies are not only amateur cooks but also amateur scientists. Preparing this scientific cuisine requires equipment (such as a Thermomix or Pacojet) and ingredients (such as sodium alginate or liquid nitrogen) that are not commonly found within domestic kitchens—or non-molecular restaurant kitchens for that matter. As Mary exclaimed, "You need like a lab as well as a kitchen to make it all!" This different equipment, combined with different levels of skill and experience, affects the different levels of competence that foodies can gain in professional culinary styles like molecular gastronomy. For as Matthew Watson and Elizabeth Shove suggest, competence is best understood not as the sole characteristic of the human subject but "*as something that is in effect distributed between practitioners and the tools and materials they use*" (2008: 77, original emphasis). Foodies recognize the differences between themselves and professional chefs in terms of formal training (or the lack thereof) and different types and levels of skills, as well as the different contexts of professional and domestic kitchens, and the different equipment and ingredients available.

This stands in contrast to the ordinary cooks in Short's study, who did not recognize the extensive training and experience possessed by professional chefs, but often thought that their superior culinary skills were a result of "natural ability." They also did not recognize the different range of skills and tasks involved in professional cookery (Short 2006: 45). Yet Short argues that the skill sets of the professional chef and the domestic cook are quite different. While they may share similar practical and technical skills, such as the ability to debone a chicken, an examination of the different contexts in which they cook and the resources they have available highlights other skills and knowledge that differentiate them (2006: 63). Domestic cooks tend to cook alone and are responsible for all the various tasks and dishes comprising a meal. Short argues that domestic cooks may have other skills, such as an ability to fit cooking in around other tasks and activities, to use up leftovers (and disguise them as something new), and to prepare meals that satisfy a range of tastes and dietary requirements within the household. In contrast, a professional chef "may be more likely to have the skills necessary to prepare food to consistent standards day in and day out and to share tasks with others" (2006: 63). In restaurants, chefs work collaboratively as part of a team rather than on their own, and when they work in kitchens that are organized into the parties system, each chef is responsible for a particular task (for example, roast, vegetables, sauce, fish, or pastry) rather than entire dishes or meals. As Fine's study of chefs has shown, professional cooking requires skills in teamwork and cooperation and an ability to cope with immense pressure and to work at great speed in extremely hot working conditions (1996: 40–1). My informants demonstrated an awareness of these different demands of professional cookery—informed partly by television programs such as *Ramsay's Kitchen Nightmares*—and often used these demands to explain why they preferred to keep cooking as a leisure pursuit rather than pursuing it as a vocation. Beth, for example, described how she would prefer to remain an amateur cook (and a professional patron) in her self-formation through food:

> From a professional perspective, I don't think I have what it takes to cook in a commercial kitchen, or do something of that nature. I have great respect for people who do. And I love to cook, and I love to eat, but I don't think I'm of the right personality type to be in a commercial kitchen cooking all of the time ... I think it's a really hard job. Being creative, as well as working in a confined space where the temperatures are physically hot, you know very hot, and there's lots of sharp objects, and there's lots of frayed tempers, and everything is being done to an almost unrealistic time frame, and you've got personalities from one end of the spectrum to the other—I think I'm probably nuts enough without having that!

Short argues that the lack of recognition by ordinary cooks of the different training, skills, experience, and equipment possessed by professional chefs may lead to a lack of confidence among such cooks (2006: 46). In contrast, the amateur foodies in my research, who did recognize these differences between chefs and themselves, and were aware of their different potentials and limitations, were generally confident in their cooking. Amelia, who was in her twenties, said: "It's one of only a few things I do with real confidence. I don't really have that many skills or hobbies other than cooking so this is my hobby. I like being experimental and mostly I like serving up good food to people I love." Likewise, Raymond, a retiree in his sixties, said: "I feel confident in my knowledge for my purposes and enjoy experimenting and trying different things." These experiences and expressions of confidence by amateur cooks stand in contrast to the experience of amateurs in many other activities, who Stebbins argues are generally characterized by a lack of confidence in comparison to their professional counterparts. He observes that confidence "is a prominent quality of experienced professionals, but absent in most amateurs," who are instead ridden with insecurities and nervousness; the amateur "doubts his abilities, expresses them timidly" (1979: 38). The amateur foodie cooks in my research seem to be an exception to this rule, perhaps because unlike amateur actors or sportspeople, the products of their serious leisure are generally not for anonymous publics but for friends and family.

While foodies displayed confidence in their cooking, this is not to say that it was always a success and that they didn't have failures. As George said, "I like experimenting a lot more as well, like I was quite happy to bake a loaf of bread that didn't work, over and over again, just to experiment and sort of try different things." Foodies are often happy to keep persevering because the pleasure and rewards they find in cooking come just as much—or even more so—from the process of material production as they do from the end result.

MORALITIES OF MATERIAL PRODUCTION: COOKING, CRAFT, AND CREATIVE PRODUCTION

Almost all of the foodies in my research reflexively thought of themselves as producers of food, not just consumers. As Rosa put it, "I think being a foodie encompasses a bit more [than just consumption]. It's not just the enjoyment of food; it's the enjoyment of food production, well for me anyway." Being a producer of food was crucial to foodies' self-formation through this object, and such material production held a higher moral value in their self-making because of anxieties over consumerism and the worth placed in productive pursuits. Indeed, there was a shared moral belief that you *had* to cook, or *should* cook, in order to "be" a foodie. This was central to their moralities of productive leisure that shaped their relationship with food. As Ruth described it: "For me, I think of being a foodie as not just the appreciation of good food or good cooking, or the consuming of it, it's actually the doing of it as well, the practice of it, so—yes, it's got to be practice, rather than just theory." Maureen went even further, saying "I think 'foodie' should only apply to people who like more than just eating good food"; they also need to enjoy preparing it. Ruth differentiated herself from a friend who she didn't consider to be a foodie because "she loves eating but she doesn't cook." Yet it was not only those who *did* cook who thought that producing this material object was vital to being a foodie but also those who *didn't*. Only two of my informants—Surat and Mathew—were not serious cooks, but they too shared this moral belief that foodies *should* cook. Surat didn't really consider himself to be a foodie for this reason, as he explained: "A foodie, apart from consuming food, you should also be able to produce it at the same time; you should be able to cook ... I don't consider myself a good cook at all, so as such, I don't think I deserve the term foodie." Thus, there was a shared sense that "foodie" was a title that needed to be earned through being productive— Surat and Mathew atoned for their lack of material production of food in their self-making by being productive in other ways, through the production of material media, as I explore in the following chapter. But this sense of self as a food producer, common to most foodies, is something they share with professional chefs. As Fine observes, "Cooks are producers. They create products that can be beautiful and appealing to the senses. Anyone who can produce such things has the 'right to feel proud'—to recognize his or her accomplishments" (1996: 43). While foodies engage in cooking as a form of productive leisure rather than productive labor, they too feel an enormous sense of reward from this practice of making material things.

Production, then—and the moral value it holds—was a critical conceptual unit around which foodies' discussions of cooking circulated. Yet it was not alone in this respect; rather, it was crucially connected to a second concept, that of creativity. What is important about cooking for foodies is not only that it is a means of producing material things but also that the process of material production is a creative one, that it offers an outlet for creative expression in everyday life. As Rowena, a human resources manager, described: "I find cooking to be a creative outlet—I'm not much of an artist or writer, but cooking allows me to experiment and try new things." Similarly, Thomas, who worked as a manager in community services, said that "cooking is my primary creative outlet ... It's creativity that you can eat, and because you have to eat and thereby destroy it, you can do it all over again tomorrow." Within academia, and society more generally, creativity has long been associated with the exclusionary realm of high art and the exclusive figure of the artist. As Paul Willis observes, this situation "seems to exhaust everything else of its artistic contents"; in contrast, he advocates a more democratic approach that recognizes the creativity of ordinary people in their "everyday life, everyday activity and expression" (1990: 1). He refers to instances of such creativity as "grounded aesthetics" (1990: 21), of which the cooking undertaken by foodies is an example. However, my informants were not comfortable describing their cooking with terms like "aesthetic" or "artistic," precisely because of the elite connotations of these words. The immorality of distinction in foodies' self-formation made them uncomfortable with using the discourse of art often employed by haute cuisine chefs for fear of sounding like a "wanker." Instead, they preferred to use the more down-to-earth term "creative" to describe their cooking. This forms part of the morality of production in their self-making: one should not appear elitist or wanky but should represent one's cooking in more modest terms.

For foodies, then, cooking constitutes a form of what I call *creative production.* This concept emerged from the language my informants used to describe their practices of producing material culture. For it was not only the production of material objects—cooking—that was spoken about in these terms; as I show later, the production of material media—food blogging—was also understood in this way in their self-making. But the concept also developed from the ways in which both these forms of production in leisure were distinguished from and contrasted to their modes of production at work. For the emphasis and value placed on producing something—be it a meal or a blog—and expressing creativity in these leisure activities was opposed to the sense of a lack of opportunity to do so in their professional knowledge work. The concept of creative production thus links the worlds of postindustrial work and leisure. It describes how people pursue leisure practices that involve creating and producing material culture, at least in part, as a counterbalance to the modes of production in their work. For foodies, this creative production involves making dishes and food blogs; for others, it may involve making jewelry, a garden, a website on fashion, or a YouTube clip on DIY. These forms of creative production do not only provide a balance to modes of production in work, but they also offer a balance to consumption in leisure, and both these aspects are significant in postindustrial self-making.

The type of production commonly associated with both creating and producing things is craft; indeed, creativity and production constitute its two essential elements. In his history of craft, Paul Greenhalgh (1997) highlights the nebulous nature of this category, which was historically a *salon de refuse* that included all aesthetic objects that did not have the high status of fine art. It was not until the late nineteenth century that craft was defined "as a thing *in itself*" by the members of the Arts and Crafts movement: "craft stood exactly *for* the making of things. Artistic expression *through* the making process was at the heart of craft aesthetics and politics" (Greenhalgh 1997: 36, 43, original emphasis). It was the additional element of producing that came to distinguish craft from art and design in the twentieth century; making was no longer considered an essential element of the latter two endeavors. It was also amateur or hobbyist crafts—particularly feminine textile crafts or handicrafts—that became the dominant meaning of the term in the twentieth century (Greenhalgh 1997: 37), although there has been a resurgence of the term among professionals in the early twenty-first century (see Levine and Heimerl 2008).

Cooking is not commonly categorized as a craft, and it was not a term that my informants used to describe their cooking because of its general connotation of textile crafts within the Australian vernacular. However, Colin Campbell has recently theorized cooking in terms of craft. While he acknowledges that cooking is "a production activity as much as (or, indeed, rather than) a consumption one" (2005: 33), he develops his argument about cooking as craft not within a discussion of production but within one of consumption, where he theorizes it as a form of what he calls "craft consumption." Campbell draws on the idea of craft as a way of theorizing modes of consumption in late modernity. He is interested in consumption not in the sense of purchase but that of using up. Thus cooking, while being a practice that produces a material product, also involves using up ingredients. It is a hybrid practice, both productive and consumptive, which the term "craft consumption" suggests. For Campbell, it is not only that the consumption of goods is productive but also that the final material product is then consumed by the self. Craft consumption refers specifically to cases where individuals combine a number of material goods to create a new "ensemble" product that they themselves consume, such that the "product" is designed, made, and consumed by the same person (Campbell 2005: 33–4). In addition to cooking, the other examples he gives include gardening and interior decoration.

While the concept of craft consumption is useful as a means of highlighting and understanding the consumption of material objects that occurs within practices such as cooking, DIY, and gardening, it is not clear why these social practices themselves should be thought of as craft consumption and not just, more simply, as crafts. For more traditional crafts, such as knitting or quilting, also involve purchasing a range of raw materials and creating a new product that is consumed by the self. The amateur textile craftswomen in Enza Gandolfo and Marty Grace's study described how they loved going to shops to look at and purchase materials for their craft (2009: 20). Moreover, the characteristics they associated with craft were similar to the meanings and values foodies associate with cooking: "the use of craft as personal creative expression; the importance of the process of making; the skills that can be learned and developed with practice; and the functionality of the made objects" (Gandolfo and Grace 2009: 9).

For my purpose here, then, it is more useful to think of cooking as craft rather than craft consumption. For while Campbell does genuinely attempt to understand the meaningfulness of practices such as cooking, DIY, and gardening in people's lives in postindustrial society, naming such practices as craft *consumption*—while useful as an exercise in abstract theorizing on consumption—distorts the very meaning and value these practices hold in their practitioners' self-formation, which is integrally concerned with *production.* This is not limited to the foodies in my research but has also been found among gardeners (Taylor 2008) and DIY enthusiasts (Rosenberg 2011b). Both the motivation and the reward for participating in such practices come from the fact that they are materially productive, that they are not merely consumption.

The politics of work is one of the key ideological and intellectual threads that have underpinned craft since industrial modernity (Greenhalgh 1997: 25). As Campbell observes, Marx and Veblen believed the preindustrial mode of labor undertaken by the craftsperson, which was expressive and creative, to be "ennobling, humanizing and, hence, the ideal means through which individuals could express their humanity" (Campbell 2005: 25). They saw the replacement of craft production by factory production in the industrial revolution as dehumanizing and leading, in Marx's terms, to the alienation of labor. The key distinction generally made between craft work and factory work is the mode of production: craft work is associated with hand production (hence the term handicraft), while factory work is associated with machine production. Yet Campbell plays down the significance of "working with the hands" to craft, and instead, he emphasizes the fact that both factory production and craft production use machines; for example, the traditional crafts of pottery and weaving use the potter's wheel and the loom. What distinguishes these two modes of production, he argues, is the different power relations between human and machine: the contrast is "between a production system in which the worker is in control of the machine and one in which the machine is in control of the worker" (2005: 28). While cooking may be aided by machines such as blenders and food processors, I argue that there is a greater significance of working with the hands than this theory acknowledges.

MAKING SOMETHING WITH YOUR OWN HANDS: MANUAL LEISURE AND MATERIAL PRODUCTION

The manual, or specifically hand-based, nature of production in cooking is central to its appeal as a form of productive leisure in postindustrial self-making. For when I asked foodies what they liked about cooking, I found that it was not only that cooking was a form of production, or creative production, but also that it was a form of manual material production, of working with the hands to produce a material object. For example, Fran, an executive assistant, said what she liked about cooking was the "satisfaction in producing by hand labor something that has pleasing qualities to enjoy." Similarly, Belinda, a business consultant, said: "I love the hands-on activity after a day of head stuff, and the fact that you can see quick results, smell them, and eat them." The significance of hand production to cooking is also demonstrated visually in the representations of home cooking on foodie blogs. For example, Rosa's blog post on making Gnocchi di Patate included nine close-up photographs of her hands that document different stages of making this pasta from scratch. Thus, the hand-based nature of cooking clearly holds immense significance in self-making for foodies, as it does for some other home cooks (Giard 1998; Hernandez and Sutton 2005).

As Belinda's statement that she loves the "hands-on activity after a day of head stuff" suggests, the significance of hand production in cooking, for foodies, lies not in the difference between hand production and machine production but between hand production and mental production. Cooking and producing something with the hands provides foodies with an alternative to their professional knowledge work. For not only is there a general lack of opportunity to make something and be creative in most work in postindustrial society, but in particular, there is a lack of opportunity to make something material, and to make it manually. Cooking, then, functions as a form of what I call *manual leisure,* which is pursued to redress the lack of manual labor and material creative production in work. Where manual labor is working class, manual leisure is middle class. Adam, an accountant by trade, described this need to engage in manual leisure in detail:

> I think the interesting thing about food culture is that when you think of what society is like now, because most people, you know, they work in offices, and people are professionals—it's different from fifty years ago, when more people worked with their hands ... I sort of think that people in general have this need to do something with their hands, to create something, whether it's cooking, whether it's painting, doing the gardening, or something like that. Because, you know, I think the human need to be able to touch and to do something and say like, "I've *done* that"—you can't get that from watching a video, you can't get that in most work situations, because a lot of stuff is intangible, you can't touch it, you can't really feel it. And I think most people are sort of looking for that, and a lot of people are finding food as one way of, you know, getting that experience of making something with your own hands.

For many foodies, then, the importance of "making something with your own hands" in the practice of cooking stems in part from its contrast to their professional knowledge work: Cooking is a form of manual leisure that compensates for their mental labor. Yet such manual leisure is more than just compensatory. It is not only satisfying a desire to do something different to work, but it is seen as fulfilling a fundamental human need to make things, and to make them manually, to feel materially connected to the world. As this need is not fulfilled in postindustrial work, it must be fulfilled in leisure.

It appears that in late modernity, as Adam suggests, a lot of people are looking for such an experience, and they are finding it not only in cooking but also in other forms of manual leisure based around material objects such as DIY (Rosenberg 2011b), gardening (Taylor 2008), and textile crafts (Gandolfo and Grace 2009), which have become increasingly popular over the last decade, particularly among the middle class. Gandolfo and Grace's study shows how crafts, such as knitting and embroidery, provide an outlet for manual leisure, particularly for professional women. As Gandolfo herself states, "I cannot go too long without the urge to make something tactile; to use thread or fabric; to make something from scratch" (2009: 6). The hand-based nature of this material creative production is of utmost importance and provides a balance to Gandolfo's knowledge work. For her informants, like many foodies, such manual leisure was seen as fulfilling a human need to be able to create and produce material things in everyday life. In a response reminiscent of Adam's, one of Gandolfo and Grace's informants, Karen, stated: "We don't grow our vegetables. We don't raise our own chickens anymore, so where's your opportunity to nurture, and to say at the end of the day, this is something I did ... I need to do something. I need to create something ... my outlet is craft" (2009: 40).

This expression of a need to engage in creative and productive activity voiced by foodies and other amateur craftspeople is not new. Greenhalgh argues that in the late nineteenth century, William Morris was responsible for generating a "politics of craft" based on "the need to engage in creative work" (1997: 33–34). Morris's dream was for all workers to be employed in craft work, not factory work, in this "vision of craft, as unalienated labor" (1997: 34). However, this utopic world of work was not to be realized. Instead, such creative expression would need to be found elsewhere, in leisure. Craft hobbies were promoted as a substitute for craft work to modern factory workers. Gelber shows how in industrial modernity, craft hobbies were popular among the working class, for whom these hobbies emulated the materially productive nature of their factory work, yet compensated for the lack of creativity and hand-based nature of such mechanized work (1999: 4–5). For factory workers, crafts as productive leisure *were* based around the difference between hand production and machine production.

In postindustrial society, however, it is often members of the middle class who are turning to crafts and expressing their own politics of craft reminiscent of that of Morris in the nineteenth century. Like Morris, they emphasize the human need to engage in creative and productive activity, yet unlike Morris, they do not advocate craft as unalienated labor but as unalienated leisure. In this postindustrial politics of craft of the middle class, manual leisure is seen to compensate not only for a lack of creativity and hand production (as it did with the industrial working class) but also for a lack of any material production in mental labor. This middle-class politics is also tied to neoliberal models of citizenship. The late modern state "emphasizes that citizens be not only active, but also "enterprising" in the pursuit of their own empowerment and well-being" (Ouellette and Hay 2008: 12). It appears that many people feel that their well-remunerated mental labor denies them the opportunity to acquire and express manual skill and to have a sense of making the material world in which they live; this makes them feel disempowered, as though an essential part of their humanity were missing. If they are not to find such material creative production in their work, these enterprising individuals take charge of their life and empower themselves by acquiring and expressing manual skills in their leisure time as a means of maximizing the "life of one's own" (Beck and Beck-Gernsheim 2001: 22).

While this manual leisure may be pursued in part as a counterbalance to mental labor, it is important to note that cooking is also still a form of knowledge-based leisure in my understanding, as it involves the expression of the practical knowledge and skill that foodies acquire from material media (see also Heldke 1992). Indeed, this form of practical knowledge of material production, or manual skill, is the most highly valued in knowledge-based leisure, precisely because of its exclusion from knowledge work. The reason why materially productive leisure, such as cooking, holds the highest moral value in these postindustrial forms of self-making is because it combines the morality of knowledge *and* material production in one practice.

The production of material things has again become central to our self-identity formation in postindustrial societies, but this time, it is not in the realm of work but in productive leisure. It is because of the decline of material production in work that these forms of manual leisure are so highly valued in self-making, but also because of the moral value they hold compared to simply consuming material objects. In a late modern era of risk and flux, people have a strong desire—or as many put it, an essential human need—to be connected to the material world in which they live, but in a way that is felt to be more substantial than just using their taste in commodities to communicate who they are. They want to be—and communicate themselves to be—a *producer* of material objects not just a consumer. This is considered more substantial because it involves injecting the self into the material object through the production process—developing a new relationship to the object by shaping it directly with one's hands—rather than just associating off-the-shelf commodities with the self. As a result, this form of material production is of utmost importance, and has the highest moral value, in the new modes of self-making through material culture in postindustrial society.

8

Blogging: Digital Leisure and Material Media Production

In late modernity, individuals increasingly go about constructing a life of one's own not only in the material world but also in the digital world. The Internet has become a primary site of self-formation in the twenty-first century, as millions of people around the world make and shape their selves on websites such as *Facebook, MySpace, YouTube, Twitter,* or *blogger.* The development of this digital world has opened up new opportunities for shaping the self through material objects in postindustrial society that weren't available in the past. Now, people also construct their self through material objects online, engaging with these objects in digital ways in their project of the self. The Internet is the site of the newest forms of self-making through material culture, which are productive rather than consumptive. It offers the potential for a different kind of production of material culture in postindustrial self-formation. For it is not only the production of material objects—such as food—that are used in self-formation today, but increasingly, the production of material media—such as food blogs—that are personal, amateur, and digital. In late modernity, then, it is not only professional experts, such as TV chefs and food writers, who share their knowledge of this material object with the public via old material media but also amateur foodies via new media.

A blog (or weblog) is a user-generated website that consists of regular dated entries in reverse-chronological order. Most have a single author but allow audience members to post comments. Blogs first emerged around 1996 (Lovink 2008: x) and became increasingly popular as a site of self-making in the early twenty-first century. In 2004, the blog search engine and indexer *Technorati* was tracking around 2 million blogs; by the end of 2011, NM Incite was tracking over 180 million (Herring et al. 2007: 5; Nielsen Company 2012). Blogs cover a range of topics and genres, including material media. The most popular category continues to be the journal blog or lifelog, followed by topical blogs on technology, politics, and news; *Technorati*'s directory lists 10,340 technology blogs and 7,762 politics blogs. These genres have attracted the greatest amount of scholarly attention (Reed 2005; Bruns and Jacobs 2006; Atton and Hamilton 2008). However, food blogs—which like most material blogs, have not been the focus of research—come in very close behind with 7,683 listed. Food is by far the leading genre of material media in *Technorati*'s directory, which lists 1,583 home and garden blogs and 448 fashion blogs (Technorati 2010).

PRODUCTIVE LEISURE AND PERSONAL MEDIA

In postindustrial society, the media do not only educate in productive leisure but have increasingly become the object of such leisure, as people spend their free time producing forms of personal digital media. The social practice of blogging has predominantly been undertaken as productive leisure rather than work. *Technorati*'s report on the blogosphere found that 72 percent of bloggers are hobbyists, while the remainder are professionals—defined as people for whom blogging relates to, or constitutes (all or part of), their paid work (McLean 2009). Most blogs, then, are not professional; they represent "the mass amateurization of publishing online" (Bruns and Jacobs 2006: 3). Marika Lüders categorizes such publications as "personal media," which she distinguishes from mass media. She argues that with the development of digital technologies, forms of personal media may now facilitate mass communication. The key difference between the two is that mass media content is made within institutionalized and professionalized structures, whereas personal media is deinstitutionalized and deprofessionalized. She observes that "the combination of the internet, PC and evolvement of less expensive and more manageable media production tools give leeway for the amateur media producer... 'Anyone' becomes qualified to be a media producer and is likely to have an audience to their productions" (Lüders 2008: 693–94).

In terms of categories of productive leisure, we can distinguish between different types of blogging as being hobbyist or amateur practices. For example, journal blogging or lifelogging—the most popular genre—is more hobbyist in nature, as it continues the tradition of diary writing and is not invested in a system of relationships with professionals and the public. In contrast, political, news, and food blogging are amateur practices, as they are situated in a relationship with the professional media they seek to emulate, supplement, or replace. Some amateur bloggers have successfully transformed their leisure pursuit into a career in professional publishing. This has been the case for a number of food bloggers, including France's Clotilde Dusoulier (*Chocolate & Zucchini*), America's Molly Wizenberg (*Orangette*), Britain's Niamh Shields (*Eat like a Girl*), and Australia's Sandra Reynolds (*The $120 Food Challenge*). But the most famous is America's Julie Powell, whose blog *The Julie/Julia Project*—which documented her goal of cooking all the recipes from Julia Child's book *Mastering the Art of French Cooking* (Beck et al. 1961) in one year—led to a book deal (Powell 2007), followed by a movie deal for *Julie & Julia* (2009), starring Meryl Streep and Amy Adams.

The boom in blogging as a form of knowledge-based productive leisure—combined with other forms of user-generated content—has seen the Internet become the main battleground for the culture wars between amateurs and professionals in postindustrial knowledge society. Some celebrate the new cultural power afforded to amateurs by these technologies and see them as making an important contribution to knowledge society; others see them as destroying it. In a report for the British think-tank Demos, *The Pro-Am Revolution: How Enthusiasts Are Changing Our Economy and Society* (2004), Leadbeater and Miller embrace the rise of "Pro-Ams," a new generation of amateurs shaped by the Internet, who are "knowledgeable, educated, committed and networked, by new technology" (2004: 12). They view the shifting power relations between amateurs and professionals in postindustrial society in a positive light, arguing that professionals "shaped the twentieth century through their knowledge, authority and institutions. They will still be vital in the twenty-first century. But the new driving force, creating new streams of knowledge, new kinds of organisations, new sources of authority, will be the Pro-Ams" (Leadbeater and Miller 2004: 71). The opposite view is put forward by Andrew Keen in *The Cult of the Amateur: How Today's Internet Is Killing Our Culture* (2007). He observes that the Web 2.0 revolution is celebrated on behalf of the "noble amateur," who will democratize "the dictatorship of expertise"; in contrast, he views such democratization as leading to a "dictatorship of idiots" (Keen 2007: 35). He argues that on today's Internet, "amateurism, rather than expertise, is celebrated, even revered...The professional is being replaced by the amateur, the lexicographer by the layperson, the Harvard professor by the unschooled populace" (Keen 2007: 37). Keen critiques the celebration of amateur knowledge on collaborative sites such as *Wikipedia,* as well as citizen journalism on blogs, arguing that the information created by amateurs can rarely be trusted because they lack the credentials of professionals.

Yet while they may not be professionals, research shows that bloggers are not idiots or unschooled. Rather, the majority of bloggers, like those in my research, are well-educated members of the knowledge class, who engage in both knowledge work and knowledge-based leisure. *Technorati's* report found that 75 percent of bloggers have degrees and 40 percent have postgraduate degrees (Sussman 2009). And while they may not be professional experts in the areas they blog about, in the case of foodies at least, they have acquired a level of amateur-expertise in various professional practices through their productive leisure.

FOOD BLOGS: AMATEUR MATERIAL MEDIA

Food blogging has become increasingly popular in recent years (de Solier 2006, 2010), so much so that the international blogging awards, the

"Bloggies," have a separate category for the Best Food Blog. The classical food blog consists of a combination of writing and photographs, with the two main categories of entries focusing on home cooking and restaurant dining. These amateur material blogs share similarities with both hobbyist lifelogs and amateur citizen media blogs on news and politics. Like the latter, food blogs have a public function as they seek to "inform and influence people" like the professional media they emulate (Atton and Hamilton 2008: 123). On food blogs, this takes the form of sharing knowledge and lifestyle advice on both the consumption of material objects (where to dine and what to eat) and their production (what to cook and how) in self-formation and self-improvement, like professional material media. Although these types of blogs share a public function, the foodie bloggers in my research differed significantly from news and political bloggers in terms of their relationship to the mainstream media and their professional counterparts. The latter bloggers are generally politically motivated by a critique of mainstream media and have an antagonistic attitude toward their professional counterparts (Singer 2006; Atton and Hamilton 2008). In contrast, the food bloggers in my research had a great deal of respect for professional food writers. They were not opposed to the mainstream media; indeed, they were avid consumers of it. Nor did these food bloggers see themselves as superior (or even equal) to or seeking to replace such gastronomes; rather, they sought to complement professional material media with their own amateur perspectives.

These amateur material blogs share more in common structurally with hobbyist lifelogs than with amateur political and news blogs. The latter are generally filter blogs—a collection of links to other Web content on which bloggers may offer their opinion (Herring et al. 2004)—whereas food blogs and lifelogs are primarily based around original content, such as writing and photographs. They also share a personal function of documentation and "presentation of the self" (Goffman 1959), which is something they have in common with social networking sites like *Facebook* and *My Space* (Horst 2009; D. Miller 2011). Yet where lifelogs, like the latter, tend to document all aspects of one's everyday life, food blogs focus on documenting the formation of the self through this material object in productive leisure practices like cooking and dining out. While food blogs are autobiographical, they are generally not inward looking and concerned with expressing private thoughts and feelings as journal blogs tend to be (Reed 2005). The style of writing on some food blogs, or on particular entries, is similar to the personal musings characteristic of lifelogs. Yet unlike the latter, it is not so much the personal genre of diary writing that such food blogging cites but the professional genre of gastronomic writing, associated with authors like Elizabeth David, M.F.K. Fisher, and Anthony Bourdain. Such food writing is literary and erudite; it often takes the form of gastronomic memoirs or tales of culinary travels and focuses nostalgically upon memorable meals (see Mennell 1996; Jones and Taylor 2001;

Sutton 2001; Duruz 2004). While some food blogs are primarily written in this style, most are more advice-driven and combine literary style (to a lesser or greater degree) with the more instructional genres of the recipe and restaurant review, even within a single entry.

Foodie blogs, then, are a form of amateur material media that have both a personal function of documenting the self (like journal blogs) and a public function of sharing knowledge (like citizen media blogs), both of which focus upon the material object of food. They thus blur the distinction that scholars commonly make between personal blogs and public blogs (see Cenite et al. 2009), as they do not fit neatly into either category. What is it, then, that motivates foodies to create these material media?

FOOD BLOGGING: MATERIAL MEDIA
AND DIGITAL CREATIVE PRODUCTION

While food blogging was not as common among my informants as cooking, it was highly valued by those foodies who used it in their self-making because it offered another mode of production to engage in with food as a material object. Like cooking, food blogging involves the production of material culture, but in this case, it is the production of material media based around the object rather than the object itself. Just as the production of food in cooking holds a higher moral value than its consumption in foodies' self-formation, so too the production of material media in blogging holds a higher moral value than just the consumption of food television and cookbooks for those who participate in it. While it is tied to the morality of knowledge in foodies' postindustrial self-making, blogging holds an even higher value than their other knowledge-based leisure because it involves sharing material knowledge, not just acquiring it, giving information about food, not just receiving it.

Like cooking, food blogging was experienced more specifically as a form of creative production by foodies and tied to the morality of this process in their self-making. It was spoken about in remarkably similar terms to cooking, such as "being creative" and "making something" as a way of connecting to the material world, and it was likewise seen as fulfilling a need to engage in such activities that were felt to be missing in their postindustrial work. When I asked Rosa, a public servant, why she blogged, she said: "I do it for me, yeah, it's that creative—because I need to, you know, do something, you know, out of the regular, ordinary work that I do, so I like that outlet." Likewise, Mary, a business manager, said the reason she made her food blog was because "it's another way to, you know, be creative about the whole thing," to have the opportunity to create and produce in her self-formation through food. As with cooking, it was both the process of creative production and its product that motivated foodies to engage in this practice.

But the making of material media in blogging offers a different mode of creative production to the making of material objects in cooking. As I have shown, the specific appeal the latter holds is in the process of making something material with one's hands, of engaging in manual creative production. Food blogging, on the other hand, does not involve such manually creative processes, but it holds a different appeal, of making material media with words and images. Rosa described this appeal, saying, "I love to write, I love food, and I love taking photos, so all together it seemed like the perfect outlet." As her statement highlights, blogging involves a number of creative processes, including writing, photography, and combining words and images, all of which are performed using digital technologies, such as the digital camera and importantly, the personal computer. Thus, food blogging may be considered a form of digital creative production that involves making new material media through digital technologies.

Axel Bruns has suggested that "produsage" is a better term than production to describe the making of user-generated new media, such as blogs. He argues that such media are not made by dedicated individuals or teams but by a broad-based distributed community of Web-savvy "produsers" (Bruns 2007: 3), who "engage with content interchangeably in consumptive *and* productive modes (and often in both at virtually the same time)" (Bruns and Jacobs 2006: 6, original emphasis). This concept seems more applicable to collaborative environments such as *Chowhound* (see Naccarato and LeBesco 2012) and *Yelp* (see Rousseau 2012a) than to blogs, particularly those composed mostly of original content, like food blogs, where the majority of the production is still undertaken by a dedicated individual, one to whom such production is of crucial importance in his or her self-identity. Moreover, despite the rhetoric of interactivity that dominates media studies work on the subject, empirical research shows that most blogs are not so interactive: A study undertaken in the United States found that the majority of posts did not receive any comments or contain links to external content (Herring et al. 2004: 8). This suggests that a more traditional notion of production and consumption *is* at work in relation to blogs, compared to other forms of new media.

The computer-based nature of blogging means that this form of creative production based around food is structurally closer to the knowledge work most foodies undertake than is cooking. Thus, while it compensates for the lack of creative production in such work, blogging can also be understood as a more substantial form of spillover leisure, as it carries over not just the work ethic and the expression of knowledge but also the skills in writing and information technology required by knowledge work. As Gelber highlights, compensation and spillover are often found together in forms of productive leisure: "Both the copyeditor who writes novels and the assembly line worker who builds a boat may be compensating for lack of creativity on the job and spilling over their job-related skills" (1999: 16). He goes on to explain that the two can coexist because they operate at different levels of awareness: "Compensation is, for the most part, self-conscious. People know what they do not like at work and choose the opposite in leisure. Spillover is often unintentional. Workers instinctively gravitate to leisure activities that allow them to use skills and attitudes that have brought them success on the job" (1999: 20).

This experience of blogging as both compensatory and spillover leisure does not appear to be limited to the foodies in my research, nor to material or food blogging, but may be more characteristic of blogging as a productive leisure pursuit in general. In his ethnography of journal bloggers in the United Kingdom, Adam Reed found that most were technophiles for whom blogging carried over their professional skills in information technology but compensated for the "repetitive, uninspiring office demands" they resented having to apply their time and skills to at work. He highlights how "individuals contrast weblogs to the artefacts they are required to produce at work—spreadsheets, corporate websites, well maintained IT systems. Blogging is presented as an antidote to the necessity of their employment, which for many involves sitting in front of a computer terminal all day" (Reed 2005: 229). Thus, blogging spills over skills from paid work, yet it is also reflexively pursued and experienced as a form of compensatory leisure that makes up for the lack of creative production on the job.

In that it involves both creating and producing—the two essential elements of craft—blogging might also be considered a form of craft in late modernity. This may be a somewhat provocative statement, considering the machine-based nature of blog production and the common conception of craft production as hand-based. Yet in considering this, it is useful to return to Campbell's (2005) argument that many traditional crafts did involve machines, but the worker was in control. David Gauntlett has recently extended discussions of craft from the material world into the digital world, where he suggests that "making things to share online," such as blogs, "is very much a craft process" (2011: 80). My research found that the processes of making and creating— and the human need to engage in such processes—that are at the heart of the philosophy of craft were central to how blogging, like cooking, was experienced by foodies. Food blogging is similarly invested in foodies' postindustrial politics of craft, based on their need to engage in creative production as unalienated leisure. For these enterprising individuals, blogging offers another way of taking control of the life of one's own by using leisure time to engage in forms of creative production not found in paid work, as a means of self-maximization.

This sense of self-empowerment through blogging is not only confined to foodies. In relation to the journal bloggers in his research, Reed observes that "in home and work situations where individuals claim they too often feel disempowered (an index of the agency of the boss, kin or friends), weblogs are taken to provide evidence of autonomy and self-distinction" (2005: 230). Indeed, most scholarly discussions of blogs focus on the capacity of such media to "empower citizens" by providing "the opportunity for 'ordinary' people to tell their own stories without the formal education or professional expertise and status of the mainstream journalist" (Atton and Hamilton 2008: 77; see also Meyers 2012).

This notion of ordinary people being empowered to tell their own stories brings me to the other two reasons why foodies make material media, which expand upon that of creative production. Foodies are driven by a desire to make something that both documents their own process of self-formation through food and shares their knowledge of this material object with others. As I have suggested, the former purpose of self-documentation is something food bloggers share with lifeloggers and can be considered a personal function of the food blog. The second purpose, of sharing knowledge, is something food bloggers have in common with citizen journalists, such as news bloggers, and can be considered a public function of the food blog. For some of my informants, the personal function was primary, while for others, the public function was of greatest importance in their self-making. The different prioritizations of these functions lead to different attitudes toward the creative processes through which foodies produce these material media.

PERSONAL MEDIATIONS: DOCUMENTING THE MATERIAL SELF

Food blogging is a practice through which foodies produce material media that document their self-formation through an object, and in so doing, form part of their material self-making. As Heather Horst observes, some people's engagements on the Internet are "purposefully non-material"; while for others, including the food bloggers in my research, "engagement in the digital world is only significant in that it reinforces the same physical and material objects" that shape their lives offline (2009: 108). For such foodies, the focus of their online presence is their relationship with food; it is a digital homage to this material object and the significant role it plays within their lives.

Blogging offers foodies a creative means of making memories of their material food experiences and practices, of which restaurants they've dined in, of what dishes they've cooked and eaten. Food blogs are forms of "mediated memories", which José van Dijck defines as *the activities and objects we produce and appropriate by means of media technologies, for creating and recreating a sense of past, present, and future of ourselves*" (2007: 21, original emphasis). She suggests that blogs represent the "digitization of personal memory" (2007: 42) and that the archival function on blogs "signals a desire to build up a personal repository of memories" (2007: 72). In this process of memory-making, amateur food blogs cite the professional genre of gastronomic memoirs—such as M.F.K. Fisher's *The Gastronomical Me* (1943) or Julia Child's *My Life in France* (2006)—which generally take the form of literary gastronomic writing, but for bloggers, may take this form along with the more advice-driven writing of recipes and restaurant reviews, as well as photographs. The production of these digital gastronomic memoirs is driven in large part by the ephemeral nature of food as a material object: photographing or writing about a gastronomic experience fixes it in time, and it gives the foodie something concrete to which they can return. These literary and visual texts operate to stabilize and document the ephemeral object of foodies' self-making.

For some of my informants, this personal function of the food blog was of primary importance. This was the way Surat felt. He was one of only two of my informants who were not serious cooks, so blogging played a particularly important role in his self-formation through food as it offered a mode of production to engage in with this material object, so that his relationship with it was not merely consumptive. This took the form of a photoblog, where he posted images of the dishes he had consumed in haute cuisine restaurants. For Surat, this was undertaken as a productive way of documenting his career in serious dining and "memorable meals" for the self rather than displaying it to others. He said: "I use it as an archive...It's mainly for me, I do not publicize—that website is mainly for me, for record-keeping purposes." Like the photobloggers in Kris Cohen's research, Surat's blog gave him the sense of "having assembled a collection, a visual memory of one's life and activities" (2005: 895–6). Slater describes the important function that photography serves in the creation of such personal records, writing that "domestic photography provides me with that existential sense of my personal past which Barthes so poignantly described, that rich but weird 'tense' of 'having-been-there' into which the most banal snapshot moves me. This sense of the past is crucial to one's sense of identity, and we accomplish it very largely through photographs" (1991: 49).

For foodie bloggers, photographs of food provide this existential sense of "having-been-there": I cooked that; I ate that. Yet in contrast to the family snapshots Slater discusses, foodies themselves are conspicuously absent from the photographs on their blogs: the images are generally close-ups of the material object itself. While some photographs of home cooking may include the foodie's hands, the genre conventions of food blogs refrain from showing the faces or bodies of foodies in photographs of food. This may be due to the public nature of the blog as opposed to the domestic photo album. However, this does not appear to be the main reason for the absence of the foodie from their photographs of food as most included a head shot in their blogger profile. Rather, the foodie is absent because such photographs emulate the genre conventions of close-ups of food within professional photography in cookbooks and magazines. Although they are generated to serve a personal function, then, these photographs use the public genre conventions of professional food photography, which in turn reflects the self-identity of the foodie as an amateur. Thus, the photographs on food blogs are strange forms of gastronomic memoirs from which foodies themselves are absent: these images provide a visual record of the material object, the memorable meal, rather than the foodie cooking or eating the meal.

Like Surat, Rosa felt that the personal function was of primary importance in her food blog, and this shaped her approach to the creative process of writing, which differed from that of foodies for whom the public function was of greater importance. Her preferred mode of writing was similar to that of lifeloggers, which as Reed describes, is governed by an "ethos of immediacy" (2005: 227); lifeloggers insist that people "should type as they think or feel" (2005: 228). However, Rosa described how when she began her blog, she took an adult education course on food writing with a professional journalist, which she disliked because she "became aware" of what she was writing: "I didn't really like that, because normally I just write . . . But now I've sort of come back to just recording, you know, what I'm eating, and recipes, and what have you." Approaching writing too professionally and putting the audience first means that she loses the sense of creativity, which is the reason she makes the blog in the first place. Yet while Rosa prioritized the personal function, this is not to say that the public function was not also important, as she put it: "I'd say the purpose of my blog is more selfish, I do it more for me, just to document it. But I also enjoy the fact that other people read it."

PUBLIC MEDIATIONS: SHARING MATERIAL KNOWLEDGE AND LIFESTYLE ADVICE

As well as documenting one's own self-formation and self-improvement through the material object of food, blogs are also a means by which foodies share their knowledge and expertise in this process with the public, like the professional material media they emulate. This public function of the blog was of greater importance for Mathew, who had migrated to Australia from Singapore as a child. Now in his thirties, he worked as a policy advisor in the public service. Mathew was the second of my two informants who were not serious cooks. Therefore, like Surat, Mathew's production of material media on food was vitally important in his self-formation. His blog was based around reviews of the restaurants he had dined in, and he adopted a very work-like approach to writing these reviews. Mathew described the sense of reward he gained from such work-like leisure—from turning his material consumption into material media production—but also the satisfaction he gained from offering lifestyle advice on this material object to others and having them agree with his opinion:

> I get satisfaction from writing a good piece, you know, I like to read it and say, "Well, that's quite well written." But I also like it more when other people read it and enjoy it, and get a laugh out of it, and go to a place and actually find that it's to their liking as well. So I actually get satisfaction from recommending a place, I think that's a good experience as well. Yeah, my writing is more, to be honest, for other people to enjoy.

Placing the primary importance on the food blog's public function, as Mathew did, led to a different approach to writing from that of Rosa. This is something he shared in common with Adam. They both tried to write to more professional standards, and they invested a significant amount of time and effort crafting their writing before posting it on their blogs. As Mathew said, "for a single piece, I will actually spend quite a bit of time on it, just getting the language right as well." Mathew and Adam were both concerned with issues of structure in their writing, and Mathew described how he had developed a particular structure for his restaurant reviews: "There are certain things that I stick to, like I like to start with an analogy, then describe the décor, and then the food, and then wrap it up a bit like that, so there's that structural element there." However, he described how this structure could sometimes be more of a hindrance than a help: "Well I get stumped, because if I can't think of an analogy, then I tend not to write about it."

With their more professional approach to food writing and their emphasis on the public function of their material media, Mathew and Adam also had greater professional aspirations than Rosa, yet these aspirations were mostly daydreams of the ideal job rather than a career they were actively pursuing. However, before he began his blog, Mathew had written restaurant reviews for a news website that paid authors $100 for each review. He described how the formal requirements demanded by this professional media affected his process of food writing: "I tried to write quite formally, as you would if it was going to be published in *The Good Food Guide,* or something like that, which sort of conflicted me in a way, you know, I wanted to—because I was being paid for it, so I sort of made my writing more formal in tone." Although Mathew already took a more formal and professional approach to his food writing than Rosa, he too found that the standards of professional media stifled his creative process of writing. After the news website stopped publishing restaurant reviews, he continued to write them but posted them on his blog instead, which he felt offered greater freedom for creative expression.

Sharing their material knowledge and lifestyle advice on food via digital media is another way in which foodies participate in postindustrial knowledge society. This constitutes a different type of knowledge-based leisure—not the acquisition of knowledge from professional media or its application in food practices, but the sharing of acquired knowledge and of how it has been deployed. Ruth Finnegan (2005) has highlighted the potential that digital media hold for communicating the skills, knowledge, and expertise that amateurs and hobbyists have acquired in their chosen pursuits. Indeed, foodies are not the only such enthusiasts to use the Internet to share knowledge and advice with others. Rhiannon Gainor has explored how hobbyist quilters develop personal websites and blogs as information resources: they "come home from work at the end of the day and spend their leisure time creating information repositories for public access" (2009: 5). Like food blogs, she suggests that the production of such sites is motivated by "a relationship between expressing creativity and willingness to supply information and teaching resources" (2009: 8). But where quilting blogs concentrate on knowledge of material production, food blogs generally share knowledge on both the production and consumption of this material object, with the main genres of entries being culinary and restaurant blogging.

CULINARY BLOGGING: MEDIATING MATERIAL PRODUCTION

Blogging about their home cooking allows foodies to document their manual leisure and material production and share the knowledge and skills they have acquired in their culinary education. For Adam, culinary blogging was an online extension of his earlier practice of keeping material records of his cooking:

> I had a notebook, before I did the blog, where I would actually write down what I'd cooked for dinner parties, and what recipes I used and little notes about why a recipe worked, or didn't work. And there were two things, I think it was a learning tool, so you know, I could amend a recipe the next time, and it was also so I knew what I'd cooked for certain people.

Adam's notebook resembles the culinary journals kept by some of the hobby cooks in Jenna Hartel's (2006) research into information resources within this practice. She describes how cooks used these journals—which often contained detailed notes as well as photographs—to memorialize and evaluate the meals they had cooked for different occasions. By making such culinary journals, she argues, the *"gourmet cook is an active producer and manager of information resources"* (Hartel 2006, original emphasis). Like these journals, Adam's notebook served the personal function of documenting his culinary practices and operating as a self-learning tool. This may not be dissimilar from the techniques used by some professional chefs to document their culinary creations, as they record their recipes and keep a portfolio of photographs to preserve "the memory of accomplishments in this perishable art form" (Peterson and Birg 1988: 69).

Other foodies had material precursors to their culinary blogging that served a more public function of sharing their knowledge of food production with others. For example, Mary said:

> I gave eight of my girlfriends a recipe book of sorts, which was basically a folder and then all these recipes that are mine that I put together. Because every now and then they say, "Oh Mary, I'm having people over for dinner, what should I make?" and so I end up scribbling out all these recipes. So I thought, "Well why not be a bit cute and do that for them?" Oh, three out of the eight of them cried when I gave it to them!...I'd done little illustrations all through it, and I'd done it in a very conversational style. So instead of just ingredients and method, it was all about, how to enjoy it while you're cooking it, and what wine to have with it, so it was like I was standing next to them in the kitchen telling them what to do!

Thus, culinary blogging was not seen as an entirely new practice for such foodies but as a continuation of their production of culinary notebooks and amateur cookbooks, forms that served personal or public functions.

Rosa, for whom the personal function of blogging was most important, nevertheless stressed the importance of the public function of culinary blogging. She said that while it was partly about documenting her home cooking for herself, "it's to share as well. Because I like sharing recipes, I like learning recipes off other people's blogs, so I like to give something back." In terms of its focus on material production in leisure, as well as this philosophy of sharing knowledge between practitioners, culinary blogging is very similar to the quilting websites made by the hobbyists in Gainor's research. Like culinary blogs, these sites often contained photographs of the material objects the hobbyist had made and shared instructions on how to make them (Gainor 2009: 6). Gainor discusses how this sharing of knowledge online continues the strong tradition of knowledge sharing that has existed within the culture of quilting, a tradition that has also existed in the culture of cooking, as recipes have been shared and passed down, generally among women.

Some foodies use culinary blogging not to share their own recipes but to document their reproduction of recipes from cookbooks, the most famous being Julie Powell's replication of Julia Child's recipes on *The Julie/Julia Project*. Others have sought to replicate the most difficult dishes of haute cuisine, using their blog to document their reproduction of molecular gastronomy recipes from elBulli's cookbooks and demonstrate their acquisition of more professional culinary skills (de Solier 2010). In such cases, the entries generally take the form of gastronomic writing, as the foodie describes the dish and some of its ingredients and methods but does not provide the exact recipe due to potential copyright issues. Of those in my research, Adam's came closest to this, as he listed what dishes he had made for certain occasions, documented which cookbook the recipe came from, and described his experience of cooking each dish.

Rosa and Mary, on the other hand, mostly used their blogs to share their own recipes. Rosa also posted recipes that she had altered from cookbooks, such as those of Jamie Oliver, but stressed that she never reproduced them verbatim; she posted her own version of the dish with her directions and instructions and attributed its origins: "I normally say, 'This is inspired by so-and-so's recipe,' but I'd never copy it word for word." Thus the ethical principle of attribution was important for Rosa, as it is for most bloggers in general (Cenite et al. 2009: 586). Where Mary's recipes on her blog—unlike those in the cookbook she gave her close friends—were generally purely instructional, consisting of a list of ingredients followed by method, Rosa often couched this instructional format within some gastronomic writing that gave the context of her recipe. By communicating their own recipes on their blogs, these foodies become the authors of their own amateur digital cookbooks, as they offer readers lifestyle guidance in what to cook and how. But what do readers think of this amateur advice in culinary production?

As I showed earlier, most of the foodies in my research did not read food blogs, precisely because of the amateur nature of these material media and the trust foodies placed in professional experts. Those who did read them—including those who were bloggers themselves—tended not to leave comments. Rosa's blog did attract a fair degree of traffic and comments though. The comments made on her culinary posts, which appeared to be from fellow amateurs and laypersons rather than professionals, showed that such audiences did respect her amateur culinary expertise. For example, in response to her recipe for Gnocchi di Patate, one commenter wrote, "I love this post! I actually got to learn how fresh gnocchi are actually made! Thank you Rosa," while another simply said "Excellent tutorial!" These responses position Rosa in the authoritative role of the teacher or expert and suggest that her audience has learnt from her lifestyle advice. One commenter went further, complimenting Rosa on her culinary skills and signaling their intention to put her advice into practice: "I will definitely be giving your recipe a go next time I feel like gnocchi." Another had already done so: "Thanks heaps for posting up your recipe—we just tried it for dinner (with napoli sauce and parmesan). We don't regularly make gnocchi, so the pics were really helpful." These responses show that those people who do read and comment on foodie blogs place trust in the culinary advice offered by these amateurs and appreciate their generosity in sharing their knowledge of food production. Their advice about consumption, though, is more hotly contested.

RESTAURANT BLOGGING: MEDIATING MATERIAL CONSUMPTION

Earlier, I explored how some foodies emulate restaurant critics not only in their serious approach to consumption when dining out but also in their documentation of their judgments, such as Sarah's annotation of *The Good Food Guide.* This served a personal function, as she recorded her opinions for her own future reference and was embarrassed when a friend read it and poked fun at her. In contrast, the restaurant reviews published by foodie bloggers, while written partly to document the experience for the self, are also intended to be public texts. These amateurs thus take their emulation of professional restaurant critics even further, making their judgments public via material media in this creative production based around their serious consumption.

While the most famous food blog *(The Julie/Julia Project)* is culinary, it is restaurant blogging that has attracted the greatest debate and criticism, particularly within mainstream media. It is here that debates over the democratization of media production and its effects on the relationships between professionals and amateurs emerge for food blogs. While the democratization of culinary media into the hands of amateurs has not been a significant cause for concern, the democratization of restaurant media certainly has been. As one newspaper article put it, "The once-genteel discipline of restaurant reviewing has turned into a free-for-all, celebrated by some as a new-world democracy but seen by others as populist tyranny" (quoted in Semenak 2007).

The key criticism of restaurant bloggers within the mainstream media concerns the expertise that entitles them to make judgments. For example, in an article titled "The Self-Appointed Critics" in the Montreal newspaper the *Gazette*—which fuelled debate around the world, including Australia—Susan Semenak (2007) argues that bloggers have "no official credentials" to undertake food criticism. Credentials are central to claims to expertise in knowledge society (Frow 1995: 117), as well as to contestations over knowledge. While it is true that amateur bloggers do not hold credentials in food criticism, neither do professional critics, for such a qualification does not exist. As Jay Rayner (2007), food critic for the United Kingdom's *Guardian* newspaper, admitted in his contribution to the debate, the only qualifications most professionals, such as Rayner himself, hold are in journalism.

Thus, expertise in judging food—for professionals and amateurs alike—is based on experience rather than formal training and qualifications. It is for precisely this reason, I argue, that restaurant blogging has become the site of such contention. In contrast, culinary blogging has not been seen as posing a threat to its professional counterparts because there *are* qualifications in cooking; most mediated culinary experts are credentialed chefs, which distinguishes their expertise from amateur bloggers. Moreover, it is only recently, at the height of knowledge society, that professional restaurant criticism has separated itself off from its amateur counterpart, perhaps as a means of shoring up its claims to expertise. For historically, restaurant guides have included reviews by amateurs alongside those of professionals: The first restaurant guide, Grimod de la Reynière's *Almanach des Gourmands,* contained recommendations by amateurs in early nineteenth-century France, as did Raymond Postgate's first British *Good Food Guide* in the 1950s and the early editions of *The Age Good Food Guide* in Melbourne in the 1980s. The *Zagat* guide, which began in New York in the same period, has been based on amateur reviews ever since. Through their inclusion of user-generated content, these publications share more similarities with blogs than do most contemporary guides, which tend to be written exclusively by professional critics.

Through restaurant blogging, foodies have gained a degree of cultural power to shape tastes and influence consumer behavior. The debate within the mainstream media is not only over whether these amateurs deserve such power but also whether they will use it responsibly. The potential power of reviewers to make or break a restaurant—or even a person, as in the case of French chef Bernard Loiseau's suicide after dropping two points in the *Gault Millau* guide in 2003—is well known. Amateur bloggers have been criticized within mainstream media for a perceived lack of ethics; as Allen Salkin (2007) argues, "ethical standards are all over the map. Restaurant critics for established publications generally give a new establishment a few weeks or months to settle in and visit several times, spending their employers' money." Yet the amateur blogger's experience is far more representative of that of the average diner, in that they visit the restaurant once (whether new or old) and spend their own money. None of the foodie bloggers in my research accepted free food in return for their reviews, and they were also anonymous to restaurateurs, unlike well-known professional critics. Moreover, while they did not have to account for their opinion to an editor or employer, these bloggers believed the ethical responsibility of restaurant reviewing to be very important. Indeed, the ethical burden of publishing a negative review weighed heavily on their shoulders, as there was a degree of unease concerning the potential impact it could have on a restaurant's reputation. The ethical principle of minimizing harm to others was extremely important to these foodie bloggers, as it is for many other bloggers (Cenite et al. 2009). Rosa described how she felt guilty about the only negative review she had published, as she knew that a lot of people read it after Googling the restaurant. She had considered deleting it from her blog but said that it was an honest review, and that with the various positive and negative comments left by others, the restaurant "came out on par," so she thought readers could make up their own minds based on both the review and the comments. Yet since then, she has decided to publish only positive reviews on her blog: "I must admit, if I don't have a good experience, I don't write about it. I only blog what's good these days." This sentiment was echoed by other foodies, such as Mathew, who said, "I tend to write only good reviews." This did not mean they gave positive reviews where they were not deserved; rather, if they thought a restaurant was bad, they would not publish the review.

This ethical and moral stance distinguishes the amateur critics in my research from their professional counterparts, who are generally willing to publish a negative review if they believe a restaurant is not up to scratch. There are different moral orders at work in restaurant reviewing as leisure and labor then: where professionals have a moral duty to critique where necessary, for these amateurs, restaurant reviewing as a moral practice involves publishing positive reviews. Some professional reviewers develop a reputation as being particularly critical in their judgment of restaurants, which may in turn affect their ability to review. For example, after the opening of Jamie Oliver's restaurant Fifteen Melbourne—the setting for the television program *Jamie's Kitchen Australia*—a stir was created when one of the city's high-profile critics, Stephen Downes, from the tabloid the *Herald Sun,* was asked to leave. As he described in his newspaper column, "Fifteen Melbourne would not serve me. When asked why, he [the sommelier] said the owners and managers of Fifteen had no respect for my opinion and reputation" (Downes 2006). A day after his column, Rosa published her review of Fifteen Melbourne on her blog. She described to me how Downes then responded in a comment on her post: "He got chucked out of Fifteen, and I got in quite early and did my blog review, and because he got chucked out he wrote a little comment on my blog that as food bloggers—no, as food *writers,* and then he put in brackets, even *bloggers*—we should all unite together and not write about Fifteen!" This demonstrates the more direct negotiations that are occurring between professional and amateur restaurant critics, as the former struggle with the emergence of a large number of amateurs in their field and attempt to establish protocols for how the two can work (or leisure) together. It also demonstrates professionals' attempts to assert power over amateurs—to get amateurs to do as they say and not write about the restaurant—because they have in effect lost power to the amateurs. Whilst Downes does not appear to think highly of amateurs, he nevertheless believes they should support professionals, such as himself, and bond together as critics against restaurateurs and chefs. In regards to Downes's comment on her blog, Rosa said, "I actually felt quite angry about that, you know, that we should all ban it [Fifteen] just because he's got a rather unsavoury reputation in the restaurant community." Thus, in response to his call for solidarity between amateur and professional restaurant critics, she replied in a comment of her own:

> Mr. Downes. I do not heed your call to arms for all food writers—even bloggers (ahem)—to ignore Fifteen. Whatever their reason, well, that is between you and Fifteen. I am certainly not going to deprive myself of a culinary experience just because you have created for yourself a reputation that is less than popular in the restaurant world (no offence intended). So chill.

It is not only professional critics who have had to respond to the rise of amateur bloggers but also chefs and restaurateurs. At an industry conference on the future of food media, chefs and restaurateurs spoke of how they read reviews of their restaurants on blogs and take the opinions of amateur critics seriously. This stands in contrast to many fields in entertainment and art, where there is a tendency for professionals to ignore the criticism of amateurs and brush it off as uninformed (Stebbins 1992: 40). Indeed, these food industry professionals appear to be less hostile than professional critics toward amateur bloggers. For example, Will Goldfarb (2007), restaurateur and pastry chef at New York's Room 4 Dessert, argued that bloggers are not necessarily less knowledgeable than professional critics. He described how he uses the comments function on blogs to respond to any negative reviews, apologizing for the bad experience, and sometimes inviting the blogger to return to the restaurant free of charge.

While some chefs and restaurateurs use the comments section on amateur blogs legitimately, this function can also be used for more manipulative purposes, as Rayner (2007) describes, through "shilling, where restaurants get friends and family to pepper the site with positive reviews." Rosa believed that this had occurred in the comments responding to her review of a new fine dining restaurant, when after some fairly critical comments, four extremely positive comments were posted in a row on the same day, naming and praising the chef's cookbooks, and including links to the restaurant's website. She responded to them with this comment of her own: "Is it just me or do I detect something a little fishy about the last four comments? Is someone trying to do some stealth marketing on my blog? If so, then I'm not friggin' happy about it! My bullshit detector is going right off." When I asked her what aroused her suspicions, she said:

> Well I know they all came from the same site, because I can tell what IP [Internet protocol address] they're coming from. It was just the way they were all written, the way they used their pseudonyms. Because it's very rare to get that, you either get anonymous, or a blogger profile, not often do you get someone write their

name. Yeah, and it just seemed a bit *suss*...And it was just because there were quite a few negative reviews and then suddenly it got all these positive reviews, yeah, so I just called it. Because that's the one thing that I'm always a bit iffy about, is whether people use my blog for viral marketing.

One of the fundamental differences between the reviews on blogs and those in professional media is that in the latter, the judgment of the expert is final; the verdict of the amateur, by contrast, is open to debate through comments, thus transforming the restaurant review into a more dialogic genre. While this interactive function may be used by fellow diners to genuinely debate the quality of a restaurant, it may also be used by food industry professionals to serve their own financial benefit. This demonstrates one of the limits of restaurant blogs, and of blogs in general: their democratic and participatory nature means that they can be manipulated to serve particular interests. Restaurant blogging, then, is the main site of conflict over the material object of food—and more specifically, knowledge of this object—between amateur foodies and professional experts. It is through this practice that foodies come closest to approximating professionals and have the greatest power to influence professional practices surrounding this material object.

It is clear that in postindustrial society, then, people do not just construct a reflexive DIY self through the consumption of material culture, as is commonly thought, but also—crucially—through its production, which holds a higher moral value and is considered more substantial in self-formation. The production of material objects, such as food, in manual leisure is of vital importance to many people as a way of connecting to the material world in a nonconsumptive manner, in an era when we no longer produce such objects at work. But increasingly, this is also achieved through the production of material media focused on objects, which foster a similar sense of connection to the material world but via digital means. In late modernity, material media is not only the means by which people acquire knowledge of material objects from experts to use in their self-formation and self-improvement, but with the advent of new media, it is increasingly the means by which people share their own knowledge of material consumption and production with others, by producing amateur media such as food blogs. This has led to contestations over material expertise and knowledge of objects—especially knowledge of material consumption, which lacks credentials—between amateur and professional material media producers in postindustrial knowledge society.

Afterword

Materializing Moral Selves

We live in a world full of material things, from mobile phones and computers to homes and cars, clothes and food. This material world is intricately inter-twined with our social world, with how we form our individual selves and our relationships with others. It has a significant impact on what kinds of selves are formed and how they are formed. This book has explored how changes in the material world engendered by postindustrialism have led to changes in the way we reflexively shape our sense of self in and through this world. How do we make our selves through material culture, when we no longer produce ma-terial things at work? While most answers to this question have concentrated solely on consumption, this book has redirected our attention to production and examined how it has taken on new forms and meanings in self-formation in leisure as a response to the changing nature of work.

MAKING THE SELF IN A POSTINDUSTRIAL MATERIAL WORLD

The cultivation of the self, as Foucault (1986) has shown us, is an age old question, one that stretches back more than two thousand years. Today, in the early twenty-first century, it takes on specific resonances and pressures in the context of institutionalized individualism and neoliberalism in late moder-nity, when it becomes not a choice but an obligation. Where social theories of individual self-identity have remained speculative in nature to date (Gid-dens 1991; Beck and Beck-Gernsheim 2001; Bauman 2008), this book has sought to develop a theory of the self that is grounded in empirical, ethno-graphic research. This approach puts the lived experiences of real people at the forefront of theory. My theoretical claims are based on the experiences of ordinary people and the complexities they face as they go about shaping a re-flexive self in a late modern, postindustrial world. The value of adopting such an empirical approach to theory is that it gives us an understanding of what really matters in people's lives and what should, therefore, matter to social theory—as opposed to what we presume matters or what we think ought to matter. While the material objects that surround us in our everyday life are often dismissed as trivial and unimportant, one of the key findings of my research is that material culture *does* matter in self-identity formation—not in superficial ways but in ways that are highly profound—and therefore needs to be incorporated into theoretical understandings of late modern DIY selves. This book, then, has sought to rematerialize social theories of self-identity by theorizing the role of material culture in self-making in postindustrial society.

How do we materialize individual selves today? If one were to develop a speculative theory of the role of material culture in self-identity based on observations about the state of the postindustrial world, one would likely observe that we are surrounded by more material goods than at any other time, yet we produce less goods than ever before; one could therefore conclude that consumption is of prime importance in self-formation. Indeed, this has been the case in theories to date (Featherstone 1991; Baudrillard 1998). This speculative approach assumes that there is a direct correlation between the state of the material world and what is most important to the people living in it—in short, we are surrounded by consumer goods, so we must all be consumerist and value consumption above all else. However, by taking an ethnographic approach, I found the opposite to be true: it is the production of material culture that matters more to people and holds a higher moral value in postindustrial self-formation. This evidence overturns the speculative theories through which we have understood the role of material culture in self-identity to date and presents us with a new approach to understanding this relationship in late modernity. It means that we cannot presume to know how people shape their identities simply from observing the state of material culture in society. Rather, it's only through engaging with people and closely examining them that we can understand the significance and moralities of material culture in the self in postindustrial society.

What does it mean to be postindustrial? The term suggests being postproduction, or at least postmaterial production. Yet, as I have shown, many people today are anything but. Where material production has become less important at the level of society, it has become more important at the level of the individual. To be a producer of material culture, such selves *have* to be materialized in leisure—productive leisure—because there are few opportunities to do so in work. More people than ever before are spending their spare time shaping their selves through forms of creative production of material culture. We are seeing a significant growth in people wanting to make things, to be creative, not just to consume things. For most, it involves making material objects through manual leisure, such as DIY, gardening, or craft, or in the case of foodies, cooking. There is a strong desire to make something tangible and to make it with one's hands, to have a sense of creating the material world in which one lives. But it is not just material objects that people are producing in their leisure time. Increasingly, they are also producing forms of material media through digital creative production—whether it be a YouTube clip on how to sew a dress or a food blog, as it is for many foodies. Through these amateur forms of material media, ordinary people share the knowledge and expertise they have acquired about particular categories of material objects. In some cases, such as food or gardens, the creation of these material media play a particularly important role as memoirs because of the ephemeral nature of the material object that is the focus of self-making. Whether it is material objects or media, individuals inject their self into these forms of material culture through producing them, such that they then come to reflect and narrate the self. These forms of production are considered to be a more substantial—and more moral—way of shaping the self through material culture in late modernity. To be a moral postindustrial individual, one must be a producer of material culture, not just a consumer.

Postindustrial society was originally forecast to be the leisure society, where work would take up less of our time and be less important than leisure (Jenkins and Sherman 1979). As this book has shown, only part of this came true. Now, in the early twenty-first century, most people in postindustrial societies continue to work long, inflexible hours. If one were again to speculate as to the relative importance of work and leisure in self-identity based on this fact, one would undoubtedly conclude that work is of greater significance. Indeed, while there has been some discussion of work in theories of individualization and self-identity (Beck and Beck-Gernsheim 2001), the question of leisure has been largely overlooked—as it has been in the social sciences and humanities, more generally, oft considered not serious enough to be worthy of study. But my ethnographic research shows that regardless of the time spent working, paid work *has* become less important in self-identity formation for many people in postindustrial society. It is in leisure that such individuals are their "true" or "real" selves: a foodie rather than a teacher or perhaps a gardener rather than a public servant. My research has shown leisure to be the key site of self-making today. This is a result, in part, of the control we have over leisure and who we make ourselves through it, as opposed to work: we may not get that promotion or new position, but we may become a blogger or an accomplished cook. Just as many people take their leisure seriously, so should we as scholars if we are to understand the late modern self.

While leisure has indeed assumed increased importance and become central to identity as the leisure society thesis predicted, it has not taken the form that was envisaged. Where visions of the leisure society imagined it as a society of play, what my research shows is that it is productive leisure—work-like leisure—that has taken hold because of the moral value it possesses, particularly as a way of shaping the self through material culture. Rather than being post-work then, postindustrial society is one in which many people work long hours *and* engage in highly privileged forms of work-like leisure. Indeed, as I have shown, for growing numbers of people, such productive leisure is not just work-like but actually emulates the approach professionals take to material culture by shaping the self as an amateur. This may take the form of constructing the self as an amateur fashion designer or a DIY home renovator. For foodies, it involves shaping themselves as amateur chefs and food critics. The amateur is considered a moral self to form through material culture because it is work-like, professional, and productive, not just consumptive. It epitomizes the moralities of productive leisure that guide the new forms of self-making through material culture in late modernity. Postindustrial society, then, is shaping up to be less of a leisure society per se and more of a productive leisure society.

Postindustrial society has also been understood as the knowledge society. Scholars have highlighted the role of knowledge as the new force of production in late modern work, as material production and manual labor have been replaced by knowledge production and mental labor (Lyotard 1984). Where discussions of knowledge society have concentrated on this realm of work, what my research shows is that the dimensions of late modern knowledge society extend beyond work into leisure. To be postindustrial, then, is not just to engage in knowledge work but also to participate in knowledge-based leisure. Knowledge is the key characteristic of productive leisure in postindustrial society, as the morality of knowledge as the new productive force is carried across into leisure. This morality of knowledge shapes the approach to material culture in shaping the self, as people want to learn about material objects, not just consume them. They acquire this education from the experts of material media. Expert systems are central to knowledge society. Yet where social theories have highlighted the decline or lack of trust placed in experts in late modernity as a result of the decline of grand narratives, competing voices of authority, and continually revised truths (Lyotard 1984; Bauman 1987; Giddens 1991), my research reveals that many people place a significant amount of trust in professional experts of material culture, such as food. Making the self through material culture amid a diversity of lifestyle options can be an anxious and risky undertaking. The late modern individual is faced with a world where they are expected to craft their own biography among a plethora of options, a world in which they are surrounded by material objects—commodities they didn't produce—and face the problem of how to relate to this world, how to be in, and of, this world. With the freedom to choose comes the obligation to actively shape one's self, and what Giddens calls "existential anxiety" (1991). As a result, people place trust in the experts of material media for guidance in how to use the consumption and production of objects in their self-formation in order to help them navigate this process; previously, such guidance (in what to eat or how to cook) came from cultural traditions and the family. Thus, material media—and their experts—are central to late modern self-formation through material objects.

Where existing theories of material lifestyle media in general and food media in particular suggest that they only teach audiences how to construct and improve the self through consuming objects (Chao 1998; Deery 2006), I have argued that these media also teach audiences how to produce objects; I also argued that material production is represented as having a higher moral value in the models of self-improvement such media convey. Moreover, my ethnographic research reveals how people acquire both knowledge of consumption, such as good taste, and practical knowledge of production, such as culinary skills, from material media. For people such as foodies, acquiring material knowledge—especially knowledge of production—is considered a moral approach to consuming material media in self-formation. For where the socially defined realm of knowledge work excludes manual skill in material production, knowledge-based leisure includes it; indeed, it is the most highly prized form of knowledge in productive leisure because of its lack in work. But people do not just acquire knowledge of objects from the experts of professional material media in late modernity; I have shown how, increasingly, individuals also share their own knowledge and expertise via amateur material media, such as food blogs. Professional experts coexist alongside new amateur experts of material objects and the self in the democratization of expertise brought about by digital media technologies. This, I have shown, has led to struggles between amateurs and professionals over expertise in material objects in postindustrial knowledge society.

The main way in which postindustrial society has been thought of, though—especially in relation to identity—is as a consumer society (Baudrillard 1998; Featherstone 1991; Lury 1996). The research presented in this book places this common understanding in question. Can postindustrial society still be a consumer society when what many people find more meaningful in their lives is production? The term "consumer society" purports to summarize our key drives and motivations, what we do, and who we are in late modernity: consumers. But is this an adequate description, when many people want to produce material culture and learn how to do so at least as much as—or even more than—they want to consume it? The example of the foodie, which I have explored here, suggests that we may have moved through an obsession with consumption in selfhood and into a new phase in postindustrial society where both the consumption *and* production of material culture (in productive leisure) are used to shape a moral selfhood, one through which people get a strong sense of value from their material practices and their lives. This demands a more complex title than consumer society and a rethinking of some of our central assumptions about late modern life and identities.

As well as challenging the overarching status of consumption in self and society, the example of the foodie also unsettles and reconfigures common understandings of consumption itself. In particular, it challenges binary understandings of consumers as docile fools or playful postmodern subjects, for as my research has shown, the foodie is neither. Foodies' approach to consumption in their self-formation is reflexive, serious, and work-like. Indeed, the new forms of self-making through consumption that are exemplified by the foodie involve more work than simply mobilizing systems of taste or the sign-value of goods and brands to speak for the self, and these forms are more serious and substantial than the superficial pursuit of distinction (Bourdieu 1984; Baudrillard 1998). They involve questions not only of who we are or who we want to be but also who we *should* be, as foodies attempt to consume material culture in a meaningful and moral way. This involves reflexive decisions about what categories of material objects are appropriate for self-making, what levels of consumption are considered proper, and what mode of consumption should be adopted. The morality of production comes to shape the foodie's consumption in the form of serious consumption, which is knowledge-based, productive, and work-like. This mode of consumption also upsets binaries between consumerism and ethical consumption, for while it is moral, it is not *necessarily* ethical, political, or resistant.

Thus, where the individual selves shaped by material culture in postindustrial modernity are often thought to be selfish and immoral, my research shows this not to be the case. While religion may have declined in importance for many people in late modernity, my study of foodies suggests that there is still a strong moral order in contemporary self-formation—in particular, in our relationship to material culture in that process. This does not mean that people are worshipping commodities in "cathedrals of consumption," as has been suggested (Ritzer 2005). Rather, this new secular material morality is about trying to carve out a meaningful sense of identity in a world full of commodities; the way people do this is through moral regimes of consumption—such as serious consumption—but also through production, which is considered the most sacred. But these new moralities are not religious, nor are they directly ethical (that is, showing concern for others before the self); rather, they are concerned with the good and bad behavior of the self more broadly. They may, however, be replacing religion in a certain way by providing a sense of being a good person for the secular. These new moralities stem from the shifting relationship to material culture in postindustrial society, combined with processes of individualization and the freedom to create a life of one's own. What we see in the example of the foodie is not so much the "remoralising of social life" that Giddens discusses (1991: 224), but what we might think of as a *remoralizing of individual life.*

In late modernity, then, many people try to form a moral sense of self through material culture. But why is material culture so important in late modern self-formation in the first place? It is because, I argue, material culture provides people with a way of feeling embedded and connected in an individualized, globalized, runaway world. With the decline of traditional social structures, such as the family and religion, we each now have the responsibility to create a meaningful, individual, "life of one's own" (Beck and Beck-Gernsheim 2001). There is a common feeling of being disembedded and disconnected among individuals in global modernity and a desperate need to re-embed the self in some way. People seek solutions to this existential problem, and material culture is one solution that many, like foodies, find particularly meaningful. Material objects literally give us something to hold on to, to hang our identities on; they provide something constant to define us in a world of flux. Moreover, they offer a more permanent, ongoing bond, and a source of self-creation we can control in a world where much of the life of one's own is beyond control: while we may lose loved ones, friends, or jobs, material culture may operate as a continuous thread in the biographical narrative of the self throughout these tumultuous changes we confront. Through forging connections with material objects, we gain a sense of control over life in the risky and runaway world of late modernity: material objects provide us with what Giddens calls "ontological security" (1991: 36). As we see in the case of foodies, food binds together their personal narrative, their own DIY biography, while at the same time providing a sense of connection to, and security in, the world in which they live.

MAKING THE SELF THROUGH MATERIAL CULTURES OF FOOD

In late modernity, certain things come to matter more for certain people. Attachments are formed, and particular kinds of material objects gradually come to play a central role in self-formation. They enable the materialization of particular kinds of selves and particular kinds of belonging and affiliation. Food is one of those things. Food has always been central to who we are, but for many people, it has become increasingly so. While the importance of food in maintaining more traditional identities—such as those based around the category of ethnicity—is well established in academic research, this book has explored the significant role food plays in forming post-traditional individual identities—in particular, how it is used to materialize the elected self-identity of the foodie. The role of food in such identities is often perceived as less authentic and more superficial than its role in ethnic identities, as simply a middle-class consumerist affectation, a search for cultural capital and status (Johnston and Baumann 2010). However, my research shows the material object of food and its practices to be a source of profound meaning and identification for foodies. The example of the foodie demonstrates how in late modernity identifications are coalescing, for some, less around social categories of gender, race, or ethnicity than around forms of material culture and leisure: Two people may find they share more in common because they are both foodies than because they are both women or of the same ethnicity. While this elected self-identity exists alongside an individual's multiple social identities, it may speak more about who they are or who they feel themselves to be.

This book has developed a material culture studies approach to studying food. Where research in food studies often tends to play down the significance of the materiality of food—focusing instead on its symbolic dimensions through discourse and representation—the perspective of material culture studies directs our attention to these questions through ethnography, exploring the interconnections between the material and the symbolic in why food matters in people's lives. I argue that the answer to why foodies choose to shape their selves through food lies in its potential to construct what people feel to be a meaningful and moral self through material culture in postindustrial societies. For foodies, food itself holds a higher value than other categories of objects in the moralities of material culture that guide their self-formation. I have argued that the ephemeral nature of food's materiality is also central to its appeal for those who are anxious about being materialistic, as it offers a way of consuming material objects without accumulating. My research shows that the discursive construction of the self as an omnivore is central to the formation of what foodies consider to be a moral self through food consumption, as is their belief in the immorality of distinction. However, I argue that most foodies are not true omnivores, because while they consume highbrow haute cuisine and middlebrow authentic ethnic cuisine, they repudiate lowbrow industrial foods, such as fast food and processed supermarket food.

My approach to material culture in this book has also expanded our understanding of the material cultures of food to include not only food itself but also food media. I have shown food media to be central to the foodie's relationship with this material object and to their self-making through it. In addition to examining what foodies eat, this book has focused in depth on what they *do* with food and food media—that is, their material cultural practices. By focusing on the practices through which foodies form their selves, we see that different moral regimes operate within their material consumption practices of shopping and dining out. Yet we also see that the appeal of food is not only that it offers a more moral means to shape the self through the consumption of material culture, but even more importantly, it also offers the potential to construct the self through the production of material culture—in cooking and food blogging—which carries a higher moral value and is felt to be a more substantial way of connecting with the material world in postindustrial society. Thus, food offers people a means of shaping moral selves through both the production and consumption of material culture. It provides a way of feeling connected to both the local material world as well as the global material world, of feeling part of something larger. By engaging in production as well as consumption and by taking a work-like professional approach to both as forms of productive leisure, foodies shape the self as an amateur, which is considered a more moral self to form through material culture than simply that of a consumer.

Some people argue that foodies are conspicuous consumers and selfish gluttons (Myers 2011). But when we take an ethnographic approach as I have here, we find that this is far from the case. For me, the example of the foodie is most important because of how it speaks to what is a collective experience of life in late modernity: a feeling of being disembedded—socially and materially—in an individualized, postindustrial, runaway world, and the struggle to grasp onto something that gives meaning and a sense of belonging to the life of one's own. This is a struggle we all share. For foodies, the material culture of food provides a way of re-embedding their lives and a sense of ontological security. This is neatly summarized in the words of the world's most famous foodie, Julie Powell, in *Julie and Julia* (where she is played by Amy Adams). At the beginning of the film, we see her walking the anonymous streets of New York to her job at the Lower Manhattan Development Corporation, where she works in a cubicle fielding phone calls about the redevelopment of the World Trade Center site from people who lost loved ones in the September 11 terrorist attack. At home that evening, making chocolate cream pie, she says to her husband:

> You know what I love about cooking? I love that after a day when nothing is sure—and when I say "nothing," I mean *nothing*—you can come home and absolutely know that if you add egg yolks to chocolate and sugar and milk, it will get thick. It's such a comfort.

Bibliography

Adema, P. (2000), "Vicarious Consumption: Food, Television and the Ambiguity of Modernity," *Journal of American & Comparative Cultures*, 23/3: 113–23.

Adrià, F., Soler, J., and Adrià, A. (2008), *A Day at elBulli: An Insight into the Ideas, Methods, and Creativity of Ferran Adrià*, London: Phaidon Press.

Albala, K. (2012), *Routledge International Handbook of Food Studies*, London: Routledge.

Alexander, S. (1996), *The Cook's Companion*, Ringwood, Vic.: Penguin Books Australia.

Allon, F. (2008), *Renovation Nation: Our Obsession with Home*, Sydney: University of New South Wales Press.

Apelgren, J. (2010), *The Age Good Food Guide 2011*, Camberwell, Vic.: Penguin.

Appadurai, A. (ed.) (1986), *The Social Life of Things: Commodities in Cultural Perspective*, Cambridge: Cambridge University Press.

Appadurai, A. (1988), "How to Make a National Cuisine: Cookbooks in Contemporary India," *Comparative Studies in Society and History*, 30: 3–24.

Ashley, B., Hollows, J., Jones, S., and Taylor, B. (2004), *Food and Cultural Studies*, London: Routledge.

Atton, C., and Hamilton, J. F. (2008), *Alternative Journalism*, London: Sage.

Australian Bureau of Statistics [ABS] (2011a), *Arts and Culture in Australia: A Statistical Overview, 2011* [website] <http://www.abs.gov.au> accessed August 7, 2012.

ABS (2011b), *Migration, Australia, 2009–10* [website] <http://www.abs.gov.au> accessed June 11, 2012.

Bailey, P. (1978), *Leisure and Class in Victorian England: Rational Recreation and the Contest for Control, 1830–1885*, London: Routledge & Kegan Paul.

Banwell, C., Dixon, J., Hinde, S., and McIntyre, H. (2006), "Fast and Slow Food in the Fast Lane: Automobility and the Australian Diet," in R. Wilk (ed.), *Fast Food/Slow Food: The Cultural Economy of the Global Food System*, Lanham, MD: AltaMira Press.

Barnett, C., Cloke, P., Clarke, N., and Malpass, A. (2005), "Consuming Ethics: Articulating the Subjects and Spaces of Ethical Consumption," *Antipode*, 37/1: 23–45.

Barnett C., Cloke, P., Clarke, N., and Malpass, A. (2010), *Globalizing Responsibility: The Political Rationalities of Ethical Consumption*, Oxford: Blackwell.

Barr, A., and Levy, P. (1984), *The Official Foodie Handbook: Be Modern—Worship Food*, London: Ebury Press.

Baudrillard, J. (1998), *The Consumer Society: Myths and Structures,* London: Sage.

Bauman, Z. (1987), *Legislators and Interpreters: On Modernity, Post-Modernity and Intellectuals,* Cambridge: Polity Press.

Bauman, Z. (2008), *The Art of Life,* Cambridge: Polity Press.

Beardsworth, A., and Keil, T. (1997), *Sociology on the Menu: An Invitation to the Study of Food and Society,* London: Routledge.

Beck, S., Bertholle, L., and Child, J. (1961), *Mastering the Art of French Cooking,* Harmondsworth, UK: Penguin.

Beck, U., and Beck-Gernsheim, E. (2001), *Individualization: Institutionalized Individualism and its Social and Political Consequences,* London: Sage.

Beeton, I. M. (1861), *The Book of Household Management: Also Sanitary, Medical, and Legal Memoranda; with a History of the Origin, Properties, and Uses of All Things Connected with Home Life and Comfort,* London: S. O. Beeton.

Belasco, W. (2008), *Food: The Key Concepts,* Oxford: Berg.

Belk, R. W. (1995), *Collecting in a Consumer Society,* London: Routledge.

Bell, D., and Hollows, J. (eds) (2005), *Ordinary Lifestyles: Popular Media, Consumption and Taste,* Maidenhead, UK: Open University Press.

Bell, D., and Hollows, J. (eds) (2006), *Historicizing Lifestyle: Mediating Taste, Consumption and Identity from the 1900s to 1970s,* Aldershot, UK: Ashgate.

Bell, D., and Valentine, G. (1997), *Consuming Geographies: We Are Where We Eat,* London: Routledge.

Bennett, L. (1998), "The Uncivic Culture: Communication, Identity, and the Rise of Lifestyle Politics," *PS: Political Science and Politics,* 31: 740–61.

Bennett, T., Emmison, M., and Frow, J. (1999), *Accounting for Tastes: Australian Everyday Cultures,* Cambridge: Cambridge University Press.

Beriss, D., and Sutton, D. (eds) (2007), *The Restaurants Book: Ethnographies of Where We Eat,* Oxford: Berg.

Binkley, S., and Littler, J. (2008), "Cultural Studies and Anti-Consumerism: A Critical Encounter," *Cultural Studies,* 22/5: 519–30.

Black, W. (2007), *Plats du Jour: A Journey to the Heart of French Food,* London: Bantam Press.

Blumenthal, H. (2009), "Heston Blumenthal's Tasting Notes," *Australian Gourmet Traveller* [online magazine], (June), <http://gourmettraveller.com.au/hestonblumenthals-tasting-notes.htm> accessed July 26, 2012.

Bonner, F. (1994), "Representations of the Female Cook," in K. Ferres (ed.), *Coastscripts: Gender Representations in the Arts,* Brisbane: Australian Institute for Women's Research and Policy, Griffith University.

Bonner, F. (2000), "Lifestyle Programs: 'No Choice but to Choose'" in G. Turner and S. Cunningham (eds), *The Australian TV Book,* St. Leonards, NSW: Allen & Unwin.

Bonner, F. (2005), "Whose Lifestyle is it Anyway?" in D. Bell and J. Hollows (eds), *Ordinary Lifestyles: Popular Media, Consumption and Taste,* Maidenhead, UK: Open University Press.

Bonner, F. (2009), "Early Multi-Platforming: Television Food Programmes, Cookbooks and other Print Spin-offs," *Media History,* 15/3: 345–58.

Bourdieu, P. (1984), *Distinction: A Social Critique of the Judgement of Taste,* London: Routledge.

Bower, A. (ed.) (1992), *Recipes for Reading: Community Cookbooks, Stories, Histories,* Amherst: University of Massachusetts Press.

Bowlby, R. (1997), "Supermarket Futures," in P. Falk and C. Campbell (eds), *The Shopping Experience,* London: Sage.

Brillat-Savarin, J.-A. (1970), *The Physiology of Taste,* London: Penguin.

Brownlie, D., Hewer, P., and Horne, S. (2005), "Culinary Tourism: An Exploratory Reading of Contemporary Representations of Cooking," *Consumption, Markets and Culture,* 8/1: 7–26.

Bruns, A. (2007), "Produsage: Towards a Broader Framework for User-Led Content Creation," *Proceedings of the 6th ACM SIGCHI Conference on Creativity & Cognition,* Washington, DC, Queensland University of Technology Digital Repository <http://eprints.qut.edu.au/archive/00006623/> accessed October 23, 2008.

Bruns, A., and Jacobs, J. (2006), "Introduction", in A. Bruns and J. Jacobs (eds), *Uses of Blogs,* New York: Peter Lang.

Brunsdon, C. (2003), "Lifestyling Britain: The 8–9 Slot on British Television," *International Journal of Cultural Studies,* 6/1: 5–23.

Brunsdon, C. (2004), "Taste and Time on Television," *Screen,* 45/2: 115–29.

Buchli, V. (ed.) (2002), *The Material Culture Reader,* Oxford: Berg.

Burns, C., Sacks, G., and Gold, L. (2008), "Longitudinal Study of Consumer Price Index (CPI) Trends in Core and Non-Core Foods in Australia," *Australian and New Zealand Journal of Public Health,* 32/5: 450–53.

Campbell, C. (1997), "Shopping, Pleasure and the Sex War," in P. Falk and C. Campbell (eds), *The Shopping Experience,* London: Sage.

Campbell, C. (2005), "The Craft Consumer: Culture, Craft and Consumption in a Postmodern Society," *Journal of Consumer Culture,* 5/1: 23–42.

Campion, A., and Curtis, M. (2009), *The Foodies' Guide to Melbourne 2010: More than 400 Butchers, Bakers, Food Stores and Chocolate Makers,* Prahran, Vic.: Hardie Grant Books.

Caraher, M., Dixon, P., Lang, T., and Carr-Hill, R. (1999), "The State of Cooking in England: The Relationship of Cooking Skills to Food Choice," *British Food Journal,* 101/8: 590–609.

Caraher, M., Lang, T., and Dixon, P. (2000), "The Influence of TV and Celebrity Chefs on Public Attitudes and Behavior Among the English Public," *Journal for the Study of Food and Society,* 4/1: 27–46.

Carrier, J. G., and Luetchford, P. G. (eds) (2012), *Ethical Consumption: Social Value and Economic Practice,* New York: Berghahn Books.

Cenite, M., Detenber, B. H., Koh, A.W.K., Lim, A.L.H., and Soon, N. E. (2009), "Doing the Right Thing Online: A Survey of Bloggers' Ethical Beliefs and Practices," *New Media & Society,* 11/4: 575–97.

Chan, A. (2003), "'La Grande Bouffe': Cooking Shows as Pornography," *Gastronomica,* 3/4: 47–53.

Chao, P. S. (1998), "Gendered Cooking: Television Cook Shows," *Jump Cut,* 42: 19–27.

Charles, N., and Kerr, M. (1984), *Attitudes towards the Feeding and Nutrition of Young Children,* London: Health Education Council.

Charles, N., and Kerr, M. (1988), *Women, Food, and Families,* Manchester: Manchester University Press.

Child, J. (2006), *My Life in France,* New York: Alfred A. Knopf.

City of Melbourne (1997), *The History of the City of Melbourne* [website] <http://www.melbourne.vic.gov.au/AboutMelbourne/History/Pages/HistoryofaCity.aspx> accessed May 25, 2012.

Clark, S. (2011), Review of *Foodies: Democracy and Distinction in the Gourmet Foodscape,* by J. Johnston and S. Baumann, *Food, Culture & Society,* 14/3: 433–36.

Clarke, J., and Critcher, C. (1985), *The Devil Makes Work: Leisure in Capitalist Britain,* Houndmills, UK: Macmillan.

Cohen, K. R. (2005), "What Does the Photoblog Want?" *Media, Culture & Society,* 27/6: 883–901.

Collins, H., and Evans, R. (2007), *Rethinking Expertise,* Chicago: University of Chicago Press.

Collins, J. (2002), "High-Pop: An Introduction," in J. Collins (ed.), *High-Pop: Making Culture into Popular Entertainment,* Malden, MA: Blackwell Publishers.

Collins, K. (2009), *Watching What We Eat: The Evolution of Television Cooking Shows,* New York: Continuum.

Commonwealth of Australia (2008), *Australian Food Statistics 2007,* <http://www.daff.gov.au/agriculture-food/food/publications/afs/australian_food_statistics_2007> accessed August 9, 2009.

Counihan, C. M. (2004), *Around the Tuscan Table: Food, Family, and Gender in Twentieth-Century Florence,* New York: Routledge.

Counihan, C. M., and Van Esterik, P. (eds) (1997), *Food and Culture: A Reader,* New York: Routledge.

de Certeau, M. (1984), *The Practice of Everyday Life,* Berkeley: University of California Press.

de Solier, I. (2004), "'Save the Universe of Flavours': Slow Food and the Politics of Taste," *Antithesis Forum* [online journal], 2, <http://pandora.

nla.gov.au/pan/66374/20070301-0000/www.english.unimelb.edu.au/antithesis/forum2004/deSolier.html> accessed April 19, 2010.

de Solier, I. (2005), "TV Dinners: Culinary Television, Education and Distinction," *Continuum,* 19/4: 465–81.

de Solier, I. (2006), "Foodie Blogs: Cookbooks, Recipes and Gustatory Identities," paper presented at the Cookery Books as History Conference, University of Adelaide, July.

de Solier, I. (2008), "Foodie Makeovers: Public Service Television and Lifestyle Guidance," in G. Palmer (ed.), *Exposing Lifestyle Television: The Big Reveal,* Aldershot, UK: Ashgate.

de Solier, I. (2010), "Liquid Nitrogen Pistachios: Molecular Gastronomy, elBulli, and Foodies," *European Journal of Cultural Studies,* 13/2: 155–70.

de Solier, I. (2013), "Making the Self in a Material World: Food and Moralities of Consumption," *Cultural Studies Review,* 19/1: 9–27.

de Solier, I., and Duruz, J. (eds) (2013), "Food Cultures," special issue of *Cultural Studies Review,* 19/1.

Deery, J. (2006), "Interior Design: Commodifying Self and Place in *Extreme Makeover, Extreme Makeover: Home Edition,* and *The Swan,*" in D. Heller (ed.), *The Great American Makeover: Television, History, Nation,* New York: Palgrave Macmillan.

DeVault, M. (1991), *Feeding the Family,* Chicago: University of Chicago Press.

Douglas, M. (1966), *Purity and Danger,* New York: Praeger.

Dover, C., and Hill, A. (2007), "Mapping Genres: Broadcaster and Audience Perceptions of Makeover Television," in D. Heller (ed.), *Makeover Television: Realities Remodelled,* London: I. B. Tauris.

Downes, S. (2006), "Fifteen Reasons I was Shown the Door," *Herald Sun* [online newspaper], (Oct. 12), <http://www.news.com.au/heraldsun/story/0,21985,20565752–2862,00.html> accessed October 21, 2008.

Dubin, R. (1992), *Central Life Interests: Creative Individualism in a Complex World,* New Brunswick, NJ: Transaction Publishers.

Duruz, J. (2004), "Adventuring and Belonging: An Appetite for Markets," *Space and Culture,* 7/4: 427–45.

Duruz, J. (2011), "Four Dances of the Sea: Cooking 'Asian' as Embedded Cosmopolitanism," in T. Chee-Beng (ed.), *Chinese Food and Foodways in Southeast Asia and Beyond,* Singapore: Singapore University Press.

Erickson, B. H. (1991), "What Is Good Taste For?" *Canadian Review of Sociology and Anthropology,* 28/2: 255–78.

Erickson, B. H. (1996), "Culture, Class and Connections," *American Journal of Sociology,* 102/1: 217–51.

Escoffier, A. (1907), *Le Guide Culinaire: Aide Mémoire de Cuisine Pratique,* Paris: E. Colin.

Featherstone, M. (1991), *Consumer Culture and Postmodernism,* London: Sage.

Ferguson, A. (2011), "Melbourne Judged World's Most Liveable City," *The Age* [online newspaper], (Aug. 30), <http://www.theage.com.au/business/melbourne-judged-worlds-most-liveable-city-20110830–1jjaq.html> accessed June 11, 2012.

Ferguson, P. P. (1998), "A Cultural Field in the Making: Gastronomy in 19th-Century France," *American Journal of Sociology,* 104/3: 597–641.

Ferguson, P. P. (2004), *Accounting for Taste: The Triumph of French Cuisine,* Chicago: University of Chicago Press.

Ferguson, P. P., and Zukin, S. (1998), "The Careers of Chefs," in R. Scapp and B. Seitz (eds), *Eating Culture,* Albany: State University of New York Press.

Fine, G. A. (1996), *Kitchens: The Culture of Restaurant Work,* Berkeley: University of California Press.

Fine, G. A. (1998), *Morel Tales: The Culture of Mushrooming,* Cambridge, MA: Harvard University Press.

Finkelstein, J. (1989), *Dining Out: A Sociology of Modern Manners,* Oxford: Polity Press.

Finnegan, R. (2005), "Introduction: Looking Beyond the Walls," in R. Finnegan (ed.), *Participating in the Knowledge Society: Researchers Beyond the University Walls,* Basingstoke, UK: Palgrave Macmillan.

Fisher, M.F.K. (1943), *The Gastronomical Me,* New York: Duell, Sloan & Pearce.

Floyd, J. (2006), "The Restaurant Guide as Romance: From Raymond Postgate to Florence White," in D. Bell and J. Hollows (eds), *Historicizing Lifestyle: Mediating Taste, Consumption and Identity from the 1900s to 1970s,* Aldershot, UK: Ashgate.

Floyd, J., and Forster, L. (eds) (2003a), *The Recipe Reader: Narratives— Contexts—Traditions,* Aldershot, UK: Ashgate.

Floyd, J., and Forster, L. (2003b), "The Recipe in Its Cultural Contexts," in J. Floyd and L. Forster (eds), *The Recipe Reader: Narratives—Contexts— Traditions*, Aldershot, UK: Ashgate.

Foucault, M. (1986), *The Care of the Self: The History of Sexuality Volume 3,* London: Penguin.

Foucault, M. (1988), *Technologies of the Self: A Seminar with Michel Foucault,* ed. L. H. Martin, H. Gutman, and P. H. Hutton, Amherst: University of Massachusetts Press.

Friedberg, A. (1993), *Window Shopping: Cinema and the Postmodern,* Berkeley: University of California Press.

Frow, J. (1995), *Cultural Studies and Cultural Value,* Oxford: Clarendon Press.

Fyfe, M., and Millar, R. (2012a), "Small Grocers Target Big Two," *The Age* [online newspaper], (June 11), <http://www.theage.com.au/national/small-grocers-target-big-two-20120610–204gn.html> accessed June 14, 2012.

Fyfe, M., and Millar, R. (2012b), "What They Do to Food," *The Age* [online newspaper], (June 9), <http://www.theage.com.au/victoria/what-they-do-to-food-20120608–201su.html> accessed June 14, 2012.

Gabaccia, D. R. (1998), *We Are What We Eat: Ethnic Food and the Making of Americans,* Cambridge, MA: Harvard University Press.

Gainor, R. (2009), "Leisure Information Behaviours in Hobby Quilting Sites," [web extract] *Proceedings of the Canadian Association for Information Science Conference* <http://www.cais-acsi.ca/proceedings/2009/Gainor_2009.pdf> accessed November 11, 2009.

Gallegos, D. (2005), "Cookbooks as Manuals of Taste," in D. Bell and J. Hollows (eds), *Ordinary Lifestyles: Popular Media, Consumption and Taste,* Maidenhead, UK: Open University Press.

Gandolfo, E., and Grace, M. (2009), *. . . It Keeps Me Sane . . . Women Craft Wellbeing,* Carlton North, Vic.: The Vulgar Press.

Gans, H. (1999), *Popular Culture and High Culture: An Analysis and Evaluation of Taste,* New York: Basic Books.

Garval, M. (2001), "Grimod de la Reynière's *Almanach des Gourmands:* Exploring the Gastronomic New World of Postrevolutionary France," in L. R. Schehr and A. S. Weiss (eds), *French Food: On the Table, on the Page, and in French Culture,* New York: Routledge.

Gauntlett, D. (2011), *Making Is Connecting: The Social Meaning of Creativity, from DIY and Knitting to YouTube and Web 2.0,* Cambridge: Polity Press.

Gaytán, M. S. (2004), "Globalizing Resistance: Slow Food and New Local Imaginaries," *Food, Culture & Society,* 7/2: 97–116.

Geertz, C. (1983), *Local Knowledge: Further Essays in Interpretive Anthropology,* New York: Basic Books.

Gelber, S. M. (1999), *Hobbies: Leisure and the Culture of Work in America,* New York: Columbia University Press.

Giard, L. (1998), "Doing-Cooking," in M. de Certeau, L. Giard, and P. Mayol (eds), *The Practice of Everyday Life, Volume 2: Living and Cooking,* Minneapolis: University of Minnesota Press.

Giddens, A. (1990), *The Consequences of Modernity,* Cambridge: Polity Press.

Giddens, A. (1991), *Modernity and Self-Identity: Self and Society in the Late Modern Age,* Cambridge: Polity Press.

Giddens, A. (2002), *Runaway World: How Globalization is Reshaping our Lives,* London: Profile.

Gigante, D. (ed.) (2005), *Gusto: Essential Writings in Nineteenth-Century Gastronomy,* New York: Routledge.

Glaser, B. G., and Strauss, A. L. (1967), *The Discovery of Grounded Theory: Strategies for Qualitative Research,* Beverly Hills: Sage.

Glasse, H. (1747), *The Art of Cookery, Made Plain and Easy: Which Far Exceeds Anything of the Kind Ever Yet Published / By a Lady,* London: Printed for the Author.

Goffman, E. (1959), *The Presentation of Self in Everyday Life,* Garden City, NY: Doubleday.

Goldfarb, W. (2007), Panel discussion at Out of the Frying Pan: Future of the Food Media Conference, Melbourne Food and Wine Festival, Melbourne, March.

Goodman, D. (2002), "Rethinking Food Production-Consumption: Integrative Perspectives," *Sociologia Ruralis,* 42/4: 271–77.

Goodman, D. (2003), "The Quality 'Turn' and Alternative Food Practices: Reflections and Agenda," *Journal of Rural Studies,* 19: 1–7.

Goodman, D., DuPuis, E. M., and Goodman, M. K. (2012), *Alternative Food Networks: Knowledge, Practice, and Politics,* London: Routledge.

Goodman, M. K., Maye, D., and Holloway, L. (2010), "Ethical Foodscapes? Premises, Promises, and Possibilities," *Environment and Planning A,* 42: 1782–96.

Goody, J. (1982), *Cooking, Cuisine, and Class: A Study in Comparative Sociology,* Cambridge: Cambridge University Press.

Greenhalgh, P. (1997), "The History of Craft," in P. Dormer (ed.), *The Culture of Craft: Status and Future,* Manchester: Manchester University Press.

Gregson, N., and Crewe, L. (2003), *Second-Hand Cultures,* Oxford: Berg.

Grimod de la Reynière, A.B.L. (1803), *Almanach des Gourmands, Servant de Guide dans les Moyens de Faire Excellent Chère,* Paris: Maradan.

Guthman, J. (2003), "Fast Food/Organic Food: Reflexive Tastes and the Making of 'Yuppie Chow,' " *Social and Cultural Geography,* 4/1: 45–58.

Hage, G. (1997), "At Home in the Entrails of the West: Multiculturalism, Ethnic Food and Migrant Home-Building," in *Home/World: Space, Community and Marginality in Sydney's West,* Sydney: Pluto Press.

Hamilton, C., and Denniss, R. (2005), *Affluenza: When Too Much Is Never Enough,* Crows Nest, NSW: Allen & Unwin.

Hannerz, U. (1990), "Cosmopolitans and Locals in World Culture," *Theory, Culture & Society,* 7: 237–51.

Hartel, J. (2006), "Information Activities and Resources in an Episode of Gourmet Cooking," *Information Research* [online journal], 12/1, <http://informationr.net/ir/12–1/paper282.html> accessed March 28, 2009.

Hastings, K. (2008), "Delia's How to Cheat at Cooking Causes Stir," *The Telegraph* [online newspaper] (Feb. 11), <http://www.telegraph.co.uk/news/uknews/1578259/Delia's-How-to-Cheat-at-Cooking-causes-stir.html> accessed August 19, 2008.

Heldke, L. M. (1992), "Foodmaking as a Thoughtful Practice," in D. W. Curtin and L. M. Heldke (eds), *Cooking, Eating, Thinking: Transformative Philosophies of Food,* Bloomington: Indiana University Press.

Heller, D. (ed.) (2006), *The Great American Makeover: Television, History, Nation,* New York: Palgrave Macmillan.

Heller, D. (ed.) (2007), *Makeover Television: Realities Remodelled,* London: I. B. Tauris.

Hernandez, M., and Sutton, D. (2005), "Hands That Remember: An Ethnographic Approach to Everyday Cooking," *Expedition,* 45/2: 30–37.

Herring, S., Scheidt, L. A., Bonus, S., and Wright, E. (2004), "Bridging the Gap: A Genre Analysis of Weblogs," *Proceedings of the 37th Hawaii International Conference on System Sciences* <http://www.computer.org/comp/proceedings/hicss/2004/2056/04/205640101b.pdf> accessed November 11, 2009.

Herring, S., Scheidt, L. A., Kouper, I., and Wright, E. (2007), "Longitudinal Content Analysis of Blogs: 2003–2004," in M. Tremayne (ed.), *Blogging, Citizenship and the Future of Media,* New York: Routledge.

Hicks, D., and Beaudry, M. C. (eds) (2010), *The Oxford Handbook of Material Culture Studies,* Oxford: Oxford University Press.

Hill, A. (2005), *Reality TV: Audiences and Popular Factual Television,* London: Routledge.

Hockey, J. (2002), "Interviews as Ethnography? Disembodied Social Interaction in Britain," in N. Rapport (ed.), *British Subjects,* Oxford: Berg.

Holloway, L., and Kneafsey, M. (2000), "Reading the Space of the Farmers' Market: A Case-Study from the United Kingdom," *Sociologia Ruralis,* 40: 285–99.

Hollows, J. (2003a), "Feeling Like a Domestic Goddess: Postfeminism and Cooking," *European Journal of Cultural Studies,* 6/2: 179–202.

Hollows, J. (2003b), "Oliver's Twist: Leisure, Labour and Domestic Masculinity in *The Naked Chef," International Journal of Cultural Studies,* 6/2: 229–48.

Hollows, J., and Jones, S. (2010), "*Please* Don't Try This at Home: Heston Blumenthal, Cookery TV and the Culinary Field," *Food, Culture & Society,* 13/4: 521–37.

Horst, H. A. (2009), "Aesthetics of the Self: Digital Mediations," in D. Miller (ed.), *Anthropology and the Individual: A Material Culture Perspective,* Oxford: Berg.

Horst, H. A., and Miller, D. (eds) (2012), *Digital Anthropology,* Oxford: Berg.

Hosking, W. (2012), "Melbourne Rated World's Most Liveable City in Economist Intelligence Unit's Global Liveability Survey," *Herald Sun* [online newspaper], (Aug. 15), <http://www.heraldsun.com.au/news/victoria/melbourne-rated-worlds-most-liveable-city-in-economist-intelligence-units-global-liveability-survey/story-e6frf7kx-1226450004273> accessed August 15, 2012.

Humphery, K. (1998), *Shelf Life: Supermarkets and the Changing Cultures of Consumption,* Cambridge: Cambridge University Press.

Humphery, K. (2010), *Excess: Anti-Consumerism in the West,* Cambridge: Polity Press.

Intergovernmental Panel on Climate Change (1999), *Aviation and the Global Atmosphere* [online report], Cambridge: Cambridge University Press <http://www.ipcc.ch/ipccreports/sres/aviation/index.htm> accessed February 24, 2010.

Jackson P., Ward, N., and Russell, P. (2010), "Manufacturing Meaning Along the Chicken Supply Chain: Consumer Anxiety and the Spaces of Production," in M. K. Goodman, D. Goodman, and M. Redclift (eds), *Consuming Space: Placing Consumption in Perspective,* Aldershot, UK: Ashgate.

Jeffries, S. (2006), "Art of Cooking," *The Guardian* (May 6).

Jenkins, C., and Sherman, B. (1979), *The Collapse of Work,* London: Eyre Methuen.

Jenkins, H. (2006), *Convergence Culture: Where Old and New Media Collide,* New York: New York University Press.

Johnston, J., and Baumann, S. (2010), *Foodies: Democracy and Distinction in the Gourmet Foodscape,* New York: Routledge.

Jones, M. (2008), *Skintight: An Anatomy of Cosmetic Surgery,* Oxford: Berg.

Jones, S., and Taylor, B. (2001), "Food Writing and Food Cultures: The Case of Elizabeth David and Jane Grigson," *European Journal of Cultural Studies,* 4/2: 171–88.

Keen, A. (2007), *The Cult of the Amateur: How Today's Internet Is Killing Our Culture,* New York: Doubleday.

Kneafsey, M., Cox, R., Holloway, L., Dowler, E., Venn, L., and Tuomainen, H. (2008), *Reconnecting Consumers, Producers and Food: Exploring Alternatives,* Oxford: Berg.

Koch, S. L. (2012), *A Theory of Grocery Shopping: Food, Choice and Conflict,* Oxford: Berg.

Korsmeyer, C. (1999), *Making Sense of Taste: Food and Philosophy,* Ithaca, NY: Cornell University Press.

Korsmeyer, C. (ed.) (2005), *The Taste Culture Reader: Experiencing Food and Drink,* Oxford: Berg.

Kwan, S. (2009), "Individual versus Corporate Responsibility: Market Choice, the Food Industry, and the Pervasiveness of Moral Models of Fatness," *Food, Culture and Society,* 12/4: 477–95.

Labelle, J. (2004), "A Recipe for Connectedness: Bridging Production and Consumption with Slow Food," *Food, Culture & Society,* 7/2: 81–96.

Lane, C. (2010), "The Michelin-Starred Restaurant Sector as a Cultural Industry: A Cross-National Comparison of Restaurants in the UK and Germany," *Food, Culture & Society,* 13/4: 493–519.

Lang, T., and Caraher, M. (2001), "Is There a Culinary Skills Transition? Data and Debate from the UK about Changes in Cooking Culture," *Journal of the Australian Institute of Home Economics,* 8/2: 2–14.

Langland, E. (1995), *Nobody's Angels: Middle Class Women and Domestic Ideology in Victorian Culture,* Ithaca, NY: Cornell University Press.

Laudan, R. (1999), "A World of Inauthentic Cuisine," in M. W. Kelsey and Z. Holmes (eds), *Cultural and Historical Aspects of Foods: Yesterday, Today, and Tomorrow,* Corvallis: Oregon State University.

Laudan, R. (2001), "A Plea for Culinary Modernism: Why We Should Love New, Fast, Processed Food," *Gastronomica,* 1/1: 36–44.

Leadbeater, C., and Miller, P. (2004), *The Pro-Am Revolution: How Enthusiasts are Changing our Economy and Society* [online book], London: Demos. <http://www.demos.co.uk/publications/proameconomy> accessed October 28, 2008.

Lehtonen, T.-K., and Mäenpää, P. (1997), "Shopping in the East Centre Mall," in P. Falk and C. Campbell (eds), *The Shopping Experience,* London: Sage.

Leitch, A. (2003), "Slow Food and the Politics of Pork Fat: Italian Food and European Identity," *Ethnos,* 68/4: 437–62.

Leonardi, S. (1989), "Recipes for Reading: Summer Pasta, Lobster à la Riseholme, and Key Lime Pie," *PMLA,* 104/3: 340–47.

Lévi-Strauss, C. (1965), "Le Triangle Culinaire," *L'Arc,* 26: 19–29.

Lévi-Strauss, C. (1969), *The Raw and the Cooked,* London: Cape.

Levine, F., and Heimerl, C. (2008), *Handmade Nation: The Rise of DIY, Art, Craft, and Design,* New York: Princeton Architectural Press.

Lewis, T. (2008a), *Smart Living: Lifestyle Media and Popular Expertise,* New York: Peter Lang.

Lewis, T. (2008b), "Transforming Citizens? Green Politics and Ethical Consumption on Lifestyle Television," *Continuum,* 22/2: 227–40.

Lewis, T. (ed.) (2009), *TV Transformations: Revealing the Makeover Show,* London: Routledge.

Lewis, T., and Potter, E. (eds) (2011), *Ethical Consumption: A Critical Introduction,* London: Routledge.

Linnell, G. (2008), "Gordon Ramsay to Open First Aussie Restaurant in Melbourne," *Herald Sun* [online newspaper], (June 23), <http://www.heraldsun.com.au/entertainment/tv-radio/melbournes-f-wow-ramsay/story-e6frf9ho-1111116706638> accessed July 26, 2012.

Littler, J. (2009), *Radical Consumption: Shopping for Change in Contemporary Culture,* Maidenhead, UK: Open University Press.

Lockie, S., Lyons, K., Lawrence, G., and Mummery, K. (2002), "Eating 'Green': Motivations Behind Organic Food Consumption in Australia," *Sociologia Ruralis,* 42: 23–40.

Lovink, G. (2008), *Zero Comments: Blogging and Critical Internet Culture,* New York: Routledge.

Lüders, M. (2008), "Conceptualizing Personal Media," *New Media & Society,* 10/5: 683–702.

Luetchford, P. (2008), "The Hands That Pick Fair Trade Coffee: Beyond the Charms of the Family Farm," *Research in Economic Anthropology,* 28: 143–69.

Lury, C. (1996), *Consumer Culture,* Cambridge: Polity.

Lyotard, J.-F. (1984), *The Postmodern Condition: A Report on Knowledge,* Manchester: Manchester University Press.

MacDonogh, G. (1987), *A Palate in Revolution: Grimod de la Reynière and the Almanach des Gourmands,* London: Robin Clark.

McGee, H. (2003), *On Food and Cooking: The Science and Lore of the Kitchen,* New York: Simon & Schuster.

McLean, J. (2009), "State of the Blogosphere 2009 Introduction," *Technorati State of the Blogosphere 2009* [website], (Oct. 19), <http://technorati.com/blogging/article/state-of-the-blogosphere-2009-introduction/> accessed November 20, 2009.

Mennell, S. (1996), *All Manners of Food: Eating and Taste in England and France from the Middle Ages to the Present,* Urbana: University of Illinois Press.

Meyers, E. A. (2012), "'Blogs Give Regular People the Chance to Talk Back': Rethinking 'Professional' Media Hierarchies in New Media," *New Media & Society,* 14/6: 1022–38.

Miele, M., and Murdoch, J. (2002), "The Practical Aesthetics of Traditional Cuisines: Slow Food in Tuscany," *Sociologia Ruralis,* 42/4: 312–28.

Miller, D. (1987), *Material Culture and Mass Consumption,* Oxford: Blackwell.

Miller, D. (1998), *A Theory of Shopping,* Cambridge: Polity Press.

Miller, D. (2001a), *The Dialectics of Shopping,* Chicago: University of Chicago Press.

Miller, D. (2001b), "The Poverty of Morality," *Journal of Consumer Culture,* 1/2: 225–43.

Miller, D. (2008), *The Comfort of Things,* Cambridge: Polity Press.

Miller, D. (ed.) (2009), *Anthropology and the Individual: A Material Culture Perspective,* Oxford: Berg.

Miller, D. (2010), *Stuff,* Cambridge: Polity Press.

Miller, D. (2011), *Tales from Facebook,* Cambridge: Polity Press.

Miller, D., Jackson, P., Thrift, N., Holbrook, B., and Rowlands, M. (1998), *Shopping, Place and Identity,* London: Routledge.

Miller, D., and Slater, D. (2000), *The Internet: An Ethnographic Approach,* Oxford: Berg.

Miller, J., and Deutsch, J. (2009), *Food Studies: An Introduction to Research Methods,* Oxford: Berg.

Miller, T. (2001), "Screening Food: French Cuisine and the Television Palate," in L. R. Schehr and A. S. Weiss (eds), *French Food: On the Table, on the Page, and in French Culture,* New York: Routledge.

Miller, T. (2006), "Metrosexuality: See the Bright Light of Commodification Shine! Watch Yanqui Masculinity Made Over!" in D. Heller (ed.), *The Great American Makeover,* New York: Palgrave Macmillan.

Miller, T. (2007), *Cultural Citizenship: Cosmopolitanism, Consumerism, and Television in a Neoliberal Age,* Philadelphia: Temple University Press.

Miller, T. (2008), "Afterword: The New World Makeover," *Continuum,* 22/4: 585–90.

Mills, C. W. (1956), *White Collar: The American Middle Classes,* New York: Oxford University Press.

Mol, A. (2012), "Mind Your Plate! The Ontonorms of Dutch Dieting," *Social Studies of Science,* September: 1–18.

Montagné, P. (1961), *Larousse Gastronomique: The Encyclopedia of Food, Wine and Cooking,* London: Hamlyn.

Moseley, R. (2000), "Makeover Takeover on British Television," *Screen,* 41/3: 299–314.

Moseley, R. (2001), "'Real Lads Do Cook...But Some Things are Still Hard to Talk About': The Gendering of 8–9," in C. Brunsdon, C. Johnson, R. Moseley, and H. Wheatley, "Factual Entertainment on British Television: The Midlands TV Research Group's '8–9 Project'" *European Journal of Cultural Studies,* 4/1: 29–62.

Museum Victoria (n.d.), *Origins: Immigrant Communities in Victoria* [website] <http://museumvictoria.com.au/origins/> accessed June 11, 2012.

Myers, B. R. (2011), "The Moral Crusade Against Foodies: Gluttony Dressed Up as Foodie-ism Is Still Gluttony," *The Atlantic* [online magazine] (Feb. 9), <http://www.theatlantic.com/magazine/archive/2011/03/the-moral-crusade-against-foodies/8370/> accessed July 21, 2011.

Naccarato, P., and LeBesco, K. (2012), *Culinary Capital,* Oxford: Berg.

Nielsen Company (2012), "Buzz in the Blogosphere: Millions More Bloggers and Blog Readers" [newswire article] <http://blog.nielsen.com/nielsenwire/online_mobile/buzz-in-the-blogosphere-millions-more-bloggers-and-blog-readers/> accessed October 5, 2012.

Northover, K. (2012), "Melbourne on the Menu," *The Age* [online newspaper] (Mar. 2), <http://www.theage.com.au/national/melbourne-on-the-menu-20120302–1u7gp.html> accessed July 26, 2012.

Oakley, A. (1990), *Housewife,* Harmondsworth, UK: Penguin.

Organisation for Economic Co-operation and Development [OECD] (2010), "Tertiary Education Graduation Rates" [online library] (Jun. 14), <http://www.oecd-ilibrary.org/education/tertiary-education-graduation-rates_20755120-table1> accessed August 3, 2012.

OECD (2012), "Average Annual Working Time" [online library] (Jul. 11), <http://www.oecd-ilibrary.org/employment/average-annual-working-time_20752342-table8> accessed August 2, 2012.

Ouellette, L., and Hay, J. (2008), *Better Living through Reality TV: Television and Post-Welfare Citizenship,* Malden, MA: Blackwell.

Palmer, G. (2004), "'The New You': Class and Transformation in Lifestyle Television," in S. Holmes and D. Jermyn (eds), *Understanding Reality Television,* London: Routledge.

Palmer, G. (ed.) (2008), *Exposing Lifestyle Television: The Big Reveal,* Aldershot, UK: Ashgate.

Parkins, W., and Craig, G. (2006), *Slow Living,* Oxford: Berg.

Peterson, R. A. (1992), "Understanding Audience Segmentation: From Elite and Mass to Omnivore and Univore," *Poetics,* 21: 243–58.

Peterson, R. A., and Kern, R. M. (1996), "Changing Highbrow Taste: From Snob to Omnivore," *American Sociological Review,* 61/5: 900–907.

Peterson, Y., and Birg, L. D. (1988), "Top Hat: The Chef as Creative Occupation," *Free Inquiry in Creative Sociology,* 16: 67–72.

Petrini, C. (2003), *Slow Food: The Case for Taste,* New York: Columbia University Press.

Polan, D. (2011), *Julia Child's 'The French Chef,'* Durham, NC: Duke University Press.

Pollan, M. (2006), *The Omnivore's Dilemma: The Search for a Perfect Meal in a Fast-Food World,* London: Bloomsbury.

Pollan, M. (2009), "Out of the Kitchen, Onto the Couch," *New York Times* [online newspaper] (Jul. 29), <http://www.nytimes.com/2009/08/02/magazine/02cooking-t.html> accessed September 11, 2009.

Poulantzas, N. (1975), *Classes in Contemporary Capitalism,* London: Verso.

Powell, H., and Prasad, S. (2010), "'As Seen on TV.' The Celebrity Expert: How Taste is Shaped by Lifestyle Media," *Cultural Politics,* 6/1: 111–24.

Powell, J. (2007), *Julie and Julia: My Year of Cooking Dangerously,* London: Penguin.

Probyn, E. (2000), *Carnal Appetites: FoodSexIdentities,* London: Routledge.

Raisborough, J. (2011), *Lifestyle Media and the Formation of the Self,* Basingstoke, UK: Palgrave Macmillan.

Rappaport, E. D. (2000), *Shopping for Pleasure: Women in the Making of London's West End,* Princeton, NJ: Princeton University Press.

Ray, K. (2004), *The Migrant's Table: Meals and Memories in Bengali-American Households,* Philadelphia: Temple University Press.

Rayner, J. (2007), "Critiquing the Critics," *The Guardian* [online newspaper] (Oct. 30), <http://www.guardian.co.uk/lifeandstyle/wordofmouth/2007/oct/30/critiquingthecritics> accessed October 17, 2008.

Redden, G. (2007), "Makeover Morality and Consumer Culture," in D. Heller (ed.), *Makeover Television: Realities Remodelled,* London: I. B. Tauris.

Reed, A. (2005), "'My Blog Is Me': Texts and Persons in UK Online Journal Culture (and Anthropology)," *Ethnos,* 70/2: 220–42.

Ritzer, G. (2005), *Enchanting a Disenchanted World: Revolutionizing the Means of Consumption,* Thousand Oaks, CA: Pine Forge Press.

Ritzer, G., and Jurgenson, N. (2010), "Production, Consumption, Prosumption: The Nature of Capitalism in the Age of the Digital 'Prosumer'" *Journal of Consumer Culture,* 10/1: 13–36.

Roe, E. J. (2006a), "Material Connectivity, the Immaterial and the Aesthetic of Eating Practices: An Argument for How Genetically Modified Foodstuff Becomes Inedible," *Environment and Planning A,* 38: 465–81.

Roe, E. J. (2006b), "Things Becoming Food and the Embodied, Material Practices of an Organic Food Consumer," *Sociologia Ruralis,* 46/2: 104–21.

Rose, N. (1992), "Governing the Enterprising Self," in P. Heelas and P. Morris (eds), *The Values of the Enterprise Culture: The Moral Debate,* London: Routledge.

Rosenberg, B. C. (2005), "Scandinavian Dreams: DIY, Democratisation and IKEA," *Transformations* [online journal], 11, <http://www.transformations-journal.org/journal/issue_11/article_02.shtml> accessed May 14, 2010.

Rosenberg, B. C. (2008a), "Masculine Makeovers: Lifestyle Television, Metrosexuals and Real Blokes," in G. Palmer (ed.), *Exposing Lifestyle Television: The Big Reveal,* Aldershot, UK: Ashgate.

Rosenberg, B. C. (2008b), "Property and Home-Makeover Television: Risk, Thrift and Taste," *Continuum,* 22/4: 505–13.

Rosenberg, B. C. (2011a), "Home Improvement: Domestic Taste, DIY, and the Property Market," *Home Cultures,* 8/1: 5–23.

Rosenberg, B. C. (2011b), "The *Our House DIY Club:* Amateurs, Leisure Knowledge and Lifestyle Media," *International Journal of Cultural Studies,* 14/2: 173–90.

Rosenberg, B. C. (2012), "Dangerous Houses: Scientific Lifestyle Television and Risk Management," *Home Cultures,* 9/2: 173–94.

Rousseau, S. (2012a), *Food and Social Media: You Are What You Tweet,* Lanham, MD: AltaMira Press.

Rousseau, S. (2012b), *Food Media: Celebrity Chefs and the Politics of Everyday Interference,* London: Berg.

Rubin, J. S. (1992), *The Making of Middlebrow Culture,* Chapel Hill: University of North Carolina Press.

Salkin, A. (2007), "Sharp Bites," *New York Times* [online newspaper] (Feb. 4), <http://www.nytimes.com/2007/02/04/fashion/04bloggers.html> accessed October 11, 2008.

Santich, B. (2002), "Why Study Gastronomy?" *Meanjin,* 61/4: 171–74.

Sassatelli, R., and Davolio, F. (2010), "Consumption, Pleasure and Politics: Slow Food and the Politico-Aesthetic Problematization of Food," *Journal of Consumer Culture,* 10/2: 220–50.

Schehr, L. R., and Weiss, A. S. (eds) (2001), *French Food: On the Table, on the Page, and in French Culture,* New York: Routledge.

Schofield, M. A. (ed.) (1989), *Cooking By the Book: Food in Literature and Culture,* Bowling Green, OH: Bowling Green State University Popular Press.

Schor, J. B. (1999), *The Overspent American: Why We Want What We Don't Need,* New York: Harper Perennial.

Semenak, S. (2007), "The Self-Appointed Critics," *The Gazette* [online newspaper] (Oct. 27), <http://www.canada.com/montrealgazette/story.html?id= c2a3a841–0e1f-4bcb-9af7-ef014836a80e> accessed October 17, 2008.

Sherman, Y. D. (2008), "Fashioning Femininity: Clothing the Body and the Self in *What Not to Wear*," in G. Palmer (ed.), *Exposing Lifestyle Television: The Big Reveal,* Aldershot, UK: Ashgate.

Short, F. (2006), *Kitchen Secrets: The Meaning of Cooking in Everyday Life,* Oxford: Berg.

Singer, J. (2006), "Journalists and News Bloggers: Complements, Contradictions, and Challenges," in A. Bruns and J. Jacobs (eds), *Uses of Blogs,* New York: Peter Lang.

Slater, D. (1991), "Consuming Kodak," in J. Spence and P. Holland (eds), *Family Snaps: The Meanings of Domestic Photography,* London: Virago Press.

Slater, D. (1997), *Consumer Culture and Modernity,* Oxford: Polity Press.

Slater, D. (2010), "The Moral Seriousness of Consumption," in J. B. Schor, D. Slater, S. Zukin, and V. A. Zelizer, "Critical and Moral Stances in Consumer Studies," *Journal of Consumer Culture,* 10/2: 280–84.

Slater, D., and Miller, D. (2007), "Moments and Movements in the Study of Consumer Culture: A Discussion Between Daniel Miller and Don Slater," *Journal of Consumer Culture,* 7/1: 5–23.

Slocum, R. (2008), "Thinking Race through Corporeal Feminist Theory: Divisions and Intimacies at the Minneapolis Farmers' Market," *Social & Cultural Geography,* 9/8: 849–69.

Slow Food (2010), "Our Philosophy" [website] <http://www.slowfood.com/ about_us/eng/philosophy.lasso> accessed February 24, 2010.

Smith, A. (2010), "Lifestyle Television Programmes and the Construction of the Expert Host," *European Journal of Cultural Studies,* 13/2: 191–205.

Soper, K. (2008), "Alternative Hedonism, Cultural Theory and the Role of Aesthetic Revisioning," *Cultural Studies,* 22/5: 567–87.

Spang, R. L. (2000), *The Invention of the Restaurant: Paris and Modern Gastronomic Culture,* Cambridge, MA: Harvard University Press.

Stanton, J. L., Wiley, J. B., and Wirth, F. F. (2012), "Who are the Locavores?" *Journal of Consumer Marketing,* 29/4: 248–61.

State Government of Victoria (2006), *Ten Year Tourism and Events Industry Strategy* [website] <http://www.tourism.vic.gov.au/strategies-and-plans/ strategies-and-plans/strategies-and-plans/> accessed March 15, 2009.

Stebbins, R. A. (1979), *Amateurs: On the Margin Between Work and Leisure,* Beverly Hills: Sage.

Stebbins, R. A. (1982), "Serious Leisure: A Conceptual Statement," *Pacific Sociological Review,* 25: 251–72.

Stebbins, R. A. (1992), *Amateurs, Professionals, and Serious Leisure,* Montreal: McGill-Queen's University Press.

Stebbins, R. A. (2001), *New Directions in the Theory and Research of Serious Leisure,* Lewiston, NY: Edwin Mellen Press.

Stebbins, R. A. (2002), *The Organizational Basis of Leisure Participation: A Motivational Exploration,* State College, PA: Venture Publishing.

Stebbins, R. A. (2007), *Serious Leisure: A Perspective for Our Time,* New Brunswick, NJ: Transaction Publishers.

Sussman, M. (2009), "Day 1: Who are the Bloggers? SOTB 2009," *Technorati State of the Blogosphere 2009* [website], (Oct. 19), <http://technorati. com/blogging/article/day-1-who-are-the-bloggers1/> accessed November 19, 2009.

Sutton, D. E. (2001), *Remembrance of Repasts: An Anthropology of Food and Memory,* Oxford: Berg.

Symons, M. (2007), *One Continuous Picnic: A Gastronomic History of Australia,* 2nd ed., Carlton, Vic.: Melbourne University Press.

Taylor, L. (2008), *A Taste for Gardening: Classed and Gendered Practices,* Aldershot, UK: Ashgate.

Technorati (2010), "Blog Directory" [website] <http://technorati.com/blogs/ directory/> accessed March 9, 2010.

This, H. (2006), *Molecular Gastronomy: Exploring the Science of Flavor,* New York: Columbia University Press.

Tilley, C., Keane, W., Küchler, S., Rowlands, M., and Spyer, P. (eds) (2006), *Handbook of Material Culture,* London: Sage.

Toffler, A. (1980), *The Third Wave,* New York: William Morrow.

Tourism Victoria (n.d.), *Victoria's Tourism Plan Summary: Food and Wine 2004–2007* [website] <http://www.tourismvictoria.com.au/foodandwine> accessed April 8, 2007.

Trubek, A. B. (2000), *Haute Cuisine: How the French Invented the Culinary Profession,* Philadelphia: University of Pennsylvania Press.

Turner, B. S., and Edmunds, J. (2002), "The Distaste of Taste: Bourdieu, Cultural Capital and the Australian Postwar Elite," *Journal of Consumer Culture,* 2/2: 219–40.

Turner, G. (2004), *Understanding Celebrity,* London: Sage.

Unruh, D. R. (1980), "The Nature of Social Worlds," *Pacific Sociological Review,* 23: 271–96.

van Dijck, J. (2007), *Mediated Memories in the Digital Age,* Stanford: Stanford University Press.

Veblen, T. (1934), *The Theory of the Leisure Class: An Economic Study of Institutions,* New York: The Modern Library.

Vileisis, A. (2008), *Kitchen Literacy: How We Lost Knowledge of Where Food Comes from and Why We Need to Get It Back,* Washington, DC: Island Press.

Warde, A. (1997), *Consumption, Food and Taste: Culinary Antinomies and Commodity Culture,* London: Sage.

Warde, A. (2005), "Consumption and Theories of Practice," *Journal of Consumer Culture,* 5/2: 131–53.

Warde, A. (2009), "Imagining British Cuisine: Representations of Culinary Identity in the *Good Food Guide, 1951–2007,*" *Food, Culture & Society,* 12/2: 151–71.

Warde, A., and Martens, L. (2000), *Eating Out: Social Differentiation, Consumption and Pleasure,* Cambridge: Cambridge University Press.

Warde, A., Martens, L., and Olsen, W. (1999), "Consumption and the Problem of Variety: Cultural Omnivorousness, Social Distinction and Dining Out," *Sociology,* 33/1: 105–27.

Watson, M., and Shove, E. (2008), "Product, Competence, Project and Practice: DIY and the Dynamics of Craft Consumption," *Journal of Consumer Culture,* 8/1: 69–89.

Weber, B. R. (2009), *Makeover TV: Selfhood, Citizenship, and Celebrity,* Durham, NC: Duke University Press.

Weber, M. (1930), *The Protestant Ethic and the Spirit of Capitalism,* London: Routledge.

West, H. G., and Domingos, N. (2012), "Gourmandizing Poverty Food: The Serpa Cheese Slow Food Presidium," *Journal of Agrarian Change,* 12/1: 120–43.

Whatmore, S., and Clark, N. (2006), "Good Food: Ethical Consumption and Global Change," in N. Clark, D. Massey, and P. Sarre (eds), *A World in the Making,* Milton Keynes, UK: Open University Press.

Wilensky, H. L. (1960), "Work, Careers, and Social Integration," *International Social Sciences Journal,* 12: 543–60.

Wilk, R. (2001), "Consuming Morality," *Journal of Consumer Culture,* 1/2: 245–60.

Wilk, R. (ed.) (2006), *Fast Food/Slow Food: The Cultural Economy of the Global Food System,* Lanham, MD: Altamira Press.

Williams-Forson, P. A. (2006), *Building Houses Out of Chicken Legs: Black Women, Food, and Power,* Chapel Hill: University of North Carolina Press.

Willis, P. (1990), *Common Culture: Symbolic Work at Play in the Everyday Cultures of the Young,* Milton Keynes, UK: Open University Press.

Woods, V., Meades, J., O'Conner, P., and Barr, A. (1982), "Cuisine Poseur," *Harpers & Queen* (August): 66–70, 140.

Woodward, I. (2007), *Understanding Material Culture,* London: Sage.

Woodward, S. (2007), *Why Women Wear What They Wear,* Oxford: Berg.

World's 50 Best Restaurants (2010), "The S. Pellegrino World's 50 Best Restaurants" [website] <http://www.theworlds50best.com/> accessed February 21, 2010.

Zukin, S. (2008), "Consuming Authenticity: From Outposts of Difference to Means of Exclusion," *Cultural Studies,* 22/5: 724–48.

Index

www.ingramcontent.com/pod-product-compliance
Lightning Source LLC
Chambersburg PA
CBHW062027270326
41929CB00014B/2342